Judge LANDIS

and

Twenty-Five Years *of* Baseball

JUDGE LANDIS IN HIS BOX IN CHARACTERISTIC POSE

Judge
LANDIS

and
Twenty-Five Years
of Baseball

By J. G. Taylor Spink

Publisher of *The Sporting News*

Thomas Y. Crowell Company · *New York*

MANUFACTURED IN THE UNITED STATES OF AMERICA BY
THE VAIL-BALLOU PRESS, BINGHAMTON, NEW YORK

TO MY WIFE BLANCHE

*whose patience and consideration have made possible
an active participation and many notable experiences
in a historic era of America's national game*

Introduction

BY ALBERT B. CHANDLER

Commissioner of Baseball

This book, in dealing with Kenesaw M. Landis' twenty-four-year tenure as Commissioner of Baseball, covers a highly important period in the national game.

It was a period of vital decisions and historic events in baseball, when the course of the game was shaped to a large extent by the character of one man—Judge Landis.

As publisher of *The Sporting News*, national baseball weekly, and as a close friend of Ban Johnson, president of the American League, who frequently clashed with Landis, J. G. Taylor Spink eyewitnessed and often participated in dramatic events of that period.

Recognizing the ability of Judge Landis, yet also having differences with him at times, Publisher Spink is in a position where he can draw a realistic, full-length portrait of the Commissioner. This book gives such a portrait.

As the colorful life story of a great American and as a close-hand view of his iron rule over the game for nearly a quarter of a century, this book not only gives a clearer understanding of events of the Landis regime but represents a noteworthy contribution to the history of baseball.

Contents

Judge LANDIS
and
Twenty-Five Years *of* Baseball

1 : "The Mountain" Is Born in Millville

The Judge was a tempestuous character, who led a tempestuous life from the time he took his first breath. There never was anything prosaic about him. He uttered his first bawl at Millville, Ohio, November 20, 1866. It was only a little over a year after the close of the Civil War, and memories of that fratricidal strife still were most vivid in the minds of men and women—both north and south. His father, Dr. Abraham Landis, had served as a surgeon with the Union forces, and Civil War history always was a hobby of his most distinguished son. His mother's maiden name was Mary Kumler, and Organized Baseball's future Commissioner was the sixth in a family of five boys and two girls. The dynamic Judge outlived them all.

After naming all of their earlier boys, the Landises were rather shy of masculine names when the post-war baby came along. The battle of Kennesaw Mountain, in northwestern Georgia, stood out especially in the father's mind. During this engagement in Sherman's March to the Sea, Dr. Landis had set up his military surgical headquarters in the shade of the mountain, June 27, 1864. While he was dressing the wounds of a beardless teen-age blue-clad infantryman, a nearly spent Confederate cannon ball ricocheted off a nearby tree and struck the surgeon on the leg. The limb was badly shattered.

Perhaps the good doctor was brooding over that lost leg when it came time to christen the babe, or he had a hunch that this red-faced, squalling urchin some day would be a mountain among men. "Let us call him Kenesaw Mountain," he said to Mary Kumler Landis, and being a good wife and mother, with great respect for her spouse's wisdom and judgment, she readily gave her consent. Somewhere along the route from Georgia to Ohio, Dr. Landis dropped a letter out of Kennesaw, as the Judge had one less "n" in his name than the mountain.

On one of his trips north from his former winter home at Belleair, Fla., the Judge visited the Kennesaw Mountain battle-field. He tried to visualize just where it was that his Dad had stopped that cannon ball with his leg. He expressed a wish to personal friends to have a little ground on that mountain. Some baseball-minded citizens of Marietta, Ga., heard of it, and without Landis' knowledge, purchased several acres of ground alongside the mountain.

When Landis attended the annual convention of the National Association, the governing body of minor league baseball, in Atlanta, Ga., in December, 1940, the Judge again was taken out to the battlefield, and the deed for the piece of ground was presented to him. He was pleased to the bottom of his toes. "Gentlemen, I am deeply touched," he said. "Some day, I want to settle on Kennesaw Mountain and stay awhile." America's entrance into World War II came a year later, and the Judge's death in 1944, prevented him from ever making that prolonged visit to the mountain.

The Landises were born and bred in the American traditions. The family originally was Swiss, and an early ancestor, Pete Landis, a Mennonite, was decapitated at Geneva for his religious convictions back in the sixteenth century. For a spell, the Landis clan lived in France, and then a whole boatload of them came to this country before the American Revolution. There were eight brothers on the same voyage; they settled in the fertile farm country near Lancaster, Pa. The town of Landisville, a few miles outside of Lancaster, is named after these Swiss settlers. The family of Mary Kumler, the Judge's mother, was of German origin, but the original Kumlers also came to America many years ago.

Kenesaw Mountain was the sixth of the Landis children; in the order named, they were Catherine, Frances, Walter, Charles, John, Kenesaw and Frederick. Because of his war injury, Dr. Landis early had to give up his medical practice; he purchased small farms and the boys early had to do farm chores and obtain small jobs in town. With their rich American heritage, they all turned out well. Kenesaw became the most famous of the five sons.

Walter was a crack newspaperman, and shortly after the Spanish-American War, President Theodore Roosevelt appointed him as our first Postmaster in Puerto Rico. He was there during the famous volcanic eruption which totally destroyed a neighboring island. Walter Landis was one of the first American government officials to inspect the place after the disaster; he wrote a graphic newspaper account which caused much comment at the time.

Like his father, John Landis took up medicine. As health commissioner of Cincinnati, he made a national reputation by cleaning up some of the wretched unsanitary conditions which existed in that city. He discovered a typhoid epidemic was caused by infected milk, and after a struggle forced the pasteurization of all milk coming into Cincinnati.

Both Charles Landis and Frederick Landis became Congressmen from Indiana, Frederick, the youngest boy, representing a district adjacent to that of his older brother. Both were in Congress at the time Theodore Roosevelt appointed Kenesaw to the Federal bench in Chicago, and all three were close friends and admirers of the Rough Riding Teddy. Charles won national fame as the editor of the Delphi, Indiana, *Journal*. Like William Allen White of the Emporia, Kansas, *Gazette*, he made his Hoosier publication speak louder than many big city newspapers fifty times its size. After twelve years in the House of Representatives, he became a vice president of the du Pont Company of Wilmington, Delaware.

Frederick Landis' son, the present Kenesaw M. Landis, though a member of a Logansport law firm, followed his Uncle Charles into journalism, and his widely read progressive column is syndicated nationally. While Dr. Abe Landis' children were alive, they were a pretty close corporation. Although the brothers went their various ways, they always were loyal to the clan, helped each other out whenever occasion demanded, and through the years they got together at the old family house at Logansport, Indiana, to enjoy each other and talk of their boyhood pranks, joys and sorrows.

* * *

Millville, Ohio, where young Ken first looked out on the world, was a little hamlet of less than 1,000 persons. Dr. Landis was a country doctor, and he kept his own livestock. And, at an early stage in the Judge's life, he curried the horse, helped milk the cows, called to the hogs and fed the chickens.

Quite a few years later, Judge Landis had a golfing engage-

3

ment with several of the New York baseball writers staying with the Yankees at St. Petersburg, Fla. "Will you fellows be ready to tee off at 9 o'clock?" asked the Judge, over the phone.

"That's too early, Judge," replied one of New York's lazybones. "Do you want us to get up in the middle of the night?"

"You're a bunch of damned sissies," said the Judge. "If you had been brought up on a farm as I was, you would know that 9 o'clock is the middle of the day."

When K. M. was only eight, Dr. Abraham and Mary Landis moved their brood across the state line to Indiana, first to Delhi and then to Logansport. The crippled doctor and Civil War veteran had saved a little money, and purchased a small farm on the Eel River, just outside of Logansport. Logansport is in Cass County, located in the northwestern section of the state. As a result of the moves to Delhi and Logansport, the Landises have been more famous as Hoosiers than as Buckeyes, and Kenesaw Mountain was no exception. When he was handing down some of his severe decisions in Federal court in Chicago, he often was referred to as "that tough Hoosier judge."

Kenesaw's early life in Logansport, then a town of about 15,000, was much like that of Wendell Willkie in Elwood in the southern part of the state and that of President Harry S. Truman in Independence, Missouri. Ken was willing to put his hand to anything, so long as there was an honest dollar—or a fraction thereof—in it for him.

Dr. Landis' big family ate well and regularly, but it was not opulent. Too often Dr. Abe's patients, especially those from the outlying farm country, paid off with a side of bacon or a bag of corn meal. Neither Dr. nor Mary Landis encouraged their boys to loaf when school hours were over. Both were firm believers of the old proverb: "Idleness is the Devil's handmaiden." It was a lesson well learned. All his life Kenesaw Landis had a tremendous capacity for work.

Ken early helped meet expenses by selling newspapers. He would get his bundle of Chicago papers, the *Tribune*, the old *Inter-Ocean*, the *Daily News*, at the Vandalia railroad station. He had his regular route, and delivered papers each morning before

4

going to school. He made his delivery while riding the family horse named "Buckskin." Later the younger brother, Frederick, took over the same route, riding the same horse, and earned the nickname, "Buckskin" Landis. It stuck to him even in Congress. As for Kenesaw, he never had any difficulty with his vocal chords while delivering his newspapers, and always was in good voice. Handling Chicago dailies gave him his early contact with the great midwestern metropolis, of which he was to become such a vital part. Chicago was his home during the great part of his adult life.

Ken took an early interest in all healthful sports, with baseball, the comparatively new game stimulated by former Civil War soldiers, being closest to his heart. As with the case of his successor, Senator Albert B. Chandler, baseball was an integral part of him from the time he was no higher than a grasshopper. Ken didn't grow skyward, as did many sturdy Hoosier lads he went to school with. However, he possessed that boundless Landis energy, and considerable agility. He also gave early evidence of that K. M. L. temper, and could cow young Hoosiers a foot taller by flashes from his dark brown eyes and a few brimstone-shaded words. He played ball and at seventeen managed his own team.

The National League started in 1876, when he was ten years old, and he got a great boot when his favorite Chicago White Stockings beat out St. Louis' Browns in the first race of the venerable old National. When he was a few years older, he would read all about Cap Anson, Ross Barnes, Silver Flint and Ed Williamson in his Chicago newspapers before delivering them to his customers. That old cry of the score-card hawker: "You can't tell 'em without a score card" never had much meaning to Judge Landis, not even when he wore knee pants.

He was a good student in subjects that he liked. American history was one of them, and being so close to Abraham Lincoln country, anything that even remotely touched old Honest Abe interested and intrigued him. Those who in later years have tried to decipher some of Landis' scribbled notes must wonder how any Indiana schoolmarm ever passed him in penmanship. The third of the three R's—'rithmetic—proved another stumbling block. Ken did manage to hurdle his figure problems in the lower grades, but in high school ol' Doc algebra was an evil ogre. X might be the unknown quantity, but no matter how he multiplied it by Y_2 or divided it by Z_3, it remained strangely unknown. "I just can't make that blankety-blank thing come out right," the boy who became one of the nation's foremost jurists and No. 1 baseball man for a quarter of a century would wail in disgust. Doc Algebra won the decision; Ken just couldn't strike him out, and he left Logansport high school before graduating. It was six months before his father found out what had happened, and Dr. Landis wasn't particularly pleased.

The man who drew $65,000 per annum for running baseball got his first steady job as a $3 per week handy boy around Logansport's general store. That job contributed to his study of human nature. If one couldn't learn anything from the orators and arguers who used to gather around the cracker barrel in an Indiana general store in the early eighties, he had to have pretty dull wits. And even the Judge's worst enemy never accused him of that.

He had free crackers at the country store, and got his first practice shooting tobacco-juice at the spittoon by the cider keg. But raises were slow in coming. The ambitious boy gave up the mercantile profession and went to railroading. He took a job as an errand boy for the Vandalia Railroad. His Vandalia pay didn't put him in a class with the New York Vanderbilt, and he applied to the road superintendent for a job as brakeman.

"Look at the little squirt who wants to be a brakeman," remarked the super to one of his brawny assistants, as Kenesaw swallowed the hot words which were struggling for an outlet.

There were other jobs. The late Commissioner was agile. If they wouldn't let him take the brakes off Vandalia trains, no one could stop him from loosening the brakes on his bike. Kenesaw won a state reputation as a bicycle rider, appearing in speed events at country fairs. One can imagine him huddled over the handle bars, the wind blowing through his shock of hair, as it used to when he was hunched over with his chin resting on the rails of his World's Series box.

Kenesaw's next venture was as the proprietor of a roller-skating rink. The roller-skating craze had hit the country, and Ken, always sports-minded, decided to get in on it. What he had saved from his newspaper route and from his jobs as delivery and errand boy and the prize money which he won at the country fairs went into his rink. But, as a young business man, he proved almost a 100 percent flop. There was little left of his bank roll, when he decided to leave the roller-skating business to more experienced heads.

However, there wasn't an idle bone in Kenesaw's body. And he wasn't the kind of young man one could keep down. He got a job on the old Logansport *Journal*, and found time to play amateur and semi-pro baseball on the side. While covering the courthouse for the *Journal*, he became impressed with the court reporter's facility with shorthand. In fact, he became dazzled with the man's speed in taking down testimony. Shorthand was a comparatively new art in the early eighties. Young women still were being raised by their mothers for matrimony and a lot of ambitious young fellows were taking up the course invented by Isaac Pitman. Ken Landis got hold of an old textbook, and taught himself. He became so expert that in 1883 he was appointed official court reporter for the Cass County circuit court. From his earliest youth, he had been intrigued by the law and legal niceties.

His experiences in the Cass County court led to an ambition to be a full-fledged lawyer. Taking down testimony, he was impressed by the stupidity of some of the lawyers. He heard one case where a lawyer blew three chances to win it for his client. "If I couldn't have handled that case better than that shyster, I would try mending shoes," he said in disgust to a crony. "That poor devil (the defendant) should have walked out of the court scot free, instead of getting three years." Dr. Abraham Landis, who patiently had watched his young "mountain" go through his bicycle riding and roller skating periods, encouraged his legal leanings. "The law is a splendid profession, and I am sure you will do credit to the profession," he told Kenesaw.

The little matter of credits he missed by not graduating from Logansport high school were made up by night plugging, and Landis had enough to enroll in the Y.M.C.A. Law School of Cincinnati. He had an avid interest in the law courses he studied, now that he had a definite aim. There was no algebra again to trip him up, and he made quick progress. He completed his law course at the Union Law School in Chicago—now a part of Northwestern University—and was graduated with a bachelor of law degree in 1891. Ken was admitted to the Illinois bar the same year.

Landis never claimed to be a college man, was rather proud of the fact that he made his way to the bar the hard way. Once when some collegiate officials petitioned him to order professional clubs to refrain from offering contracts to likely looking college ball players until they had graduated, he remarked to Tom Swope of the Cincinnati *Post:* "You know, Tom, I never went to college myself. Mighty few persons know that, but it's a fact. I started my law course at the Y.M.C.A. Law School in Cincinnati and finished it at a similar school in Chicago.

"Because I'm a lawyer, persons naturally think I'm a college graduate. But I'm not, and I'm proud of it. I don't go around shouting that I never went to college; I just keep my mouth shut about where I acquired my knowledge of the law."

Kenesaw Landis' selection of Chicago as the town in which to practice law after getting his degree from the Windy City's old Union Law School is especially interesting in view of the fact that his Dad almost settled there in the early seventies after moving from Millville, Ohio. The Judge's nephew, the present Kenesaw M. Landis, related it in some interesting reminiscences:

"The last time I saw the Judge in good health, he told me the story of how his father happened to move to Logansport. When Abraham decided to use the small amount of money he had saved up to invest in some place west of Ohio, he looked over three principal cities—Logansport, Chicago and Omaha. Logansport was a thriving town at the junction of the Wabash and Eel Rivers, and one of the first important railroad junctions. Chicago was not much larger and was swampy. After seeing Omaha, which was a very small place, Abraham decided that Logansport was going to be the future town of the three.

"Years later when the Judge was a lawyer in Chicago, his father came to visit him, and together they located the particular block which Abraham had decided was not as desirable as the property he bought in Logansport. It turned out to be approximately the present site of the LaSalle Street Station. As the Judge told the story he turned to his father and said: 'Sir, if it hadn't been for your bad judgment, I would now be one of those young blades driving down Michigan Avenue in a carriage, instead of spending my youth cooped up in a law office.' "

2: Mr. Landis Goes to Washington

Kenesaw Mountain Landis hung out his shingle in Chicago in 1891, and took those cases which came his way. He then was just another young Hoosier lawyer, in the big town sprawled along the shores of Lake Michigan, determined to make good, but fellow attorneys and the judges before whom he practiced soon learned he was different. He wasn't just another country lawyer with hayseed in his hair. He was shrewd, determined, and fearless. If Landis had any trait which stood out more than his inherent honesty it was his absolute fearlessness. Names and reputations meant absolutely nothing to him. He barked and fumed; he appealed to the court to throw out points developed by learned and experienced rivals, and several times just escaped from being held in contempt of court.

Even as a bicycle rider and roller-skater promoter, Landis had a fine sense of dramatics. This was made evident early in his law practice. His eyes blazed; he ran his fingers through his disheveled hair when not pointing a finger at a wincing witness, much as he later pointed that untiring index digit at some unhappy, gnarled-fingered culprit in his baseball docket.

When Landis mounted the federal bench and uttered his front page-making judgments, and in his years as baseball's Commissioner, persons who didn't like him made light of some of his poses and accused him of being an actor. He was often referred to by some as a "ham." Landis was an actor, but after observing him for years at World's Series and All-Star games and at baseball hearings, I feel he was an unconscious one. He played many parts, but he always held to his one big title role—and that was playing Judge Landis.

Psychologists and psychoanalysts say that most little men, physically, suffer from some kind of an inferiority complex. They brow-beat underlings and when in authority exact the last degree of respect for their positions. They cite Napoleon as a shining example. The mental probers say that at some time in the little big man's youth, someone poked fun at his size, as when the Logansport superintendent said: "Look at the little squirt who wants to be a brakeman." If Landis ranted and lashed out at his victims to hide an early inferiority complex, I wouldn't know; I am not a psychoanalyst. I never observed any in his dealings with me. The sufferer with the inferiority complex supposedly is a first cousin to the introvert. Well, Landis never was an introvert. He was for years baseball's first extrovert. The Judge wouldn't have known how to hide an inhibition.

Ken Landis took an early interest in politics, and being the son of a G.A.R., he felt more at home on the Republican side of the fence. Yet, it took a Democratic national election, and the defeat of a Hoosier President, first to put Landis in the national limelight. Grover Cleveland, defeated for re-election by Benjamin Harrison of Indiana in 1888, reversed the order in 1892, when he unseated Hoosier Ben for a second sojourn in the White House.

In selecting his new cabinet, Cleveland named Judge Walter Q. Gresham, then sitting on the federal bench in Chicago, as his Secretary of State. Judge Gresham had been Surgeon Abe Landis' commanding officer at the Battle of Kennesaw Mountain during Sherman's march through Georgia. When it came time for appointing a secretary to accompany him to Washington, Judge Gresham thought of Dr. Abe Landis' enterprising young lawyer son, Kenesaw. Naming Ken for the post gave the new Secretary of State an opportunity to do something nice for the son of his old friend and battle associate, but Ken didn't get the job solely through what then was known as "pull." Landis had many qualifications for the post. Judge Gresham had followed Ken's activities in his two years as a practicing attorney, and had a chance to observe him at close range when Abe Landis' boy argued cases in his own court. He recognized that the young Indiana attorney was different; most decidedly he had something on the ball. He knew of Ken's intensive patriotism, and his great love of his country. Landis' knowledge of shorthand, enabling him to take down Secretary Gresham's confidential notes, was another valuable asset. Few young lawyers of that time were so gifted.

Judge Landis was twenty-six years old when he went to Washington. He stayed there only two years, leaving the capital after Secretary Gresham's death in 1895, but they were two big years

11

in his life, and remained imbedded in his brain until his death in 1944. Cleveland and Gresham pursued a strong foreign policy, especially in defense of the Monroe Doctrine, and both Britain and Germany were advised to leave South American republics alone, or else. Landis took down some of Gresham's strong-worded notes; he was in the thick of things and enjoyed it.

When Secretary Gresham became ill, young Landis attended Cabinet meetings in his place, a duty usually carried on by the Under Secretary of State. The young man made such an impression on President Cleveland that he offered Landis the post of Minister to Venezuela. However, it did not appeal to K. M., and he turned it down.

Years after he left Washington, Landis would sit back at his Chicago desk, or in a hotel suite, leave baseball discussion for the moment and reminisce on his two years in the Cleveland administration. A life-long Republican, he had a great admiration for Grover Cleveland. "He never was meant to be a Democrat," the Judge used to say. The esteem in which he held Secretary Gresham is best illustrated by the fact that he named his only son Reed Gresham Landis.

Though Kenesaw Mountain Landis had made the Chicago papers a few times as a dramatic young attorney, his job as Gresham's secretary gave him his first real contact with the nation's press. Fifty years ago, the Secretary of State did not have the staff of secretaries and assistants that he has today. Not only did Landis handle Judge Gresham's confidential correspondence, but he took care of the Secretary's list of callers, including gentlemen of the Fourth Estate. His first brush with reporters came when he snapped that steel trap jaw at insistent reporters and barked: "I said you can't see Secretary Gresham today, and damn it, I mean you can't see him."

Washington was a leisurely town in the early nineties. It had a major league ball club, but not much of one. The National League and the old major American Association had merged into a twelve-club league in 1892, and the Senators were one of the door-mat teams of the circuit, invariably finishing deep in the second division. The city, however, was the seat of the baseball government then, as Chicago was to become during the reign of Landis. Nick Young of Washington was president of the National League, and he also was head of the so-called National Board which adjudicated cases between the National and the early minor leagues.

There was no thought of night or twilight ball in 1893, but the Washington club started its games at 4 or 4.30 P.M., to give government clerks and officials an opportunity to attend the games after the end of their work day. Old Capital Park was conveniently situated to the government buildings, and Ken Landis' Washington recreation was to root for such early baseball Senators as Orator Jim O'Rourke, Dummy Hoy, Jim McGuire, Al Selbach, Al Maul and Win Mercer. However, his big kick always came when Cap Anson, his old favorite, brought his Chicago Colts to Washington. They were called the Colts after the Players League–Brotherhood baseball war wrecked the old White Stockings.

No doubt in those days, Landis frequently rubbed shoulders in the Washington stands with a young government printer and red-hot baseball fan, John Arnold Heydler. Washington had a park in the 90's which would shame a Class B club today; it was small, but it was chummy and everybody spoke to everybody else. By yelling: "Take Maul out," or asking: "Why didn't Selbach bunt?" you became brethren. The last thing these two men on Uncle Sam's Washington pay roll thought in the early 90's was that the young government printer would become head of Nick Young's old National League and that the young secretary, Ken Landis, would be his superior as Commissioner of all baseball.

One of John Heydler's most interesting recollections is taking a proof of the President's annual message to the White House study one night for Grover Cleveland's approval and last-minute corrections. The session wound up with President Cleveland fanning with the young printer. How small the world really is! It is quite likely that the part of the Presidential message dealing with the nation's foreign policy had first been dictated by Secretary Gresham to Landis and Ken had run it off on his early typewriter. And how Kenesaw would have enjoyed that midnight fanning session at the White House with the President and young Heydler!

Romance also was in the air for Kenesaw Mountain Landis during his sojourn in Washington. It was during his years in the capital city that he courted the comely Miss Winifred Reed of Illinois. The fine looking couple was married in Chicago, July 25, 1895, and would have celebrated their golden wedding anniversary had the Squire, as Mrs. Landis affectionately called her husband, lived another eight months. For years Mrs. Winifred Landis was the Judge's gracious companion as he attended World's Series and All-Star games and on his winter pilgrimages to Florida and Arizona. Two children were born of this union, Colonel Reed Gresham Landis, a World War I ace who returned to service in World War II, and Susanne, now Mrs. Richard Phillips of Glencoe, Ill.

The late Commissioner always was intensely proud of Reed's achievements in World War I. He felt badly that he couldn't take a crack at the Kaiser himself, but felt that Reed had done a worth-while job. A piece of the propeller from one of his son's war planes was the most important decoration in the Judge's old 333 North Michigan Boulevard offices in Chicago.

In the same year, 1895, that Landis was married, Secretary of State Gresham died. Landis' appointment as private secretary was wholly personal, and he did not remain in Washington under the new Secretary. He returned to Chicago to pick up the rising young law practice which he had abandoned in 1893.

3 : "Big Stick Teddy" Makes Ken a Judge

For the next ten years, Landis was a hard-working attorney, making a living for himself and his little family. He was breaking more and more into the Chicago newspapers, and other lawyers were wary of the legal traps he set for them and of his barbed—often caustic—wit. Wherever he was arguing his case, Ken Landis never pulled his punches.

The Cubs, more or less under an eclipse in the nineties, were coming back to something like the former greatness of the old Chicago White Stockings under the able leadership of Frank Selee. Landis still hadn't taken up the game of golf, and his chief recreation was at Chicago's old West Side Park. Selee already had gathered such future greats as Frank Chance, Johnny Evers, Joe Tinker, Frank Schulte, Johnny Kling, Artie Hofman and Mordecai Brown. The memorable pitching duels between Christy Mathewson, ace pitcher of McGraw's New York Giants, and Brown already were making history.

"Can't we get a postponement of this case until tomorrow," Landis said to the learned counsel of the opposition. "Brownie is pitching against Matty, and I just can't miss that."

The young man who had been in a Democratic administration in his middle twenties plunged actively into Illinois Republican politics. Several times he was mentioned for high office, but was not particularly interested. In 1904, he managed the Gubernatorial campaign of Frank O. Lowden. Lowden was not elected that year, but later served two terms as Republican Governor of Illinois. Landis' relations with Lowden were close and intimate until the latter's death. Had Lowden been the Republican Presidential nominee in 1920, when Warren Harding was selected to break a deadlock between Lowden, General Wood and Hiram Johnson, baseball might never have known Judge Landis except as a fan. No matter who would have been the candidates, 1920 was a Republican year, and had the Presidency gone to Lowden instead of Harding, Landis' friends of that time say he would have been slated for a Cabinet post or for the first vacancy in the Supreme Court.

However, getting back to 1904, Landis' work as Lowden's campaign manager attracted the attention of leading Republicans in the nation, including President Theodore Roosevelt. The Judge also still was remembered in Washington as the aggressive young secretary of Secretary of State Gresham in 1893–1895. Teddy Roosevelt was leaning more and more to the progressive wing of his party, and like his Democratic fifth cousin, Franklin Delano, three decades later, he swung his "big stick" at the trusts and cracked down on what he termed "malefactors of great wealth." Both Lowden and Landis were outstanding Republican progressives of Illinois, and had much the same political philosophy as the impulsive and impetuous Teddy. So did Landis' brothers, the Congressmen from Indiana.

A vacancy occurred in the United States District Court for the Northern District of Illinois, covering Chicago and the surrounding industrial country. Wanting a tough judge and a man sympathetic with his viewpoint in that important court, President Roosevelt appointed the then thirty-eight-year-old Chicago attorney, Kenesaw Mountain Landis, to the vacant judgeship in March, 1905. The position paid $7,500, no more than K. M. could make in private practice, but a federal judgeship appealed to Landis and he readily accepted. In fact, being the top man in a federal court had long been one of his secret ambitions.

Teddy of the Big Stick wanted a strong man in that Chicago court, and he certainly got him. It wasn't long before Chicago writers discovered they had "a character" on the bench in the federal court. Though no one ever demanded greater respect for "the Court" from arguing attorneys, witnesses and court attendants than Landis, some other judges threw up their hands in holy horror. They accused him of violating the dignity of the judiciary, and some of his most severe critics called him a buffoon, a mountebank and a man who would do anything to make the front page. And he was making it almost as often as Ty Cobb was making the sporting pages in that interesting period of the nation's and the game's history.

Maybe he wasn't as flamboyant as Senator Albert B. Chandler, his successor, but he had his flair for the dramatic. He frequently astonished court attaches and reporters by interrupting proceedings with bits of humor or pathos. In sentencing a man, he was likely to supplement his remarks with an order to the bailiff: "Take this man up to Mabel's room," or "Take this man out to Room 33 and give him a nice easy chair."

Once he sentenced a young prisoner to two years in the "pen." "Please Judge; I can't do it! I can't do it!" exclaimed the culprit. In his most velvety tones, Landis replied: "Well, that's all right, Sonny. Just go along with the man and do the best you can."

On another occasion, he sentenced an old offender to five years. "But, your Honor; I'll be dead long before that," the felon protested. "I'm a sick man, and I can't do five years." Landis merely scowled at him, and shot back: "Well, you can try; can't you?"

But the Judge could be lenient, and humane, as well as tough and severe. No one ever knew what to expect from him; that's what made him such good press copy. After being sentenced, another prisoner turned up his coat collar as he started to leave the room. It was a cold raw day, and the penetrating Lake Michigan wind could be heard howling outside. "Where's your overcoat?" the Court yelled after him. "I haven't any; hocking my coat is the first thing I did after arriving in Chicago," said the unfortunate. "Here, bailiff, fetch my overcoat and give it to this man." The surprised bailiff brought Landis' overcoat from court chambers, helped the prisoner into it, and the latter wore the Judge's garment on his way to the Federal Penitentiary at Leavenworth, Kansas.

Quite often Landis would take a bored, or pained, look on the bench, or screw up his nose as though he were smelling something odoriferous. Reporters would sense he wasn't pleased with the progress of the case; it was dragging too much and maybe he wanted to get away to play golf, a game he had taken up by this time, or see the Cubs. Suddenly taking the questioning out of the hands of the attorneys, he would glower at the squirming witness, fix those steady eyes on him, and poke a long, menacing finger in the direction of the witness box. "Now, let's stop fooling around, and tell exactly what did happen, without reciting your life history," he would say in his iciest tones.

17

His court won the reputation of being the one "in which juries never sleep," and where Chicago court reporters had to stay on the job. Even the Indians sensed something of this little big man's dominating, domineering, dynamic power. Landis had a fishing cottage on Burt Lake, Wisconsin, located near an Indian reservation. Some of the tribesmen served as fishing guides. Their name for Judge Landis was "Sago-Ye-Wat-Ha," which in their tongue meant: "He Who Keeps Them Awake."

Landis and his unorthodox, iconoclastic procedures also kept them awake down in Washington. Many Senators and Representatives did not like Landis' judicial peccadilloes at all, and twice motions were introduced in Congress for his impeachment. He had the knack of making things hum.

A year after he was sworn in as judge in 1905, Landis had one of his greatest baseball thrills. Not only did his beloved Cubs win their first pennant in twenty years in 1906, but Comiskey's White Sox also won in the American League. It meant an all-Chicago World's Series. While the Judge attended some games at Comiskey's old South Side park, the Cubs were his first baseball love. Frank Chance had relieved the ill Frank Selee as Cub manager in 1906, and the husky Californian inaugurated his managerial regime by winning 116 games, which still stands as a major-league record. It was a season of thrills for Landis, and if people had to kowtow to him in his court, he worshiped his idols at old West Side Park. There were many of them, but those to whom he paid particular homage were the three men of that great double-play combination, "Tinker, to Evers, to Chance," and the three-fingered flinger, Mordecai Brown.

Alas for the Judge, those "Hitless Wonders" from the stockyard region, the White Sox, prevented that great season of 1906 from being one of complete bliss. They were the team of destiny that year, and upset the great Cubs in the World's Series, four games to two.

Reports have it that he got into plenty of good arguments with White Sox rooters in that series. Even after he became a federal judge, he remained a noisy, vociferous rooter. He could break out in that same sharp wit at the ball park as when seated on his bench. Only, out at the park, when the White Sox rooters came back at him, and replied in kind, he couldn't throw the book at them, but had to sit there and take it. And they made him take it, and like it, in the final Saturday and Sunday games of the series, when .205 batsmen on the White Sox behaved like a team of Ruths, Cobbs and Speakers, and in the vernacular of the diamond, "batted the Cubs' brains out" by scores of 8 to 6 and 8 to 3.

"How in the hell did they ever do it?" asked the Judge disconsolately, as those Hitless Wonder Sox tore into two of his pitching idols, "Brownie" and big Orval Overall, for fourteen hits in that final Sunday game, a contest which made Ban Johnson and Charley Comiskey, then real cronies, the two happiest men in the world.

4: The Judge Cracks Down on Standard Oil

The case that brought Landis more publicity and a bigger spot in the national limelight than any other was the fine of $29,240,-000, unprecedented in court history, which he levied against the Standard Oil Co. in 1907, his third year in office. It was on a rebate case; the trial lasted six weeks, and was highlighted by the fact that Landis compelled the founder of the Rockefeller fortune, old John D., Sr. himself, to come to Chicago and testify in Landis' court. And when Rockefeller seemed reluctant to answer some of the questions put to him by the United States attorney, Landis prodded the oil king from the bench.

For the remainder of his life, Landis was known as the man who fined Standard Oil $29,000,000. The $240,000 chicken feed was forgotten. Many persons today do not know that the United States Supreme Court overruled Landis and threw out his verdict. However, Teddy Roosevelt supposedly commented, "That's bully," when told of the fine. The decision made Landis many enemies among the conservative element in Washington, who called him a radical, a grandstand player and Chicago's "showboat judge."

Even though Standard Oil escaped the huge fine, the Judge thought his harsh penalty did a lot of good. "The imposition of that fine called attention to and ended abuses which could not otherwise have been corrected," he said.

Eventually he got pretty well fed up with being referred to as the man who plastered the big fine on Standard Oil. After he had held his baseball office for several years, he was being introduced at a dinner by a long-winded toastmaster. Among other things, he called Landis: "the man who startled the country when he had the temerity to fine the oil trusts." "Hell," said Landis to the man next to him. "Am I never going to live that down? If that's my only claim to distinction, I must be a pretty sorry figure."

How the Judge who flopped in algebra at Logansport High

reached his $29,240,000 may be of interest to present-day readers. I might say that in 1907 a million dollars still had a lot of meaning. In one year of his administration, Landis' sponsor, T. R., spent a billion dollars, supposedly the last word in profligacy.

The company stood indicted on 1,462 counts, each alleging that it had accepted a rebate from the Chicago and Alton Railroad on the shipment of one car of oil from Whiting, Ind., to East St. Louis, Ill. This was in violation of the old Elkins law. The rebates added up to $223,000, and the oil at $450 a car was valued at approximately $650,000. Well, the Judge fined Standard Oil $20,000, the maximum penalty under the law, on each count, representing one carload of oil. The court clerk multiplied the $20,000 by 1,462 counts, and then handed Mr. Rockefeller a bill for the product, or that little matter of $29,240,000. However, John D. left without even leaving an I.O.U.

Another famous Landis case was that of the Ryan baby, when he was asked to be a twentieth century Solomon in a case which had international ramifications. This matter was tumbled into his judicial lap on appeal after the late Illinois Governor, Henry Horner, then Judge of the Probate court in Chicago, had declared Margaret Ryan, a shop girl from Ottawa, Ontario, was the mother of the child.

However, Mrs. Dolly Ledgerwood Matters, widow of a Chicago banker who had died under mysterious circumstances, returned from a visit to Canada with a baby girl she claimed was the banker's posthumous heir. Banker Matters had left an estate of $250,000.

Giving her story in Judge Landis' court, Miss Ryan told of giving birth to a girl baby in an Ottawa hospital and that she was told her child had died. Later, however, she claimed the child had been given to Mrs. Matters and that the baby the banker's widow brought back to Chicago was actually Miss Ryan's baby.

Blood and other tests for determining parenthood now in use were not perfected when the Judge heard this celebrated case. Solomon Landis couldn't exactly recommend cutting the baby in half, but he was impressed with the ring of Miss Ryan's story and awarded the child to the Canadian girl. However, that testy

U.S. Supreme Court, always getting into Landis' tousled hair, which then already was getting white, threw him for another loss. Without attempting to establish the baby's parentage, the nation's highest tribunal reversed him on the ground that he had no jurisdiction in the matter.

However, Landis later had some vindication when in further litigation in Canada, an Ottawa court denied Mrs. Matters' right to the child and awarded it to Miss Ryan.

Early in 1917, Landis thought seriously of resigning from the bench and returning to private practice. Landis liked to live well, and though that $7,500 pay from Uncle Sam was adequate, it didn't permit the Judge to do many of the things he would have liked to do. He even confided to intimates that he was about ready to step down. Many of his young fellow lawyers of the nineties were now legal big shots, making as much in a week as the Judge made in a year. He dearly loved his duties as federal judge, but there was a temptation to go after the easier money.

Then the nation plunged into World War I on April 6, 1917, and all thoughts of retiring left his mind. Landis was intensely patriotic, and he felt while the war lasted he could best serve his country on the bench. He was the relentless foe of everything that smacked of pro-Germanism, and he had neither tolerance, nor patience, with any labor agitators who interfered in any way with the war effort. At the time he was just fifty, and felt rather badly that he couldn't stick one of his bony fingers in the Kaiser's eye, or smack him on the chin. He would have loved to accompany Col. (then Captain) Larry MacPhail, baseball's stormy petrel, into Holland, when Larry and some of his boys tried to kidnap the Kaiser after the 1918 Armistice.

In giving the oath of citizenship to eighteen Chicago soldiers in 1918, Judge Landis expressed the hope they would bag one or more of the Kaiser's sons.

"Damn the Kaiser, and his sons," he said. "I never knew until now the penalties of old age [he was one to exaggerate] which keep me here, when I want to be over there. But you may meet my boy over there."

He cracked down hard on William D. "Big Bill" Haywood,

then Secretary of the I.W.W. (International Workers of the World), and ninety-three of the membership. The I.W.W.'s perhaps were no worse than some of the left-wing labor elements of today, but during World War I and for some time thereafter, they had an unsavory reputation. Landis actually hated their very guts. Privately, after he retired from his judgeship, he referred to them as "scum," "filth" and "slimy rats."

Big Bill and 103 of his henchmen were hailed into Landis' court charged with obstructing the nation's war program. Haywood and ninety-three of the defendants were found guilty, and Landis sentenced them all to stiff sojourns in federal penitentiaries. Haywood and the smaller fry appealed, but when a higher court sustained Landis, Big Bill fled to Russia. The others went to jail.

Another war trial in Landis' docket which attracted international attention was the case of Victor Berger, editor and Socialist Congressman from Milwaukee, and six other Socialist leaders. They also were before Landis on charges of impeding the war effort. Landis was bitter in his denunciations, and sentenced the seven Socialists to jail. However, this decision did not stand up as well as the I.W.W. convictions. Berger and his associates were granted new trials and later discharged.

In one of his fiery patriotic public utterances around the time of these trials, he again let go at the former Kaiser with both fists. He demanded that Kaiser Bill, his six sons and 5,000 militarists be "lined up against a wall and shot down in justice to the world and to Germany."

Landis actually hoped to try Kaiser Wilhelm in his own Chicago Federal court at the end of World War I. The plan was to indict the former German Emperor for the murder of a Chicagoan who lost his life in the sinking of the *Lusitania* in 1916. The plan failed to materialize, as Secretary of State Lansing of the Wilson administration informed Gresham's old secretary that existent treaties prevented the extradition of the Kaiser. On receipt of this communication, he screwed up his face as though smelling Limburger cheese and uttered a most passionate "Bah." What a pleasure it would have been for him to have prescribed a stout piece of rope at Leavenworth or Atlanta for Herr Hohenzollern!

During the most bitter trench fighting in 1918, trenches were dug in Grant Park, Chicago, to give civilians an idea of how our doughboys were waging war and what comforts they were passing up. The fire-eating judge from the Federal court let fly the first spadeful of earth.

"These trenches will show us what an easy job we have at home," he said. "All we have to do is buy Liberty Bonds and pay a few taxes."

While Landis was conducting the I.W.W. trial in 1918, he received sacks of threatening letters. He was told he would be bumped off any time he stuck his nose out of the court building. If the reader thinks some of the baseballers called him rough, rude names when he gave decisions against them, it was Sunday School stuff compared to what some of those radicals called him.

"I didn't pay any attention to them," Landis said in court. "One was particularly uncomplimentary. [That probably was something in the way of an understatement.] I don't think such letters should be given any consideration."

Landis also was on the mailing list when bombs were sent to thirty prominent citizens in the way of a May Day celebration in 1919. He was out of town when the mail package was left on his desk in his chambers. Albert F. Baenziger, then a reporter on the Chicago *Evening American*, saw it, got suspicious and had it put aside. When Landis returned, at first he refused to surrender the package. "It was sent to me in the mail, so it is my property," he yelled.

While police exploded it, Landis stood by and gravely remarked: "I would have opened it, had I been in town when it first was received."

Wrist watches, commonly worn today, were novelties when Landis was on the bench. Officers in World War I found them useful and efficient. So, it was considered all right for servicemen or ex-officers of World War I to wear them, but foppish for others to do so. The Judge always had a contempt for anything that might look "sissy." Whenever a lawyer or witness in his court flipped up his wrist to see what time it was, Judge Landis would bellow: "What branch of the service were you in?"

24

He admitted having sympathy with anyone who had been in the war, and also admitted that defendants took advantage of it. Ex-soldiers, widows, especially those of men who made the great sacrifice, and former servicemen who stole out of need, he handled with great clemency.

Fred Still, a former coal passer on a freighter torpedoed by a German submarine in 1918, came before him on a charge of writing a threatening letter to a government official demanding $24 in back pay. When Landis learned the man was suffering from tuberculosis, partly the result of exposure after the sinking, he quickly quashed the indictment. He had the defendant sent to a hospital, and personally saw to it that Still's back pay was sent to him.

Landis was unpredictable on the bench; he could blow hot and cold, and do it within twenty-four hours. Though he flayed radical labor, his sympathies were with the underdog and the little fellow. A millionaire cattleman once was tried before Landis and was found guilty of selling diseased cattle. Under the law, Landis had it within his power to fine the man or slap him in the pen. He gave the cattleman the maximum jail sentence. President Woodrow Wilson, however, felt the punishment was too severe, and commuted the sentence a few months later.

On the day after Landis was advised that the President had commuted the cattle king's sentence, six men were found guilty in his court of stealing sugar from freight cars. In turning them loose, the Judge said: "Stealing sugar is no more deserving of a prison sentence than selling diseased cattle." That got him very much in bad with the administration in Washington, and there were reports that President Wilson would ask for his resignation, but the storm blew over.

However, the case of leniency which was most criticized by other jurists and lawyers was his verdict in setting free an eighteen-year-old Chicago youth who had stolen $750,000 worth of Liberty Bonds. The boy was a messenger employed by a Chicago brokerage house, and the stolen bonds were subsequently recovered. But it was Landis' finding which stirred up nation-wide comment, criticism, and some ridicule. "I am going to set this boy free," said Landis. "I wish I had the power to jail the men who sent him out with $750,000 in bonds."

Landis was liked and admired by many of the Chicago court writers. One of his foremost admirers was A. L. Sloan, political editor of the Chicago *Herald-American*, and former dean of the Federal Building reporters in Chicago. Sloan continued his friendship with the Judge after he left the bench, and frequently was his baseball guest in later years in the Commissioner's box at Wrigley Field or Comiskey Park.

"The Judge always was headline news," recalled Sloan. "He was a great showman, theatrical in appearance, with his sharp jaw and shock of white hair, and people always crowded into his courtroom, knowing there would be something going on. There were few dull moments."

However, one who doesn't sing the praises of Landis as a jurist is Jack Lait, editor of the New York *Daily Mirror*, and a young court reporter when K. M. L. held forth in Chicago's Federal Building. His comment gives one another picture of this many-sided man.

"Landis was an irascible, short-tempered, tyrannical despot," wrote Lait in his *Mirror* a few months after Landis' death. "His manner of handling witnesses, lawyers—and reporters—was more arbitrary than the behavior of any jurist I have ever seen before or since. He resented what we wrote; he resented what we did, and probably what we wore. He regarded his courtroom as his personal private preserve and even extended his autocracy to the corridors beyond."

Lait went on to say that late one extremely hot night, a group of reporters were awaiting a jury verdict in the famous Beef Trust trial. The court was not in session, and Landis was out getting a sandwich. The reporters sat down in the marble hallway, the nearest thing to a cool spot they could find. Landis came back and brusquely ordered the men off the floor. Lait didn't jump up, which exasperated the Judge. "I told him that court wasn't in session, and that he was off base," recalled Jack. "What's more I told him I liked it where I was. Landis couldn't do anything about it at the time; he fumed and fussed, and next day he called up my boss and demanded I be fired. Well, I wasn't."

From then on, Jack Lait was very much in Landis' "In Bad Club." The later baseball Commissioner became peeved just to see him around. "I worked for an afternoon paper," continued Lait. "More than once, Landis went so far as to adjourn court for several hours—too late for my deadline—and continue into the night, so that the morning papers would get the day's story or the cream of the copy."

Reminiscing further on his days in Landis' court, Lait added: "I have seen Landis send a federal marshal out to bring in the wife and children and minister of a witness and line them up and lecture them. He did not subpoena them, mind you. That would have been illegal. He merely 'sent for' them. What he said to them he kept off the record. They stood there, terrorized, in tears—simple people who had probably never been in a courtroom before—while he harangued them and the witness.

"I have seen him order a marshal to take a witness, who would not testify as Landis wanted him to, and order the marshal: 'Hold him in my chambers while he thinks it over.' No order of arrest, mind you. That would have been illegal. But confinement—sometimes for hours, with no charge, no commitment. That also did not go on the record. And what ordinary witness would defy a United States judge and court officer, and physically refuse, or resist them? They took it.

"I have heard him abuse attorneys and threaten them with contempt because they insisted on getting into the record prejudicial outbursts from the bench which Landis had ordered the court stenographers to delete.

"On the other hand, I saw him acquit a young fellow who had confessed that he rifled hundreds of letters, stole money orders and checks, and threw the letters and envelopes into a sewer. This is a penitentiary offense. But Landis declared him not guilty—on the ground that the government paid the boy too little and the temptation was too great. This mercy was as illegal as his severities. But that was Landis.

"By his fantastic conduct and drastic decisions—which he could not always keep off the record—he saw most of his major judgments overruled on appeal, including the two big trust cases which made him Page 1 and which probably led to his selection as Baseball Czar after the Black Sox scandal."

5 : Eleven Fed League Prayers to Landis

It wasn't the Black Sox scandal which first brought Landis to baseball's notice. On January 5, 1915, in the second year of the baseball war between so-called Organized Baseball and the independent Federal League, the Feds set off a legal bombshell which threatened to blow the very foundation from under the baseball structure. The Federal League, then fighting for recognition as a third major, directed its eleven prayers for relief from National and American League domination to the fan jurist of Chicago, Kenesaw Mountain Landis. The Federals, who had some real moneyed backers and a rather forceful, though garrulous, president in Jim Gilmore, wanted to pull down professional baseball's entire house because the big leagues wouldn't let them in.

Unless his name appeared in the form of a note, when he barked at someone as a rabid Cub fan, the first time the name of Landis ever was set on a linotype machine for *The Sporting News* was in connection with this suit. It was a whopping big story; *The Sporting News* gave a full page to it, and that was long before *The Sporting News* went tabloid. We knew there would be hell to pay in baseball if Landis, the man who fined Standard Oil $29,000,000, should decide that baseball was a gigantic trust and knock the props from under the game. He was known as a trust-busting judge, and I believe that's why the Feds sought relief in his court.

In *The Sporting News* issue of January 14, 1915, appeared the following: "In the United States District Court for Northern Illinois, Judge Kenesaw M. Landis presiding and court sitting in Chicago, the Federal League on Tuesday, January 5, 1915, filed suit against Organized Baseball, the 16 club presidents and the three members of the National Commission being cited by names as defendants. The action was brought under the Sherman Antitrust laws.

"In 11 prayers for relief, the court is asked to declare the National Agreement, under which the system known as Organized Baseball operates, illegal and is asked to dissolve the alleged com-

29

bination maintained under that agreement, to declare acts of the National Commission [then the governing body of baseball] void, declare all contracts made under the Agreement of no effect, order Organized Baseball to dismiss all suits they have instituted against contract jumpers, and to restrain them from instituting any more such suits.

"Judge Landis set the hearing of the suit for January 20, ordered summonses issued against all of the persons named in the suit and ruled that the defendants must answer to the Federal League petition before January 16.

"It will be the duty of Judge Landis after hearing affidavits and testimony of both sides to decide that Organized Baseball is an illegal combination and order its dissolution, or to dismiss the suit on the ground that the Federals have made no case or have no cause for action."

Ban Johnson, the strong man president of the American League, gave out this statement: "This suit is an offshoot of the Gallagher resolution in the House of Representatives a few years ago to investigate the 'baseball trust,' which was pigeon-holed. We said then we would welcome congressional investigation, and we feel the same way about it now.

"Organized Baseball has won the confidence and support of the American public. It continues to hold that respect. When the American League was launched, we never voluntarily went into court to air our troubles. We were dragged into court, but we went along on our merits and won the support of the baseball-loving public. Recognition by the National League followed, and we continued on our merits.

"The American League never violated contracts or countenanced the violation of contracts. We were content to take conditions as we found them and built up our organization on its merits. We fought our battle at the gate, not in the courts."

John K. Tener, president of the National League and then winding up his term as Governor of Pennsylvania, had this to say: "I have no fear as to the outcome of the legal proceedings, or that the validity of the National Agreement will be upheld by the court. I only regret that because of any exigent circumstances, the

Federal League has been impelled to undertake to annul an agreement which the members of that league, as supporters and advocates of the national game, know full well has materially contributed to the uplift and betterment of the game, been of great benefit and protection to the players and in its operation has given general satisfaction to the public.

"I can hardly believe that the institution of such litigation by the Federal League will redound to their credit or meet with the approval of the tens of thousands of patrons of our national game."

Looking back from the perspective of three decades, I think the statement of David Fultz, former major leaguer and president of the Players' Fraternity (a ball players' union to which most big leaguers and higher minor leaguers then belonged), came closest to hitting the real core of the matter.

"The dissolution of the National Commission would leave the players free to dispose of their services in the open market and to the highest bidder," said Fultz. "Professional baseball, without proper organization and control, would result in complete disruption of playing and business standards. Such conditions would be the forerunner of baseball chaos.

"The officers of the Fraternity will follow the action carefully and will be ready to step in at any time if the rights of its members are threatened."

I have good reason for remembering the Federal League war, and this litigation in Judge Landis' Chicago court. I had become associated with *The Sporting News*, started by my father in 1886, less than a decade before. When the Feds first made their bid for major league status in the winter of 1913–'14 and started their raids on the two major leagues, my dad, Charles C. Spink, was inclined to give the newcomers what in newspaper circles we call "a break." He had had the sagacity to string along with American League when Ban Johnson's fresh, vigorous young league made its successful fight for major recognition in the first years of this century. It was a great thing for baseball, also for *The Sporting News*.

Perhaps that's why my father thought there was room for a third

major league, and that it would further stimulate baseball interest. I couldn't see it, and we had several arguments on the subject.
For one thing I grew up with a tremendous admiration for Ban
Johnson. From the start Mr. Johnson fought the third league with
the full force of his powerful nature.

Unfortunately, the tragic hand of death determined our policy.
While I was on my honeymoon, I was called back by the illness of
my father. It was the irony of fate that he became seriously ill
shortly after attending the opening Federal League game in St.
Louis in 1914 and died of intestinal complications, April 22. It
meant that the responsibility of getting out the national baseball
weekly fell on my shoulders, and I was little more than a kid of
25. My policy was to print the Federal League box scores and their
news, but editorially we were hostile. Joe Vila, our New York
correspondent, and a particular friend of Ban Johnson, fired our
heaviest barrages against them. Joe always referred to them as
the "Lunchroom League," or the "Flap Jack Circuit," as Charley
Weeghman, backer of the Chicago club, owned a string of restaurants; the Ward brothers, who had the Brooklyn franchise, were
the wealthy bakers; and Otto Stifel, the original backer in St.
Louis, was a brewer.

Despite the fact that Johnson and Tener gave out brave statements, when the Feds went into Judge Landis' court in Chicago
in January, 1915, there long had been a dread in baseball that the
reserve and ten-day clauses, and other phases of the game's contracts, would not stand a test in the higher courts. A lot of baseball's leaders at the time feared for the worst. Fultz put his finger
on it, when he recognized the danger of Landis making free agents
of all National and American League players by an adverse decision years before he freed the St. Louis Cardinal and Detroit Tiger
farmhands.

The immediate reason for the Federal League litigation was the
big leagues going into lower courts, seeking to restrain contract
jumpers from their leagues from playing with the Feds. Walter
Johnson, the big ace of the Washington club, signed with the
Chicago Feds. Clark Griffith jumped on a train for Kansas, convinced Walter he was not doing right by Clark, and by offering

him the same money induced him to stay with the Senators. Hal Chase jumped the White Sox to go to the Buffalo Feds, after serving ten days' notice on the elder Comiskey that he would abrogate his Chicago contract. Hal claimed the ten-day clause had to work both ways to be equitable. This contention later was upheld by a Buffalo jurist, after Comiskey sought to restrain Chase from playing with that club. The Cincinnati club restrained the Cuban, Armando Marsans, from playing with the St. Louis Federals, and Schuyler Britton, the Cardinal owner, went into Cincinnati, Lee Magee's home town, to try to prevent him from playing with and directing Ward's Federal League team in Brooklyn.

When the legal battle got under way, January 21, George Wharton Pepper, later Republican United States Senator from Pennsylvania, was chief counsel for the National League, George W. Miller for the American, and Edward E. Gates for the Federal. All three were legal big shots, and their advice cost plenty. In view of Landis' eventual disposal of the case, it is interesting now to note that newspapers of that time expected a quick verdict. They based that view on the fact that Landis ordered hearings fifteen days after the action was filed. It is most unusual for a case to get such right of way in a Federal district court. There is no doubt that what Landis had in mind was to clear up the matter by the time the clubs started training.

The Sporting News of January 21 ran this paragraph: "Hearing of the evidence was set by Judge Landis for January 20, and because his action is hastening its presentation, the inference is that he expects to give an early decision in the case. That, however, does not mean that his decision will be made known immediately. There is a mass of evidence to be considered and a conclusion may not be reached by the jurist on it for a week or more."

They were just 100 percent correct about that mass of evidence, and though Landis had been a fan since his days as a Logansport newsboy, he got a liberal education in what goes on under the baseball surface; no doubt it came in most handy in later years. The Judge smirked, smiled, growled, grinned and made wry faces as the witnesses—the high, low and jacks of the game—paraded before his judicial reviewing stand.

33

At the very start of the proceedings, Leopold Hoernschmeyer (Lee Magee) asked the court to admit him as a party to the Federal League suit as a plaintiff "that he might be given an opportunity to secure justice and relief from persecution at the hands of the alleged baseball trust."

Magee (Hoernschmeyer) alleged he had been dealt with unjustly by Organized Baseball in that it had increased his pay as a player from $1,500 to only $7,200 in four years' time and utterly failed to appreciate his true worth as a player. In consequence of Magee entering the big suit, the injunction suit brought against him by the St. Louis National League club before Judge Hollister in Cincinnati was indefinitely postponed.

Some of the Judge's old Cub favorites, now Federal Leaguers, came to court to tell of some of the wickednesses of Organized Baseball. If they weren't there in person, the Fed attorneys read their affidavits. Mordecai Brown, who used to thrill Landis with his pitching duels with Matty, testified that Joe Cantillon, manager of the Minneapolis club, at one time traded a ball player for a bird dog. Landis joined in the general levity. In 1914, Mordecai had been manager of the St. Louis Federal League Club.

Joe Tinker, the Chicago Fed manager and formerly the great Cub shortstop, made a strong objection to the ten-day clause, and related that he had been sold three times in Organized Baseball without being consulted as to his wishes. Otto Knabe, the former Philly second baseman, by this time manager of the Baltimore Federals, affirmed that National and American League players were not allowed to make any suggestion relative to the printed form of their contracts.

After four days of testimony, in which the Feds recited their real or alleged grievances, Judge Landis suddenly snapped at Attorney Gates of the Flap Jacks: "I have gone just about far enough in this case. The time has come when I should ask you gentlemen just what you want me to do in issuing this injunction. Do you want me to stop the teams from going on spring training trips? Do you want me to break up the clubs or what do you want me to do?"

Gates then made denial of any intention on the part of the

34

plaintiff to bring hardship to the clubs of Organized Baseball. He contended that the sole purpose of the suit was to centralize the litigation being waged in other jurisdictions and bring them into one Federal court. Also, it was the intention of the plaintiff to prevent Organized Baseball from tying up Federal League players in injunction suits, as the Feds were sure O. B. had intentions of doing.

At another point Landis showed his love, faith and belief in baseball when he admonished both factions saying: "Both sides must understand that any blows at the thing called baseball would be regarded by this court as a blow to a national institution."

In his defense for Organized Baseball, Senator Pepper declared he did not know what the Federal League was asking to have enjoined. "Their grievance is not that we prevent them from finding the young players on the 'lot' and developing them through training in the various minor leagues as we do; they want to attain in one bound the advantage we have gained through ten years of labor; they want to profit from the skill developed by our money," said Pepper.

But when Attorney Pepper, at another point, mentioned the word "labor," as applied to the afternoon chores of ball players, Judge Landis expressed himself as shocked. "As a result of thirty years of observation, I am shocked because you call playing baseball 'labor,'" said Landis stiffly to one of Pennsylvania's great lawyers.

It showed the attitude Landis often exhibited during his Commissionership in later life. He always remained a fan-Commissioner, and ball players were heroes much as when he first came to Chicago from Logansport. Baseball was just a little more thrilling than painting a fence or putting up a brick wall. It was like Connie Mack, reminiscing of his early days in Meriden, Conn., and Hartford, saying "I still haven't quite gotten over it that some men were willing to pay you for playing ball—a game which is so much fun." Or, "Hit 'em Where They Ain't Willie Keeler," laughing over his cups at the stupidity of club owners. "The saps pay me for playing ball," said Willie. "Why, I would pay my way in to the ball park if that was the only way I had to get in a game." Of course, the Federal court judge and the later Commissioner felt the baseball worker was worthy of his hire, but there was too much glamour about the business for him to think of it as labor.

A rather humorous note appeared among short paragraphs picked up at the famous trial in *The Sporting News*. "The Judge at least came into court with 'clean hands,' for last season (1914) he refused to accept passes for the Cubs, White Sox and Chifeds. When he went to the game he paid his way in."

And in our issue of January 28, 1915, under a rather youthful and handsome picture of the already white-haired Judge were these lines: "All hands on the baseball litigation unite in praising the way Judge Landis has conducted the case. The Federal League bill of complaint was a chaotic mess of allegations, covering this, that and the other thing, but the Judge brought order out of it, found out what the Feds really wanted—which was little after all—and has in a sense started the case anew.

"Incidentally the Judge has paid a tribute to baseball by proclaiming from the bench that it is a public institution that no one shall think of harming, thus giving the game an official recognition that is highly complimentary. Judge Landis is most widely known for his famous decision in fining the Standard Oil $29,000,000 for rebating. However, he is not a stranger to the sport fraternity, for it was he who arraigned Jack Johnson (the former heavyweight champion) on a white slave indictment. He is a dyed-in-the-wool fan, has played baseball, and the game is safe in his hands."

I take a little pride that six years before Landis took his high baseball office, our publication, of which I then had been the youthful publisher only nine months, made this statement: "the game is safe in his hands."

As February came along, and the teams prepared for their training jaunts to Dixie and California, there was a little concern over Landis' failure to render a decision. It sort of left the teams up in the air. And Landis himself had expressed some concern during the trial of leaving baseball in a chaotic mess before the training season.

About this time, George S. Robbins, our Chicago correspondent, wrote: "Baseball men here have been eagerly awaiting the decision of Judge Landis in the injunction suit brought by the Feds. The fact that no decision has been forthcoming gives the impression that Uncle Sam's jurist has concluded he has jurisdiction in the case. It also tends to show that Judge Landis realizes the importance of the case and is thrashing out the evidence, pro and con, most thoroughly.

"Landis is a great fan and is conversant with baseball law and its relation to federal statutes, but is a stickler for justice. It is lucky for the game of baseball that the fate of the pastime is in such hands."

The training season came and went, and there was no decision. So did the opening of the 1915 championship season, both of the old majors and the Feds. Several times during the season, there were reports that Landis would render his decision. Once in mid-summer a report was in circulation that a decision was imminent. A bunch of reporters, apart from the regular Federal Building crowd, swarmed into Landis' court. He acted as though nothing unusual was afoot; he gave several decisions in minor cases, but said not a word about baseball. When reporters—even those who knew him well, like Sloan—asked: "When are you going to decide on that baseball business, Judge?" he merely looked the other way and said nothing.

The end of the season and the Red Sox-Philly World's Series passed and still no decision. I was one of the scorers at that Series, and I heard a lot of speculation about Landis' failure to render a decision. The question was whether it was good or bad. Obviously he felt the Federal League had a case, or he would have dismissed the case or given a ruling long before. Tinker's Chicago Whales, of Landis' home town, had won the Federal League flag in a close fight with the St. Louis club, and had built up a pretty good following in Chicago's North Side. The mayor of Chicago demanded of the old National Commission that Tinker's Whales be included in the World's Series. That would have given Judge Landis his only chance to see any of the games, as he then didn't leave Chicago for World's Series contests. However. August Herrmann, Ban Johnson and John Tener turned a deaf ear to the mayor's appeal.

After the 1915 season, the Feds made further raids on the majors and higher minors, and still the white-haired Chicago squire was silent. The Flap Jack League announced the transfer of its Newark club to New York; this club had the backing of the multimillionaire oil king, Harry Sinclair. Sinclair had the architectural plans of a big ball park he intended to build in New York's Borough of Queens prominently displayed at 42nd Street and Broadway Harry had become the big angel of the Feds, and at one time offered to stand at New York's Battery and match the big leaguers dollar for dollar, in tossing the round iron men into upper New York Bay. Between the Federal League backers and Organized Baseball, the two and a half year war probably cost around $10,000,000; Ed Barrow's International League was almost knocked out, and the baseball structure—major and minor—was pretty rocky.

However, with the first World War coming ever closer to our shores, the Feds finally threw up the sponge at the time that the National League had its December meeting in New York. But, it wasn't an "Unconditional Surrender," and the Feds were paid pretty rich sugar for agreeing to shut up shop. Charley Weeghman was permitted to buy the Cubs, and move the merged team to his North Side plant in Chicago—now Wrigley Field. Phil Ball, the St. Louis promoter, was permitted to buy the Browns, and took over Sportsman's Park. The Ward brothers of Brooklyn were given 20 annual payments of $20,000; Sinclair got ten annual payments of $10,000 for his old wooden plant near Newark and the Pittsburgh people got five annual payments of $10,000. In addition, Sinclair was permitted to sell the cream of the Federal League players, including men who had jumped big league contracts, back to the big league owners. He got $35,000 from the Giants for Benny Kauff and $22,500 from the Yankees for Lee Magee.

The National League arranged for the original peace terms, and sent Barney Dreyfuss out to Chicago to put it before the American League's annual meeting. Ban Johnson was opposed to making peace, and favored unconditional surrender. He felt certain America would enter the World War, and, after that, the Feds would die on the vine. However, he and an American League committee accompanied Barney back to New York and sat in on the final settlement.

In view of the peace settlement, the Fed suit in Landis' court was automatically dropped. Though making no public statement, Landis confided to intimates that he had put off rendering a decision, feeling that sooner or later the rival factions would come together. The general thought at the time was that Landis did not give a decision in the 11 months the case was before him because he did not wish to render an adverse verdict against Organized Baseball and its system of contracts. The general idea then was that the baseball contract would not hold in the courts of the land, and in the Chase case a New York Supreme Court Justice castigated the player's White Sox contract as an "unequitable document."

One of the reasons that considerable space has been given to this Federal League suit is that it thrust Landis forcibly on the baseball stage. Most of the club owners were witnesses in his court during the trial, and had a chance to see Landis in action, and observe him at close range. It also got fans, writers and ball players acquainted with the white-haired Chicago jurist, apart from his Standard Oil, I.W.W. and meat-packer cases.

Many persons felt that Landis saved baseball in 1915. Had he ruled Organized Baseball to be a gigantic trust, the Federal League contention, he could have thrown the whole game into chaos. There would have been no sanctity of baseball territory. Had K. M. L. decided against the legality of the reserve and ten-day clauses, the effect would have been free agencies for all the great ball players of that time, including Cobb, Speaker, Johnson, Alexander, Rucker, Eddie Collins and a rookie pitcher with the Red Sox—Babe Ruth. There would have been a wild scramble for their services between what remained of the old major leagues and the Feds. This was a possibility the legal-minded former star, Dave Fultz, had recognized.

Ban Johnson, the American League president, was not one who

joined in this chorus of Hallelujahs for the Judge. Having taken over the direction of *The Sporting News* only the year before, I saw considerable of Ban during this tempestuous year and was pretty much in his confidence. He did not say much about Landis at the time, but from the first he was not included among the Judge's admirers. Johnson termed him a "Showboat" and said his Standard Oil decision was a grand-stand play which any kid lawyer just out of college knew never would hold in a high court. As to saving baseball by failing to render a decision in the Fed suit, Ban felt the American League lawyer, George W. Miller, and Senator Pepper for the National League, had presented a clean-cut case, and that Landis should have ruled against the Feds months before they gave up.

6: Dreyfuss Goes on the War Path

There was another important happening in baseball in 1915, which was to prove an important factor in Judge Landis' election to the Commissionership of baseball five years later—the famous George Sisler case. Perhaps when Landis, the fan judge, read of the details of this case, which got reams of copy 32 years ago, he little suspected that one of its aftermaths would be a call for him to direct the game.

Sisler, a great pitcher, first baseman and all-round ball player at the University of Michigan, was signed by Branch Rickey, manager of the Browns and a former Michigan baseball coach, after George was graduated from the Ann Arbor institution in the spring of 1915.

Sisler's act in signing a St. Louis American League contract kicked up a mighty baseball fuss. Barney Dreyfuss, the wealthy and powerful president of the Pittsburgh Pirates, claimed the player and under baseball law had some justification for his claim. At a time when Sisler was a 17-year-old pitcher for the Akron High School, he foolishly attached his signature to a contract with the Akron club of the old Ohio and Pennsylvania League.

However, if he had any thought of going into baseball then, his family quickly vetoed it. They planned a college education for George. He never played a single game with Akron, nor with any other professional club, until he joined the Browns in 1915. He enrolled in Michigan in 1911, and sparkled on the Ann Arbor baseball squad almost from the day he reported. He was considered the outstanding college star of the country, when Rickey, getting the inside track through his old Michigan connections, signed George for his St. Louis team.

In the meantime, Akron, and other clubs, also had followed Sisler's brilliant performance in Michigan. That contract which George had signed with Akron suddenly was taking on value. In 1912, the Akron club sold its "title" to Sisler to the Columbus American Association club and a year later, Columbus sold its right to the player to the Pittsburgh Pirates. When Sisler was graduated from Michigan, Barney Dreyfuss instructed him to report to his team.

The case then went to the old three-man National Commission for settlement. Ban Johnson voted to award the player to the Browns; Governor Tener favored voiding the Brown contract and declaring Sisler the property of the Pirates, and the third member of the triumvirate, August Herrmann, sided with Johnson, which meant that baseball's highest authority awarded the young star to the St. Louis Americans. Among the reasons Johnson and Herrmann gave for supporting Rickey's title to the player were that he was a minor when he signed the Akron contract, that he didn't know what he was doing, and never had reported to the Akron club or the other clubs to which Akron had assigned him.

Well, Barney all but blew his topper when this decision went against him. He shouted his indignation from the Pittsburgh roof tops—and the high heavens. He got out two newspaper pages of printed matter of his grievances, which he sent to sports editors throughout the country. He recited every detail of the Sisler controversy, and left no doubt in the reader's mind that he felt he was "robbed."

Up to this time baseball had gotten along quite satisfactorily under the rule of the three-man National Commission, the two major league presidents, and the genial August (Garry) Herrmann, president of the Reds, as chairman. This form of government was adopted at the peace meeting between the two majors in Cincinnati in January, 1903, and as Herrmann had been instrumental in bringing the leagues together—and ending a ruinous baseball war—he was a natural choice for the chairmanship, even though he was a National League club president. Ban Johnson, a former Cincinnati sports writer, of course, had known Garry back in his newspaper days. In the 12 years between the Cincinnati peace and the Sisler decision, there was no serious disagreement between the two majors, and the press and baseball public were strongly behind the old National Commission.

That came to an end with the Sisler controversy. Barney Dreyfuss never forgave Herrmann for voting with Johnson in awarding the crack first baseman to the Browns. Barney was an implacable enemy, and cried for vengeance. He started his campaign for a neutral chairman for the Commission, a man with no interest in baseball. Though Herrmann was a fellow National League club owner, he charged Garry with being Johnson's man on the Commission and being strongly influenced by the powerful American League president's judgments. Of course, Garry and Ban were social companions, and at World's Series and other baseball get-togethers they enjoyed knocking off congenial highballs. After World's Series games, Garry found more conviviality in the company of Johnson than such more seriously minded National League presidents as Tom Lynch, John Tener and John Heydler.

Dreyfuss introduced his first resolution for a neutral Commission chairman at the National League meeting after the Sisler case. At first, it was a one man campaign. Garry was a friendly soul; most of his fellow club owners liked him, and some of them felt a little pride that the National League had two members on the Commission to one for its junior rival. But, Barney was not discouraged; he held to his line that Garry was "Ban's man," and gradually began to pick up converts.

During the last year of the World War, 1918, there was another celebrated player case, involving a pitcher, Scott Perry. The dispute involved the Philadelphia Athletics, the club for which Perry was pitching, and the Boston Braves. Again Johnson and Tener voted for their respective clubs, and this time Herrmann sided with the National League team. Scott was ordered to report to Manager Stallings of Boston by Herrmann as chairman of the Commission. However, Connie Mack and the Shibes went into the Philadelphia courts and procured an injunction, restraining the National Commission and its chairman from enforcing the order. Scott Perry remained with the Athletics.

That naturally burned up the National Leaguers, with Dreyfuss again being one of the most vociferous. "Herrmann decides against us, and we have to take it; he decides for us, and the American League goes to court," wailed Barney. "We need a strong man to head the game, with no connection with any club." Ban Johnson, then still absolute czar in his own league, was blamed for permitting the Athletics to go into court; some National Leaguers even felt he encouraged it.

President Tener was so irate that he requested his club owners to break off with the American League, even to the point of discontinuing the World's Series. His club owners refused to go that far, and Tener resigned in midseason. He was succeeded by the able secretary-treasurer of the league, John Arnold Heydler, who had been president of the league for a half year following Harry Pulliam's tragic suicide in 1909.

Another unhappy situation developed during the 1918 Red Sox-Cub World's Series, which gave the old National Commission another black eye. Baseball wasn't in any too good standing, as the War Department had closed the major league seasons on Labor Day with Secretary Newton Baker's Work or Fight order. The secretary gave the two champions, the Boston Americans and Chicago Cubs, a special dispensation to play the World's Series in early September. Interest in the Series had been cooled off by Baker's order, and the Commission decided not to increase the regular admission prices charged in Boston and Chicago, and the six games drew a gate of only $179,619. Unfortunately, this was the very year that the big leagues voted to include the other first division players in the World's Series players' pool.

At first the Commission felt it could pay the winning and losing players flat sums of $2,000 and $1,500, and have enough left for the second, third and fourth place players. But the receipts of the first four games showed it would go to about half of those amounts. Before the fifth game, played in Boston, September 10, the players held a meeting in which they decided not to play unless the National Commission agreed either to rule out the other first division purses or pay $1,500 to the winning players and $1,200 to the losers.

Harry Hooper, Red Sox right fielder, and Outfielder Les Mann of the Cubs, spokesmen for the players, pulled this ultimatum on the Commission, when Herrmann, Johnson and Heydler met in the umpires' dressing room at Fenway Park. As one of the official scorers, I can attest it was a nasty situation. The Commission immediately rejected the demands of the players, and the athletes

44

remained in their dugouts. There were 24,694 perplexed fans in the stands, as the start of the game was delayed nearly an hour. The Police Department, fearing a riot in the event there was no game, sent squads of cops to the ball park, while mounted police rode up and down the field in front of the bleachers. That increased the crowd's confusion.

Finally, after Ban Johnson had pointed out to Hooper and Mann the bad psychology of such a strike during wartime and its possible effect on public interest in post-war baseball, they agreed to advise the players to take the field. The players gave out a statement that they called off the strike and agreed to continue the Series "for the sake of the game, for the sake of the public, and for the sake of the wounded soldiers and sailors who are in the grandstand."

The entire incident left a nasty taste in everybody's mouth. I always have felt that mercenary-minded players on those 1918 championship teams were mostly to blame; their judgment in pulling a strike at such a time was more than deplorable—it was downright stupid. Yet, the old Commission, especially Johnson and Herrmann, took a lot of abuse, and their conduct in dealing with the strikers was termed undignified. It was felt by many that it showed the game needed a strong one-man head.

Years later, while reminiscing on the 1918 World's Series, former president Heydler of the National League remarked: "I can say now that our league went all out for the break-up of the old three-man Commission after that players' strike in Boston. From then on, we felt a strong one-man Commissioner was essential for the important post-war era of the game."

The National League was not unanimous on the subject, as Garry Herrmann, president of the Reds, wasn't ready to quit his prized chairmanship. It paid him no salary other than $12,000 a year expenses—which he spent lavishly—but he enjoyed the prestige of the office. But Barney Dreyfuss smiled; he had won half of his fight. And by one of the strange twists of fate, one of the National League club owners who favored bouncing Garry from the chairmanship was the recipient of Herrmann's favorable decision in the trouble-provoking Sisler case of three years before—Branch Rickey, by this time president of the St. Louis Cardinals.

It was the annual custom of the National League president and Johnson to go through the formality of electing Herrmann chairman each January. However, before some important post-war meetings in New York in January, 1919, Garry's goose seemed definitely to be cooked, and the chutes were greased for his exit. Certainly, *The Sporting News* predicted his exit, for the following appeared in the issue of January 16, 1919:

"Some of Garry Herrmann's dearest friends and greatest admirers—so doth each and every one of them proclaim to be—have prepared a neat little exhibition of putting the skids under Garry as Chairman of the National Commission this week. With much regret and deep sorrow, they are going to shove the harpoon into his hide and turn it around, humble him, cast him out. But there is no jealousy, no personal feeling, no animosity in the execution —it is all for high principle.

"No charges are brought against Garry. It is admitted that he has been honest, capable, painstaking and sacrificing in his work as chairman. But the times demand a change! There is deep-seated objection, we are told, to a man who happens to be interested in baseball having anything to do with its direction—the good of the game demands a man who knows less, has less interest, and will ask more for showing less. We fail to discover just where the widespread objection to Garry exists after painstaking efforts, but it must be there, for from out some dark corner an unidentified voice says it is so. Therefore, goeth Garry, and God be with him—and God be with the man who attempts to please those who have taken Garry's head."

However, no one got Garry's head at that 1919 meeting. In one of Ban Johnson's last great political victories in baseball politics, he fought and won a battle for the retention of the three-man Commission and of August Herrmann as chairman. Here was one of the strange anomalies of baseball, the American League fighting practically the combined strength of the National League for the retention of a National League club owner as the head of baseball's government.

Ban must have done it with mirrors, as Heydler and Dreyfuss were far from satisfied with the turn of events and awaited their turn. A newspaper headline after the meetings, "Ban Johnson Rules Supreme," was not inclined to soothe their ruffled feelings. If Herrmann's retention as chairman for another year meant that Johnson ruled supreme, it backed up all that had been said about Garry's being only the nominal head of baseball's government and that big Ban still was the real czar of the game.

7 Heydler First Plugs for Landis

Ban Johnson's supreme rule of the game did not last long after that January, 1919, meeting. Baseball was rocked in 1919 by a series of events that soon had the old game groggy. Though helped by the great sports boom which followed the end of World War I, it speaks volumes for the durability of the game that it not only was able to survive the punishing years of 1919 and 1920, but actually leaped forward in those years. In fact, the 1,289,422 home attendance of the 1920 New York Yankees—when they still played at the Polo Grounds—stood as the American League record until 1946, when the Yankees' home draw of 2,265,512 broke all existing baseball attendance marks. But the drama on the baseball stage, and behind the scenes, made inevitable the eclipsing of the good-natured Herrmann and the summoning of a strong man to head the game, a man who was destined to be Judge Kenesaw Mountain Landis.

Ban got into an early dispute with his erstwhile crony and associate in the formation of the American League, Charley Comiskey, owner of the White Sox. This developed into virulent hatred, far worse than the feeling Dreyfuss had for Herrmann. Barney merely wanted Garry's scalp as Commission chairman; Commie later wanted Ban driven from the game, a game to which Johnson gave so much. There are a number of stories as to what started this feud between the erstwhile friends. There is the familiar story that after Johnson spent a few days' vacation at the Old Roman's Wisconsin game lodge, he suspended one of Commie's White Sox outfielders for three days. Following his return to his office with a mess of fish, Johnson sent his prize catch to his old friend, with the notice of the suspension of Danny Greene. Comiskey sarcastically commented: "Does he think I can play that fish in left field?"

However, as Herrmann's award of Sisler to the Browns started Dreyfuss on the war-path against Garry, so Johnson's decision awarding Jack Quinn to the Yankees before the start of the 1919 season precipitated the Johnson-Comiskey break. This was another of those unfortunate cases due to the unsettled conditions during World War I. The Pacific Coast League season was suspended after July 14, 1918, and Comiskey engaged Quinn, who had been the property of the Vernon club. Jack did good work for Commie, too, winning five out of six games. With the war over, the Vernon club sold its title to Quinn to the Yankees. Both the New York and Chicago clubs claimed Quinn, and as it was an all-American League matter, Johnson alone settled it, and his award of the valuable pitcher to New York left Comiskey boiling mad.

But if there was one act in the American League which had more to do with Ban Johnson's subsequent loss of power and the eventual election of Judge Landis to the baseball Commissionership, it was Carl Mays, that stormy petrel of the old Red Sox and Yankees, walking off the field in a huff in the middle of a game between Boston and the White Sox in Comiskey Park, July 13, 1919. Reverberations of that walk were felt for years in baseball.

Mays, winner of forty-three games in 1917 and 1918 and of two 2 to 1 victories over the Cubs in the 1918 World's Series, had had rocky going in 1919, and up to the time of this unhappy incident had won only five games while losing eleven. He blamed his poor showing on the sloppy fielding behind him. There had been other errors in this unfortunate game of July 13, and at the end of an inning Mays said to his manager, Ed Barrow—later the president of the Yankees: "I'm through with this ball club; I'll never pitch another game for the Red Sox."

Barrow sent another player to the clubhouse to tell Mays to forget the incident and return to the ball game. He found Mays already dressed and about to leave the ball park. Mays took a train for Boston and he answered appeals by Harry Frazee, president of the Red Sox, and Barrow to return to his team by going off on a fishing trip. In the meantime the Yankees, as well as all four western American League clubs—the White Sox, Indians, Tigers and Browns—sent feelers to Frazee and Barrow on possible deals involving Mays.

From the start, Ban Johnson was annoyed that Frazee had not suspended Mays after the latter deserted his club, and communicated with all the club owners dickering for Mays that there could

49

be no deal involving the pitcher until Carl had returned to the Boston club. In later court testimony, he said that in a conversation in New York, Col. Tillinghast L. Huston, half owner of the Yankees, had told him the New York club would cease negotiations if the rest of the club owners would do likewise. Ban felt his wishes in the matter would be respected.

Johnson was spending a week-end at my home in the St. Louis suburbs, when the bomb fell. He was having breakfast with me, and turning to the sports page of the morning paper, his eyes popped and his hands shook when he read a head: "Carl Mays Traded to New York." Frazee had swapped the pitcher to the rich owners of the Yankees, Ruppert and Huston, for $40,000 in cash, and two other pitchers, Allan Russell and Bob McGraw. Johnson was furious; I thought he would hit the ceiling. I never saw him more riled. It was the first serious threat to his authority since he expanded the old minor Western League of the nineties into the strong major American League.

Johnson acted quickly. He suspended Mays indefinitely, notified Presidents Ruppert and Frazee of the New York and Boston clubs to that effect, and issued instructions to his umpires that under no circumstances were they to permit Mays to appear in a game in a New York uniform.

In a statement to the press, Johnson said in part: "Baseball cannot tolerate such a breach of discipline. It was up to the owners of the Boston club to suspend Carl Mays for breaking his contract and when they failed to do so, it is my duty as head of the American League to act. Mays will not play with any club until the suspension is raised. He should have reported to the Boston club before they made any trade or sale."

The Yankees immediately retaliated by getting a temporary injunction restraining Johnson, his umpires and agents, from interfering with the contract between the New York club and Carl W. Mays or with the established schedule between the New York club and the other members of the American League. The result was a feud which for bitterness and intensity exceeded anything heretofore known in baseball.

After some days of wrangling in the courts, the temporary injunction was served on Johnson's umpires before a Yankee-Brown double-header at the Polo Grounds (it was four years before Yankee Stadium), August 7, and Mays pitched and won the second game for New York, 8 to 2.

The league then split up into two factions. Frank Navin of Detroit, Connie Mack and the Shibes of Philadelphia, Jim Dunn of Cleveland, Clark Griffith of Washington and Phil Ball, the former Federal Leaguer of St. Louis, strung along with Johnson, and their clubs were called the "Loyal Five." Ruppert and Huston of the Yankees, Comiskey of Chicago and Frazee of Boston were the "Insurrectionists."

The presidents of the three insurrectionist clubs, Ruppert, Comiskey and Frazee, controlled the board of directors. The fourth director, Jim Dunn, refused to attend board meetings, saying they were "actuated only by hatred of Johnson and were called to railroad through measures to injure him." The Yankee Colonels, on the other hand, refused to attend a special meeting of the league, claiming "it was packed against them."

As the season wore on, the feud grew in intensity, and the badgering of Johnson continued. On September 5, before the New York Supreme Court Justice Robert F. Wagner, now the senior Senator from New York, the Yankee attorneys received a temporary order restraining Johnson from using league funds in defending his action in the Mays case. This injunction, as well as the earlier one, was made permanent by Justice Wagner, October 26, who found "the New York club had expended $75,000 in money and players in securing the services of Mays."

Johnson fought back the best he knew. With eight Yankee victories won by Mays, New York finished third; without those Mays games, Detroit was third. The Tigers were third in Johnson's book, and as a member of the old three-man National Commission, Johnson had Chairman Herrmann hold up the third place World's Series purse of the New York players. There then was no fourth place money. This action further angered the Yankee Colonels and got Herrmann in bad with the Insurrectionists.

The Yankees then filed a $500,000 suit against Johnson and the "Loyal Five" on the ground that "he [Johnson] conceived the idea of driving the New York club out of baseball and to this end did various acts injurious to the New York club, including the suspension of Mays, making public the plans which the New York club had for a new baseball site, preventing the acquisition on favorable terms."

However, the league was getting its fill of the family quarrel. The Insurrectionists were flirting with the anti-Herrmann faction in the National League, and there were threats of a twelve-club National League. Largely through the intervention of Frank Navin, president of the Tigers and vice president of the league, the hatchet was temporarily buried in a meeting in Chicago, February 10, 1920, and it was almost a complete defeat for Johnson. He lost everything he had been fighting for. Mays was reinstated without penalty as a member of the Yankees; New York's third place position was recognized; and third place money was ordered to be paid to the Yankee players. And, breaking Johnson's former autocratic power, a two-man committee of Jake Ruppert and Clark Griffith was appointed to review all penalties and suspensions in excess of ten days.

Now, one of the reasons the reader has been taken so fully into this Mays case in the story of Landis is to point out the sequences which brought about the final elimination of Garry Herrmann as the head of baseball's government and the break-up of the old three-man National Commission. Despite the general belief that the Black Sox scandal brought these changes about, Herrmann was out months before the scandal broke and John Heydler, the National League president, plugged Judge Landis for the Commissionership as early as the winter of 1919–1920.

I have related how Johnson saved Herrmann a year before, against the almost solid opposition of the National League. He did it because he then had the combined force of his own powerful league behind him. By January, 1920, there was a different picture. With a terrific fight within his own league, Johnson no longer could fight for his old friend, Garry. In their annual meeting in December, 1919, the National League again came out for a neutral Commissioner, a man with no baseball affiliation. And with no united American League in back of Johnson, and Garry in the bad graces of the Yankees on the third place money business, this time the National League intended to see it through.

Poor Garry! He held on to his chairmanship to the last, like a kid unwilling to give up a toy. In our December 18, 1919, edition, in the news story of the National League meeting, appears this paragraph: "August Herrmann, in explaining his position as chairman of the National Commission, said he understood the feeling that actuated some of the club magnates in protesting that a man identified with any particular club should act as judge of baseball's high court, and that he did not consider the fight on him a personal one. He would resign the office within 30 days, he said, if a majority of club owners in both leagues asked it, but the majority has never asked him to do that."

Early in 1920, John Heydler, the National League president, wrote to Herrmann, asking him to resign his chairmanship. Still trying to hold on, and perhaps thinking Johnson again might save him, Garry declined. Heydler then announced that he would not again vote for Herrmann as chairman, and Heydler and Johnson then were asked by their club owners to find a new ruler for the game. Dreyfuss and most of the National Leaguers preferred a one-man Commissioner, but they were willing to go along with the three-man National Commission so long as Ban would play ball with them and help Heydler find that new strong chairman.

I had my differences with Judge Landis, and suffered in the early years of his regime because of my friendship and loyalty to Mr. Johnson, yet I am proud that my publication was one of the first, if not the first, to bring Landis forward as the man to succeed Herrmann. On January 15, 1920, a full year before Landis signed his big league contract and eight months before the Black Sox scandal broke, we ran a picture of Landis, with a dour expression and already wearing his battered felt hat, on our front page under a head: "Called Man of the Hour."

Underneath the picture are these interesting lines: "A big campaign is being waged by admirers of Judge Landis to make him chairman of the National Commission. He is declared to be just the man to bring peace and order to Organized Baseball—a man who will have the respect of the magnates, players and public in

53

all leagues. Doubtless he is all of that, but in the East there is a strong pull for some 'native son'—meaning New Yorker—for the job.

"Judge Landis first became generally known to baseball fans by his Solomon-like attitude in the suit brought by the Federal League against Organized Baseball. Instead of giving a decision according to the law involved, which might have been disastrous, he urged the warring parties to get together and doubtless the stand he took at that time had much to do with the final agreement for peace to which only the Baltimore Feds refused to agree."

On that same front page is a two-column article by Oscar C. Reichow, former Chicago baseball writer and now business manager of the Hollywood club, quoting John Heydler as saying that the most important subject before the majors was the selection of a strong man to replace August Herrmann as chairman of the National Commission.

"We want the right man for that position," Oscar quoted John as saying. "Things have happened in baseball recently that have to be stopped. The game has an exceptionally bright future before it, and we cannot afford the future to be wrecked. Gambling has done much to hurt the sport. But that will be stopped and we are going to extremes to stop it. Club owners, of course, will have to assist us, but if they do not we will have to take it upon our own shoulders to wipe gambling out of the ball parks. And that is a part of the responsibility that will befall the new chairman of the Commission."

Further down in the article, Reichow, one of the original Landis men, and an intimate friend of the first Bill Veeck, former president of the Cubs, then swung into a strong boost for his candidate. "President Heydler speaks of desiring a man who is powerful, fearless and independent enough to reach out after any player, club owner or official who by his act or association brings the national game into disrepute. The first thought is: Who is that man? In my opinion that man is none other than Judge Kenesaw Mountain Landis. He is all that John Heydler desires and a little more. He is aggressive, and loves the game of baseball as he does no other sport and I believe, if persuaded to accept the position, would go a long way to devising some method to wipe out completely the gambling evil that threatens to ruin the game. More than that, he probably would inject some new ideas and bring the game back to the plane to which it belongs."

Oscar Reichow never pretended to be a crystal-gazer, but in that pithy paragraph, he gave a pretty good picture of the man who, a year later, would become Commissioner and what he would mean to baseball.

Early that year, after Johnson patched up his difficulties within his own league, he proposed to Heydler that they again elect Herrmann in a temporary capacity, or until such time as they could decide on someone else. But John was adamant against the man from his own league. Herrmann was out, and he intended to keep him out.

However, Heydler's effort to get together on a new Commission chairman proved of no avail. Repeatedly he wanted to get some action out of Ban, but the American Leaguer said he wouldn't be hurried. Heydler early submitted the name of Kenesaw Mountain Landis, but Ban refused to warm up to the Judge. He early called the Chicago jurist "an exhibitionist." Johnson countered Heydler's nomination of Landis by naming another Chicagoan, Harvey Woodruff, at that time sports editor of the Chicago *Tribune*. Heydler had no objection to Woodruff, but felt he wasn't sufficiently of a national figure and that his sports editor background was not so adequate as was Landis' legal and judicial training.

When Ban refused to accept the Judge, Heydler suggested several military men, Army chiefs who had held high commands in the first World War. "We went to see several of them," said Heydler, "including one who was pretty high up the ladder. We saw him privately, and at this time it wouldn't do any good to mention his name. At one time, I thought we had him, but something intervened, and we still were without a Commissioner.

"Finally, as the 1920 season was getting along, Johnson and I had a final talk at the old National League offices at 8 West 40th Street, in New York. I knew Ban since his days as sports editor of the old Cincinnati *Commercial;* I respected him for much that he had done for baseball, but I was getting pretty well fed up. I laid my cards down on the table.

"Ban, we have been dillydallying all season, and have accomplished absolutely nothing. My league is getting very tired of this situation, and unless we can get a chairman I might as well resign. Now we have seen a number of people, and gotten nowhere. So, I'll make you a proposition. Let us toss a coin; if you win, you can name the chairman and I will name the secretary. And, if I win I will name the chairman, and you can name the secretary."

Ban refused to accede to this sporting proposition. He knew if Heydler won he would name Landis. "No, I think naming the chairman is too important to hinge on the flip of a coin," he said.

So, throughout 1920 baseball had no actual head, and such controversies as arose were settled by the two league heads, Heydler and Johnson.

8: Black Sox Scandal Rocks the Game

The failure of the two league presidents to agree on a responsible head for the game stood out like a bibulous nose when the worst scandal that ever rocked baseball broke in the final week of the 1920 championship season. The fans of the nation had their eyes glued on one of the greatest American League races, as the Indians, White Sox and Yankees—strengthened that year by the purchase of Babe Ruth—came down the home stretch almost neck and neck. And then, only a few games from the finishing post, a stench bomb went off under Kid Gleason's powerful Chicago team, tore the very guts out of it and blew sordid fragments from Wisconsin to South Carolina.

On September 28, before Judge Charles A. McDonald, the Chicago grand jury voted indictments against eight of the leading players of the White Sox, and several gamblers, for conspiring to throw the 1919 World's Series, played a year before, to the Cincinnati Reds. The players were indicted on evidence submitted by Ban Johnson, and on confessions obtained from several of the players, including Eddie Cicotte, which he later repudiated in court.

The unhappy octet was made up of most of the stars of that crack team, one of the strongest in baseball history, two regular pitchers, Eddie Cicotte and Claude Williams; First Baseman Arnold (Chick) Gandil; Shortstop Charles (Swede) Risberg; Third Baseman George (Buck) Weaver; Left Fielder Joe Jackson; Center Fielder Oscar (Hap) Felsch; and Utility Infielder Fred McMullin.

It was alleged at the time that Chief Prosecutor Hoyne attempted to call off the investigation, saying it was "engineered by persons antagonistic to Comiskey," but Hoyne denied the charge and said he would push the case. Comiskey promptly suspended the eight players, and paid them off in full. The Chicago club had only three more games to play. By hastily recruiting some cast-offs, the White Sox managed to win one game of the three, enough to beat the Yankees by a game for second money, while Chicago finished two games behind the champion Indians.

Just how was this scandal hushed up for an entire year? Being one of the official scorers at that 1919 World's Series, and also enjoying the confidence of Johnson, I can understand some of the things that happened. Despite incidents which should have made a newspaperman suspicious, the average person—both in and out of the game—was so convinced of the honesty of baseball that he thought fixing a World's Series would be impossible. Why, that just was one of the things which couldn't be done!

However, we know now that had we had an alert one-man Commissioner in 1919, or even a harmonious, smooth-working three-man National Commission, the scandal either never would have happened, or, after the fix, the culprits quickly would have been rooted out and brought to justice.

We all can recall things that happened in Cincinnati and Chicago in the fall of 1919, yet most of these impressions became mental pictures later, especially after the Grand Jury investigation showed a lot of messy business had been afoot. Certainly the great majority of the men covering that Series thought it was on the up and up, and, though a few suspicious plays later came to me, I tried to convince myself that I was scoring an honest Series. Cicotte deflecting a "strike" thrown in by an outfielder that would have shot a Red down at the plate could have been due to the stress and excitement of World's Series play, and Gandil's failure to slide into third on a close play might have been just one of those boners one sees in some ball park every day of the week.

Yet, there were some circumstances of that Series which still stick in my mind after a quarter of a century. I received a dividend check from *The Sporting News* just as I was leaving St. Louis for the first game in Cincinnati, and our bookkeeper, a fan and a pretty good student of baseball, said: "If you want to make some quick money, bet it all on the White Sox." I replied, "Not me. I don't bet on ball games," adding: "I have friends and acquaintances on both sides, and it wouldn't look good."

However, he was so convinced that the White Sox were the stronger team that I got quite a surprise when I arrived in Cincinnati. I learned the odds were heavily on the Reds, despite the admitted strength of the White Sox, a team which had defeated the Giants in the World's Series of 1917. I saw gamblers going around, hocking their rings, raising any money they could, to bet on the Reds. The professionals were making their bets with the non-professionals, who thought they couldn't afford to pass up the long odds the gamblers were giving on the Sox. Somehow, that didn't add up right. The first game, of course, was the one in which the White Sox looked the worst. Cicotte was knocked out early, and Cincinnati won by a score of 9 to 1. I went to see Ban Johnson after that game, and told him some of the things I had seen and heard. He was inclined to laugh it off, but said: "Do you know, Hughie Fullerton told me the same thing."

Something happened after the second game in Cincinnati, which the Reds also won, 4 to 2, which showed the chaotic condition of baseball's government in 1919. What a strong man as Commissioner of the game would have meant at that time! Remember, Garry Herrmann then still was chairman of the old Commission, and at the same time was president of the National League's contending club.

About 2 o'clock in the morning, Charley Comiskey, president of the White Sox, called on John Heydler, the National League president, and got him out of bed, saying: "I've got something important to tell you."

John dressed and admitted Comiskey to his room. "Kid Gleason (the White Sox manager) tells me something lousy has been going on with his players in the first two games," said Commie. "He can't put his fingers right on it, but he knows some queer things are going on. Now, I can't go to Herrmann with this. He's the president of the other club, and I can't go to Johnson. You know how we stand. (It was the year of the Mays feud, and Johnson and Comiskey already were bitter enemies.) So, I am telling you, the president of the National League."

Heydler then called at Johnson's hotel, and awoke Ban out of his slumber. By this time, it was around 4 A.M. A World's Series usually was a gay time for Ban, and he had many friends in Cincinnati to celebrate with. But awakened at that time, he wasn't in an angelic mood. After Heydler repeated what Comiskey had told him, Ban replied: "That's the yelp of a beaten cur."

After that the Series became closer; by winning the third, sixth and seventh games, the White Sox reduced the Reds' margin to four victories to three. Chicago had a chance to tie it up in the eighth game, played in Chicago, October 9, but the Reds tore into Claude Williams for four runs in the first inning, and won, 10 to 5. Two of the players later accused, Joe Jackson and Buck Weaver, were the batting leaders of their club with averages of .375 and .324 respectively. In fact, Shoeless Joe led the regular players of both teams. Another of the players, McMullin, hit .500 as a pinch-hitter. The strong showing of these players—in the averages—confused the picture. Rumors still were rife. Ray Schalk, the Chicago catcher, allegedly gave out an interview that Cicotte repeatedly crossed him up in the first game, which Ray later denied. At the close of the Series, Comiskey offered $10,000 to anyone who could give him any proof that the Series wasn't on the level.

Yet, so convinced were the great majority of persons, and I include those in the writing game, of the inherent honesty of the great mass of players, that they simply would not let themselves believe anything of a crooked nature had gone on. I still must smile at the vehemence of our editor of that time, Earl Obenshain, in rushing to the defense of the accused White Sox. When Obenshain felt strongly about something, he didn't pull back his punches, or his adjectives. In our issue of October 16, 1919, the one proclaiming the victory of the Reds, Obenshain ran the picture of Comiskey on the front page, with the caption:

"Beware of Commy.
When He's 'Roused."

And then he excoriated all who were questioning the honesty of the Series, as follows: "President Charles A. Comiskey of the White Sox has made a proposition that ought to mean pretty soft picking—if the peddlers of scandal can make good. Because a lot of dirty, long-nosed, thick-lipped and strong-smelling gamblers butted into the World's Series—an American event by the way— and some of said gamblers got crossed, stories were peddled that there was something wrong with the games that were played. Some of the Chicago players laid down for a price, said the scandal-mongers.

"Comiskey has met that by offering $10,000 for any sort of a clue that will bear out such a charge. He might as well have offered a million, for there will be no takers, because there is no such evidence, except in the mucky minds of the stinkers who —because they are crooked—think all the rest of the world can't play straight.

"What Commy should have done was to offer $20,000 to any of the accusers who would meet one of the accused face to face and make the charge. There wouldn't have been any takers, unless some of the scandalmongers are a good deal better with their fists than they are with their brains."

Needless to say, if I had known as much as I did only a few weeks later, those barbed-wire lines never would have gotten into *The Sporting News*. But, attacking baseball, or casting suspicion on it, was the same to Obenshain as maligning the integrity of his country. It made him ready—and willing—to fight.

If Ban Johnson told John Heydler that Comiskey's suspicions after the second game were "the yelp of a beaten cur," it didn't take him long to take a different tack. His first reaction might have been like that of Obenshain, flaring up at anyone who questioned the honesty of a World's Series, but he was practical, and soon decided that with so much smoke there was likely to be fire.

This is Judge Landis' story, but at this date I want to give Johnson major credit for cracking that scandal, even though he knew what a black eye it would give the entire sport, and especially his league. And it was his bloodhound tactics in keeping after these "Black Sox" players until he had legal evidence, resulting in the expulsion of the octet, which brought Landis into baseball with powers that he never would have had but for the exigencies of the winter of 1919–1920.

You may have your suspicions, but you can't accuse eight ball players of crookedness, and toss them out of the game, unless you have proof. Johnson confided in me early that he was sure there was something wrong, and that he intended to get to the bottom of it. I worked with Johnson myself, and got him all the evidence I could. I was able to put him in touch with some St. Louis gamblers who had considerable information. Later I took part in the trial, and as one of the scoring board was the first witness to establish "that the Series had been played."

There were some tough mugs connected with this thing, men to whom human life meant little. But Ban was fearless, and went anywhere he thought he might get incriminating evidence. He alone was responsible for digging up Bill Burns, a former American League pitcher, who was charged with having as much to do with the fix as the guy who brought the erring ball players and the gamblers together. I recall Ban once telling me of buying a trunk for Mrs. Burns so she could make a trip to Mexico. In that way, he found Bill's hide-out. Always he was on top of the situation, and, though there were moments of discouragement when he thought he was up against a stone wall, or told of the lack of help from others in baseball, he let nothing deter him. I feel it was the strain of this scandal and the fights which accompanied its aftermath that broke down his former ruddy health.

"There are some mighty big names in this, but I don't give a damn who it hits," he told me. "When I've got the evidence to put before the prosecuting attorney, I'll not hold back a thing."

If it took nearly a year for this scandal to break, once Ban had his necessary evidence, he didn't hold it. It was late in the 1920 season, and, as I said, the White Sox again were in the thick of the race. It was suggested to hold off until the end of the race, or after the World's Series, should the Sox again get into it. But, Ban wouldn't hear of it; in fact, once he had his evidence lined up, he wanted to be sure the guilty players wouldn't get into another Series, in the event Chicago should have won.

The Chicago grand jury not only looked into the allegedly thrown World's Series, but went into all phases of baseball gambling. The investigation actually was started to look into a "queer" game pitched by the late Claude Hendrix against the Phillies in 1920. Hendrix later was dropped from league baseball. John Heydler, the National League president, gave testimony against Hal Chase and Heinie Zimmerman, of the Giants, and Lee Magee of the Reds. The names of Chase, Bill Burns, Benny Kauff, Abe Attell, former featherweight champion, Billy Maharg, a former boxer and a Philadelphia gambler; Arnold Rothstein, prince of New York's underworld—later murdered—bobbed in and out of the testimony and got into the headlines. Johnson and Comiskey had several clashes, and a heavy air hung over baseball. There was talk of calling off the Brooklyn-Cleveland World's Series of 1920, which fortunately was not done. The Series played to capacity houses in both cities, and it was Cleveland's only chance to get in the big event. But baseball had been dealt a severe wound, and no one in the game kidded himself otherwise.

Yet, in its final report to Chief Justice McDonald, November 6, the Chicago grand jury expressed its belief in baseball and its hope for the future. "The jury is impressed with the fact that baseball is an index to our national genius and character. The American principle of merit and fair play must prevail, and it is all important that the game be clean, from the most humble player to the highest dignitary. Baseball enthusiasm and its hold upon the public interest must ultimately stand or fall upon this count.

"Baseball is more than a national game; it is an American institution, having its place prominently and significantly in the life of the people. In the deplorable absence of military training in this country, baseball and other games having 'team play' spirit offer the American youth an agency for the development that would be entirely lacking were it relegated to the position to which horse racing and boxing have fallen. The national game promotes respect for proper authority, self-confidence, fairmindedness, quick judgment and self-control."

9: Quest for a Savior

Baseball men were pretty well scared. And I mean scared. So was everyone connected with the game. We didn't feel so happy about the situation in our *Sporting News* office. We talked bravely, but we saw plenty of stormy weather ahead. Thanks to Babe Ruth skyrocketing his home run record from 29 to 54 in his first season in New York, bringing about that former record Yankee home attendance of 1,289,422 and the great three-cornered American League race, baseball had enjoyed a bountiful 1920 season. The National League had done its bit in holding up the interest by staging a race in which its two New York clubs—the pennant-winning Dodgers and the Giants—came clattering down the home stretch neck and neck. Fans came out in droves in 1920; would they be back in 1921 after the public had had a winter to digest the full import of the Black Sox scandal and fuller details of the sad cases of Hal Chase and Lee Magee? No one knew the answer. Of course, there were criticism and recrimination. There was especially bitter feeling that this crisis in baseball's history had come at a time when the game had no real government or executive head. The failure of Johnson and Heydler to agree on a Commission chairman during the long months of 1920 came in for much of the criticism, with Ban taking most of the panning on his bulky shoulders. It was voiced all during the seven games of the 1920 World's Series, and picked up in vehemence in the weeks that followed.

There was a great cry for the cleaning up of the game—for the very salvation of the game. Many said the game was in need of a savior. Columns were written about it in the nation's press; the subject was discussed in the halls of Congress, from school platforms, and from the pulpits. From time to time such men as former President Taft, General Pershing, General Leonard Wood, ex-Secretary of the Treasury McAdoo, Senator Hiram Johnson had been suggested as chairmanship material. Now the name of Justice McDonald, who presided over the Chicago grand jury investigation, was added to the list. But, it was feared that baseball had waited too long to get one of the real big wigs. The Black

Sox business had given the game such an unsavory odor that there was doubt whether such men as Taft, Pershing, Johnson, Wood, McAdoo—even Landis—would touch it. Not only would the new man be called upon to govern the game, but his first duty would be to fumigate it.

Things moved quickly, and even before the start of the 1920 Brooklyn-Cleveland World's Series, Albert D. Lasker, Chicago advertising executive and a minority stockholder in the Cubs, evolved a system of baseball government which became known as the Lasker plan. On October 2, three days before the start of the series, Lasker submitted his plan to Bill Veeck and Charles Comiskey, presidents of the two Chicago clubs, John Heydler, president of the National League, Barney Dreyfuss, president of the Pirates and pioneer in the campaign for "a change," and John J. McGraw, vice president and manager of the Giants. Heydler and McGraw were in Chicago as witnesses in the grand jury investigation. It is noteworthy to recall that Lasker did not submit his original plan to Ban Johnson, a man dwelling in Chicago.

The Lasker plan, in short, recommended doing away entirely with the old three-man National Commission of baseball men and substituting in its stead a three-man board made up of "men of unquestionable reputation and standing in fields other than baseball," and in "no way connected with baseball." Again the names of ex-President Taft, Generals Pershing and Wood, Senator Johnson, former Secretary McAdoo and Judge Landis hopefully were suggested as men who came under that designation. "The mere presence of such men on the Board," said the plan, "would assure the public that public interests would first be served, and that therefore, as a natural sequence, all existing evils would disappear." Lasker proposed that this Commission of three would have sole and unreviewable power over players, managers, umpires and club owners, even to the extent of declaring an offending magnate out of baseball. It further would be empowered to establish proper relationship between the major and minor leagues, and would have the sole, unimpeachable right to prescribe the rules of the game, and to regulate the conduct of players on the field and in public. It would have provided for the most powerful and absolute tribunal ever thought up to protect and govern a sport in the history of mankind, without the baseball people having the slightest check on the men selected to be the overlords of their sport and business.

The Lasker plan met with immediate favor with the National League, and at a meeting held in Heydler's New York offices shortly after the World Series, the senior league voted unanimously for its adoption and recommended that a joint meeting of the two majors be held in Chicago, October 18, to discuss the new plans and work out the details. However, Ban Johnson, the American League head, failed to join in the enthusiasm and gave the Lasker plan the chill. Ban, of course, was a proud man; he had expanded the little Western League of the nineties into the strong American League; he once had been all powerful within his own league and the most powerful figure in baseball; he realized the plan would strip him of much of his authority, and would leave him little more than the schedule maker and director of umpires in his own circuit. Few men who have tasted great power willingly stand by while they are stripped of their authority.

However, at this late date, it is only fair to say that Johnson had some arguments on his side. He pointed out what he felt were the weaknesses of the Lasker plan. He believed that no body of civilians, no matter how high-minded, possibly could have a practical, even theoretical, knowledge of the professional game and all of the peculiar conditions that grew up as it evolved into the national sport. He further insisted the time was not ripe, inasmuch as the Chicago grand jury investigating the White Sox scandal had not completed its labor, while the Baltimore Federal League damage suit, which had been appealed, still was pending.

Then to show that the agreement which ended the Carl Mays feud in February, 1920, had been only a truce, the American League split up again as it had on the bitter Mays controversy. The powerful New York, Chicago and Boston clubs strung along with the National League in supporting the Lasker plan; the old "Loyal Five" clubs backed Ban in opposing it.

Ban Johnson refused to issue a call for his league to participate in the October 18 meeting, but Owners Ruppert and Huston of New York, Comiskey of Chicago and Frazee of Boston attended the "joint" session in Chicago with their eight National League allies. After a nine-hour conference, the meeting denounced and abrogated the then existing National Agreement, appointed a sub-committee of six to draft a new agreement on the lines of the Lasker plan. The compensation of the civilian chairman was fixed at $25,000 and that of the other civilian members at $10,000 each. The idea was these big names would take their baseball posts on a part-time basis. To enforce their demands on Johnson and the clubs loyal to him, the Lasker plan devotees issued an ultimatum that if the five other American League clubs would not come in line by November 1, the Yankees, White Sox and Red Sox would secede from the American League, and, with the addition of a twelfth club, join the National League in forming a new 12-club circuit. The session took another slap at Johnson by complimenting National League President Heydler and giving him a vote of thanks for his ceaseless efforts in trying to bring about a reorganization of baseball's government since January, 1920.

By this time, Ban Johnson had a favorable board of directors, made up of Frank Navin, Detroit; Phil Ball, St. Louis; Clark Griffith, Washington; and Tom Shibe, Philadelphia. They met in Chicago, October 29, to consider the ultimatum of the National League and their three "insurrectionist" associates from the American League. The directors looked on the 12-club league as a big bluff, rejected the Lasker plan unanimously as "wholly ineffectual to accomplish the results which its sponsors seek to accomplish," but they recognized that "there is a strong feeling prevalent among the public in favor of some reorganization in baseball," and to "work this out along sane and practical ideas" they submitted a counter-proposal that a nine-man committee be named, three from each major league and three from the minors, to study and formulate a "feasible plan of organization."

In their statement to the public, the directors said in part: "The so-called (Lasker) plan of reorganization apparently has been precipitated by reason of the gambling exposures, particularly throwing of games by players, and the idea of the sponsors of the so-called 'Lasker' plan seems to be that this evil in baseball can be entirely avoided in the future by the creation of such a commission. We have no confidence in such a commission being any more able to stamp out gambling than the National Commission has been; indeed we do not believe that such a commission could be as effective in stamping out gambling as a commission composed of practical baseball men who understand the game in all its details and know intimately the history of all its players. If baseball games have been thrown in the past, as all now know they have been in one series, it has been due to the inherent dishonesty of the players who have sold themselves to the gamblers. The thing that will stop gambling in baseball is the certainty, speed and severity of the punishment meted out to those who sell games, or do the gambling."

Dear old Ban! How he fought to the last to save something of the old order. The statement was signed by Johnson and the four directors, but the wording unquestionably was that of Ban. By this time he realized the days of the old National Commission were over, but he tried to retain a shred of his old power in baseball's government. But forces more formidable than Johnson could cope with were closing in, and Barney Dreyfuss' fight for a baseball Commissioner with no stake in the game, begun after the Sisler decision of 1915, was close to victory.

The resolution of the American League directors and the passing of the November 1 deadline without Johnson and his Loyal Five subscribing to the Lasker plan brought matters to a head, and from then on matters moved rapidly to a climax—the naming of Judge Landis as the one-man Commissioner of the game.

Following a series of telephone conversations between the National Leaguers and the rebellious heads of the three anti-Johnson American League clubs, a call was issued for a meeting in Chicago, November 8, for the organization of a new league. "We'll show them whether we were bluffing," said Heydler, Ruppert, Dreyfuss, Comiskey and the others. At the meeting the old National League was formally disbanded, and its eight clubs and the Yankees, White Sox and Red Sox organized a new circuit, called the National-American League. The twelfth franchise was awarded to Detroit. The league called for continuous ball in New York, Chicago and Boston, and elected John Heydler President-Secretary-Treasurer. And here is the most significant part of the session as far as this book is concerned. The new league voted to put the Lasker plan for civilian control of baseball into immediate effect, and Kenesaw Mountain Landis, the Chicago federal judge, was named chairman and the supreme ruler of all leagues joining in the plan. The owners hiked the original $25,000 which was suggested for the chairman to $50,000. The second and third members of the tribunal were to be selected later, and there was a stipulation that one of them would be named by the minor leagues.

Just what did Judge Landis think about all this? His name, of course, had been mentioned in connection with the chairmanship of the old National Commission all through 1920, and even before that. While the Judge later played a little coy, and seemingly had to be sold on the job, I always believe he was quite receptive—and had appreciated for some time how the trend was running. In an earlier chapter, I called attention to the fact that as early as 1917, before our entry into World War I, he contemplated resigning from the bench, as he was finding it difficult to live within his $7,500 judicial salary. I feel in the big baseball job, he saw an unquestionable opportunity for great service, also to enjoy more of the good things of life in his later years.

Oscar Reichow, one of the original Landis boosters, went to see him in his chambers around the time that the newly formed National-American League was meeting in Chicago. Oscar put it right up to the Judge whether he would be interested if the chairmanship was offered to him. The Judge shot a few questions at Oscar; that always was a favorite Landis method with interviewers. He wanted to know more about the commission, eagerly asked what could be done with the job, and what a man holding it might accomplish. He listened intently to Reichow's answers, paused a while, and then gave Oscar his answer.

"In view of my 40 years of watching baseball from the bleachers and the grandstand, and my intense love for the sport, I could not say no, if the proposition were made to me."

For a few days after the action of November 8, there were a

few bellicose signs from what was left of the American League. Ban Johnson, no doubt, would have kept up the fight, and a statement was issued that the league would put new clubs in Chicago and Boston, and possibly New York. But, it was shadow boxing, and his Loyal Five clubs had little stomach for a baseball war in which the Wrigley, Ruppert, Comiskey and other baseball fortunes would be arrayed against them. Navin especially was apprehensive of the rival club which the new league threatened to put into Detroit.

At this very same time, the National Association (the annual convention of the minor leagues) was meeting in Kansas City. On the night of November 8, Johnson left for the convention accompanied by Attorney George Miller. He was slated for a speech before the body on the 9th. Ban outlined his plan for the nine-man committee to revise baseball's government—with adequate representation from the minors—still denounced the Laskar plan and asked in the event of war, which seemed imminent, that the minors remain neutral.

By this time, most of the National and American League club owners of both factions also were in Kansas City. There were plenty of telephone calls and meetings in hotel rooms. Herrmann, for the National League, and Navin, for the Loyal Five, were the leading peacemakers. While Herrmann, the old chairman, was addressing the convention on the 10th, he was handed a note advising him that the club owners of both leagues agreed to meet in Chicago on the 12th, from which both of the major league presidents would be excluded. Herrmann finished his address; other talks were given by the gleeful Barney Dreyfuss and Charley Ebbets of Brooklyn, after which the club owners caught a train for the important final get-together. After 48 hours, the 12-club National-American League passed into history.

Two meetings were held in Chicago on the 12th. William F. Baker, the former Philly president, presided at the informal one. It was quickly apparent that four of the Loyal Five had no wish for a baseball war and were ready to climb on the Landis bandwagon. The only bolter was Phil Ball, the rugged ex-Federal Leaguer from St. Louis, but at the later regular meeting, presided over by Bill Veeck of the Cubs, Ball did not prevent Bob Quinn, his vice president and general manager, from making the vote for Landis unanimous.

The business of the meeting, which made Landis supreme ruler of baseball, was given out as follows:

"The first order of business at the formal meeting was the election of Judge Landis as the high commissioner of Organized Baseball, the vote upon this being unanimous.

"The following resolution then was unanimously adopted:

"Resolved that the chairman of the Board of Control shall be elected by a majority of the votes of the clubs composing the American and National Leagues.

"That his successor shall be elected in the same manner and this shall be incorporated in the new national agreement.

"It is agreed that upon all questions of an inter-league nature, or in any manner coming up at the joint meeting of the two major leagues that the roll be called, and after voting by clubs of each league, if there be a division, then the American League shall cast one vote and the National League another vote. Should these two votes be at variance, then the Commissioner shall cast the deciding vote and there shall be no appeal therefrom.

"Further, that the Commissioner shall preside at any and all joint meetings."

It also was decided that the presidents of the two leagues, though not permitted to attend this all-important meeting, should each appoint three men to revise the old National Agreement, or draw up a new one, and to seek the advice and assistance of a similar committee from the minor leagues.

When this business had been finished, a joint committee made up of Ruppert, Comiskey, Veeck, Griffith, Ebbets, Herrmann, Dreyfuss, Mack, Breadon, Dunn and Quinn packed into taxicabs for the Federal Building to wait on Landis. Later, they were joined by the other club presidents—all but the recalcitrant Phil Ball.

They first went into the back of the courtroom reserved for spectators, as Landis went on with the hearings in a case. The club owners did considerable buzzing among themselves, and Landis,

71

knowing the purpose of their visit, said: "Will you gentlemen wait for me in my chambers?"

Landis kept them waiting for some time before he adjourned court, and when he came into his chambers, he said almost gruffly: "Gentlemen, what is the purpose of your visit?" Yet it was no secret to him. Lasker and Col. Ruppert already had met him secretly, sounded him out, and his mood was receptive, provided the call was unanimous. Bill Veeck and Charley Comiskey, the two Chicago club presidents, were spokesmen for the larger delegation. They advised Landis of the action taken by the club owners earlier in the day, and said: "It will make us very happy if you will accept and serve us."

At first Landis refused the offer, saying: "I love my work here as judge, and I am doing important work in the community and the nation." Someone suggested that perhaps he could take on the chairmanship and still continue his work on the bench. That struck a responsive chord. In fact, I can recall that in 1920–1921, some of the club owners felt much of Landis' prestige came from the fact that he was judge of an important Federal Court. The thought was that if he descended from the bench he would be just another "former judge."

After some further conversation, Landis agreed to accept if he was given absolute control over baseball. He further said that inasmuch as he would continue on the bench he would subtract his Federal salary, $7,500, from baseball's $50,000 offer, and take only $42,500 for his baseball job.

Shortly after the club owners had their pictures taken with their new boss, Landis issued a statement to the American public: "I have accepted the chairmanship of baseball on the invitation of the 16 major league clubs. At their request and in accordance with my own earnest wishes I am to remain on the bench and continue my work here. The opportunities for real service are limitless. It is a matter to which I have been devoted for nearly 40 years. On the question of policy, all I have to say is this: 'The only thing in anybody's mind now is to make and keep baseball what the millions of fans throughout the United States want it to be.'"

At the joint meeting of November 12, and in the subsequent

talk with Landis, it had not been decided whether two civilian associates should be chosen to act with the Judge, as provided by the Lasker plan. But regardless of whether there was just a Commissioner, or a three-man commission, it was agreed that the president of each major league would be the special pleader for the clubs under him.

Johnson, the former strong man of baseball, was reduced to the role of a pleader. He even had been humiliated by being excluded from the joint meeting which selected Landis and which waited on the Judge in his chambers. And Landis had been literally jammed down his unwilling throat. I know he tried to be a good sport and make the best of it. In a statement to the Associated Press, the leading opponent of the Lasker plan said: "I am for Judge Landis, and I think these club owners have acted wisely. Baseball will be placed on the highest possible standard now and there will be no more fights. I am well satisfied with everything that took place."

John Heydler, who had been plugging Landis for some time, had greater reason for being joyful, even though he, too, was excluded from that history-making club owners' meeting. In his statement to the A.P. he said: "I am very happy over the solution of the baseball problem. It is an upward step for baseball, and forever eliminates politics from the national game. One of the chief worries of a league president was to vote fairly in the National Commission, and I am glad to be freed of that responsibility."

10: Baseball's First Commissioner

Not only baseball men, but the entire country felt pleased and gratified with the selection of Landis as ruler of the game. Baseball still was very much in the soup, and here was a man who could be depended upon to pull it out. Landis was a personality, a man of great mental strength, and one who sincerely loved America's great national sport. Of the many big shots mentioned for the Commissionership, there is no doubt the former semi-pro player and county fair bicycle rider from Logansport had a greater affection and love for the game than any of the others. And, to the very end of his days he was a fan Commissioner, and to a certain extent all ball players were his heroes.

The club owners first came to him, hat in hand, and in his long subsequent baseball career he never showed a great deal of respect for them. It almost seemed he felt a secret contempt. In days when I was on reasonably good terms with him, he often lit into one of the club owners in his pithy language and told exactly what he thought of Mr. So-and-So. I believe I can tell that, with no violation of confidence, as he frequently gave such gentlemen similar dressings down in person. I know in talks with some of my newspaper friends, he never tried to hide his feeling. He mimicked some of the owners, aggravated their lapses of grammar, colloquialisms and pronunciations. He always screwed up his face as though he were eating a particularly bitter olive when he referred to them as "magnates." I believe the club owners for whom he had most affection were men who had played big league baseball, such as Connie Mack and Clark Griffith, frequently one of his winter Florida golfing companions.

As I said before, during the Roosevelt years, he was one of the nation's most bitter anti-New Dealers. Yet, his sympathies invariably were with the little fellow and the underdog, and at heart he always remained the trust-buster that Teddy Roosevelt appointed to the Chicago federal court in 1905. He did enjoy cracking down on people.

Landis did not start on his baseball job immediately after accepting the big leaguers' offer on November 12, 1920. There was the important business of writing a new agreement between the two majors, and a new major-minor agreement. The committees appointed to draft the new agreement between the majors were made up of Herrmann, Dreyfuss and Ebbets for the National League and Frank Navin, Tom Shibe and Jim Dunn of the American League. It is significant that Johnson did not appoint the heads of any of his former three "insurrectionist" clubs.

However it was John Heydler who wrote the new agreement between the two majors. "If I never have done anything else for baseball, I am proud that this was my contribution to the game," said the genial John. It was he who suggested that the length of the agreement be 25 years. He still has his penciled notes of the agreement, which were put into more legal language by George Wharton Pepper, the National League attorney.

It is interesting to note that Heydler designated the new governing body of baseball as the "Superior Tribunal," and wrote into the agreement, "the title of Judge Landis, because of his increased powers, is raised to 'Director-General of Baseball.' " However, when Landis saw the draft of the agreement, he struck out both terms. Of the Director-Generalship he said, "That sounds too high-falutin'." He took the more simple title of Commissioner.

During the course of friendly winter discussions and negotiations, that part of the Lasker plan which provided a commission of three civilians was side-tracked, and in its stead the new Commissioner was surrounded by an Advisory Council of the two presidents of the major leagues. That was something of a sop to Johnson, though by nature Landis was not a man to ask for or take advice. He was in a position to write his own ticket, and did. As a shrewd lawyer and a judge, he knew all the loop-holes, and he plugged them.

The major leagues approved the draft of the new agreement in meetings held in New York, December 10, 11 and 12, when the joint committees' draft (still largely Heydler's handiwork) was turned over to a committee of lawyers made up of Judge Landis, George Wharton Pepper of Philadelphia, John Conway Toole of New York, and J. C. Jones of St. Louis. They gave it a final going over, and the National Association approved a similar agreement at a special meeting held in Chicago, January 10, 1921, and two days later the major leagues gave their final okay. On that same day, January 12, 1921, the Judge signed his agreement with the 16 major league clubs, and formally took charge of baseball. Again that doughty old Fed from St. Louis, Phil Ball, refused to take part in the ceremony. The signatures of 13 club presidents were put on the document. In the case of the St. Louis Browns, it again was signed by Vice President Bob Quinn.

Landis was elected for a term of seven years, and was eligible to succeed himself. His salary was fixed at $50,000 per annum, and he was officially named "the first Commissioner." He was granted autocratic power over everyone in baseball, from the humblest bat boy to a major league president, and the club owners, for themselves as well as their league, waived all recourse to the courts of the land no matter what would be the severity of the new Commissioner's discipline.

The public was pleased and the nation's press predicted a new and better era for the game. The late Will Rogers, quaint Oklahoma cowboy-philosopher, put it this way: "Baseball needed a touch of class and distinction. So somebody said: 'Get that old boy who sits behind first base all the time. He's out there every day anyhow.' So they offered him a season's pass and he jumped at it. But don't kid yourself that that old judicial bird isn't going to make those baseball birds walk the chalk-line."

In the January 20, 1921 issue of *The Sporting News,* our Chicago correspondent wrote: "Judge Landis in accepting office outlined his plans for the government of the game, dwelling particularly on the big reason for him entering into it, which is to clean out the crookedness and the gambling responsible for it and keep the sport above reproach. The Judge made it plain he would have no mercy on any man in baseball, be he magnate or player, whose conduct was not strictly honest. They must avoid even the appearance of evil or feel the iron hand of his power to throw them out of any part of the game. The Judge will be absolute ruler of the game."

Landis originally opened his baseball offices in the Peoples Gas Building on Michigan Boulevard, but later shifted his Chicago headquarters to the 333 North Michigan Building. He was un-decided for some time what to put on his office door.

"I gave it a lot of thought," he once said. "I could have put on High Commissioner, or head man of the Advisory Council, but they were high-sounding titles, and didn't mean a whole lot. So one night I had a happy thought. I thought why in the hell not call the place just 'Baseball.'" And that's what went on Landis' door, just "Baseball," and for a quarter of a century he was pretty near baseball.

He originally offered the job of secretary to John H. Farrell, of Auburn, N.Y., secretary-treasurer of the National Association. who died May 17, 1944. The full title would have been Secretary-Treasurer of the Advisory Council. John made several trips to Chicago, but turned it down. He didn't like to leave Auburn; neither did Mrs. Farrell. And Farrell at the time was a little czar of his own and pretty well ran things in the minor league world. That is one of the reasons that Landis wanted him: because of his vast acquaintance with minor league people and knowledge of minor league affairs.

I once asked genial John whether he ever regretted that he didn't hook up with Landis. After giving almost his lifetime to minor league baseball, Farrell was shuffled rather unceremoniously out of the deck at the twilight of his career. But, he had no re-grets, though he said that working with the Judge would have been a great experience.

"Perhaps I should have joined him back there in 1921, as I later was arrested with him anyway," laughed John. "George F. John-son, the millionaire shoe man, who was president of our Bing-hamton club at the time, was making a presentation to the Ameri-can Legion posts of Binghamton, Endicott and Johnson City, at Whitney's Point, N.Y. The Judge and I were motoring there to participate in the ceremonies. We didn't think we were driving fast, but a hick cop came from behind a haystack and said we had violated the law. We told him we were in a hurry, and he said he was sorry but we would have to accompany him to the Justice of the Peace.

77

"Anyway, with the Judge grumbling, the copper took us back to some farm house which had a 'Justice of the Peace' tag on it. His Honor wasn't home, and they had to call him in from the fields. When he came to hear our case, he apologized for being late, and then asked: 'Will you gentlemen have a piece of strawberry shortcake?' After we all had our cake, he proceeded with the case.

"Pointing to me, Judge Landis said: 'This man is my attorney, and he will see that my Constitutional rights are upheld.'

" 'Well, the officer says you were driving too fast, and I'll have to fine each of you $5.00,' said the Justice.

" 'We demand a trial by a jury,' I said, as counsel for our side.

" 'You're making a lot of fuss over such a little case,' said the Rube justice. 'I'd let you fellows go, but I've got to give this man (pointing to the farmer cop) half of the fines he brings in.'

"Landis then stepped in, and looking the Justice of the Peace square in the eye, he said sharply: 'I demand this case go to trial.' However, as we were losing time and had to get to Whitney's Point for the ceremony, we eventually paid our fines under protest.

"But, whenever I met Judge Landis after that, he always inquired whether that piece of strawberry shortcake was worth $5.00."

With John Farrell, a veteran experienced baseball man, turning down the secretaryship, Landis went to the other extreme. John Heydler recommended John B. Foster, former secretary of the New York Giants, who had a long career in sports journalism as a baseball writer, sports editor and editor of Spalding's Guide. Landis brushed him aside, and appointed a young Chicago attorney, Leslie M. O'Connor, who had impressed him while practicing law in his Federal court.

"A number of men were suggested to me," said Landis, "but, after Farrell rejected the job, I didn't want anyone representing some particular faction in baseball. I wanted a Landis man, and I got such a man in O'Connor."

O'Connor served Landis zealously during his entire quarter of a century in office, growing up from an eager, boyish-looking young lawyer to a middle-aged, plump, semi-baseball executive.

He did most of Landis' leg work and did the spade work in most of his big investigations. He served the Commissioner so well and faithfully that he made many enemies for himself. And, until Judge Landis breathed his last late in 1944, Leslie O'Connor was Judge Landis' man.

I met Landis for the first time when he made his first visit to St. Louis in his new role as Commissioner. He was staying at the Statler Hotel. There were a lot of other newspapermen in the room. Though I was the young publisher of baseball's publication, the new head of the game paid no particular attention to me, nor, for that matter, to any of the other St. Louis sports writers. John B. Sheridan, a popular, erudite Mound City sports scribe, who did a double column for our editorial page, did most of the talking. John was a versatile chap with an eloquent tongue as well as a gifted pen.

My only other contact with Judge Landis for years thereafter came when I asked him about publishing the findings of his office, similar to the arrangement we had for years with the old National Commission.

No one endeavored to bring us together. I would see Landis at World's Series and baseball meetings; he would see me, but we never exchanged any recognition. During that time my newspaper printed thousands of words on Judge Landis and his administration, and my editors and correspondents were in frequent contact with him. However, he seemed to soften up when I saw him at the Joe Louis-Battling Levinsky fight at the White Sox park in Chicago on August 7, 1935. As I recall it, it took Joe, then first attracting attention, about 60 seconds to flatten the Battler. I was sitting near the Judge, and the shortness of the fight seemed to hit him as amusing. "Well, Spink, they knocked that pitcher out of the box early," he laughed.

Needless to say, many pitchers were knocked out of the box, some by the Judge's decrees, between that early meeting with the St. Louis sports scribes at the Statler and the rout of Levinsky.

11 : The Judge and Ban Johnson in Early Tangle

The first big matter confronting the new Commissioner was the unfinished business of the Black Sox scandal. Melodramatic situations were springing up daily in the case as the Lasker Planners were trying to bring Judge Landis into baseball, and between November 12, when the Judge accepted the Commissionership, and January 12, 1921, when he signed his agreement with the big leaguers.

On October 22, 1920, the Chicago grand jury voted its indictments against 13 persons, including the eight accused Black Sox. On October 26, Arnold Rothstein, the New York gambler, accused by many as being the master mind in the "Big Fix," was exonerated by the grand jury. Rothstein's tale in court was that Abe Attell and Bill Burns had approached him with the proposition to finance the White Sox throwdown, saying it could be done for $100,000. Rothstein testified he turned it down flat, and was so convinced that a Series couldn't be fixed that he bet $6,000 on the White Sox. However, I always thought the unsavory Rothstein knew far more than he pretended. Certainly Hughie Fullerton always thought so, as did Frank Menke.

Joe Gedeon, second baseman of the St. Louis Browns, testified before the jury that he had bet $700 on the Reds on the tip of a White Sox player, who said the club wasn't as good as generally supposed, and Joe said he didn't know the Series was crooked until the third game. Then he admitted he foolishly attended a meeting at the Hotel Sherman in Chicago, at the instigation of two St. Louis gambler friends, where a further effort was made to raise another $25,000 for the White Sox "throwers." The story always was that these White Sox culprits were double-crossed, and never got anywhere near the money they expected to get. I always have believed this to be the case. Gedeon willingly came from Sacramento to Chicago to tell what he knew, but baseball later tossed him out for having guilty knowledge of the nasty business. The jury ended its work on October 29, and made its final report to Chief Justice McDonald, November 6.

On November 16, four days after Landis unofficially took over baseball's government, Hoyne, the State's attorney, resigned to return to private practice. Some persons thought Hoyne had been lukewarm in the matter, inasmuch as he permitted one of his assistants, Hartley L. Replogle, to conduct the gambling investigation. Then, shortly after the shift in the chief prosecutor's office, came the most startling development. It became known that all the papers in the District Attorney's office relating to the gambling cases—including the confessions of Cicotte, Williams and Jackson—had been stolen.

At first a secret was made of the mysterious disappearance of the papers. Ban Johnson seems to be one of the first who heard of it, and immediately notified Landis, and the new Commissioner quickly said that if it was found that any of the evidence had been tampered with, or was missing, he would insist that Federal action be taken against the guilty persons. Landis certainly was sincere in his remarks, but the thieves who stole the papers never were apprehended.

But copies of the indictments got around, and reached New York. About this time, the Chicago *Tribune* wrote to the new District Attorney Crowe as follows: "The New York *Herald*, through its syndicate, has offered us copies of the Grand Jury records as they concern the indictments of the crooked ball players in the World's Series of 1919. They offer this to us in eight installments, for the total sum of $25,000. What would happen if we bought the Chicago rights to this material and published it?"

Not so long thereafter, Johnson publicly charged that the papers were stolen and that Arnold Rothstein paid $10,000 for the papers. The New York gambler issued a wildly-worded denial and said he would sue Johnson for $100,000 libel.

"I hope he sues," said Ban. "Then I can get him into court, and learn a few things I want to learn."

Rothstein never filed the suit.

After Crowe found he couldn't locate the papers, he advised Johnson: "There is nothing for me to do but dismiss the indictments, inasmuch with the records gone, we have no case against the men. When that is done, it will be necessary to build up an entirely new case against those men."

If there had been any chance for Landis and Ban Johnson getting along, it blew up in a vitriolic smoke around that time. Johnson was mortified when Landis was selected in a meeting from which he was excluded; he saw his old crown as Czar of Baseball taken off his head and placed on the white, shaggy-haired dome of the Chicago judge, but I think he was prepared to play ball with Landis during baseball's troublesome time.

Several years later when the gulf between the two men became unbridgeable, I asked Ban point-blank the reason for his continuous feud with the Judge.

"When the Black Sox scandal broke, the American League voted to prosecute the crooked players," he replied. "Those men had let down the game, and our league, and I wanted them punished to the full extent of the law. Landis had just come into office, and he was given the job. After several months had passed, I asked him what he was doing about the case, and he said, 'Nothing.'

"I took the case away from him, prosecuted it with the funds of the American League, and never again asked him to help. I decided he didn't want to co-operate, and I never felt the same towards him after that."

Judge Landis no doubt had his reasons. As a fan and a Chicagoan, he was as much exercised over the cupidity of the erring players as the American League president, and while the accused athletes were awaiting trial, the Commissioner announced that regardless of the outcome of the court proceedings, the accused octet never again would play in Organized Baseball. But Landis had become the game's court. With the original Grand Jury indictments and other papers gone, perhaps he felt baseball's case would be weak, and convictions couldn't be obtained. And he resented any prodding by Johnson. If Ban didn't like the Judge, the dislike was mutual. And perhaps the Judge wanted to show Ban immediately that he was the new boss of baseball—with no divided authority.

Crowe had pointed out to Johnson that an indictment must be returned within 18 months of the time the crime was committed. The "crime," the thrown World's Series, had taken place in October, 1919, and the time limit ended in April, 1921—a matter of a few weeks.

It was this disinclination of Landis to act, while the weeks were slipping by, that further irked Johnson. He got busy, jumped on a train for Texas, induced Bill Burns to come back from Mexico, traveled 10,000 miles, and spent thousands of dollars, much of it his own, and by March 26, aided by the fine support of the new District Attorney Crowe, and his assistant, John Tyrell, he submitted enough evidence to the Grand Jury to reindict not only the original thirteen men, but five other gamblers from the middle west.

The eight Black Sox and their gambling associates went on trial in July, 1921, on a charge of criminal conspiracy. Bill Burns, former American League pitcher, was the prosecution's chief witness. He told the sordid story of the fixing in the court. However, failure to bring Abe Attell within Illinois jurisdiction, or to get his sworn statement, weakened the prosecution's case, as did inability to introduce the stolen signed confessions of the Chicago players. On August 2, the jury returned a verdict of "not guilty," in so far as criminal conduct on the part of the players and alleged gamblers was concerned.

If there was any doubt as to whom the erring players held to be their implacable foe it was revealed in a wild scene in the courtroom after the acquittal. The players had many friends in court; it was most disgusting—some of them treated the acquitted players as though they were returning heroes. There was hand-shaking, back-slapping, and other jubilation. And above the din could be heard the voice of Arnold "Chick" Gandil, the first baseman, and generally considered the leader of the Black Sox. "Boys, I want to give you a sailor's farewell," he shouted. "Goodbye; good luck; and to hell with Ban Johnson." And, in a statement to the press, Chick said: "I guess that will learn Ban Johnson that he can't frame an honest bunch of players." A rather disheartening sequel of the trial is that after the verdict the jury and the acquitted players adjourned to an Italian restaurant in Chicago's West Side and made whoopee far into the night.

Justice Charles McDonald, who directed the first Grand Jury investigation, expressed disappointment at the verdict, but felt that it had helped clear the air over baseball and saw a cleansing of the game. "The Grand Jury investigation and prosecution that followed put the fear of God and the law in the hearts of crooked gamblers and shady players and has purged baseball for a generation to come," declared McDonald. "While the club owners have sustained some monetary loss while the trial was in progress, I believe our national sport would have gone the way of horse racing and boxing due to the same baneful influence had not the strong arm of the law been extended to save it. I am pleased to note that those in control of baseball and club owners interested have decided for all time to keep shady players from the game. I am sure the young men and boys of the country will welcome the purging and will again have confidence in the great American sport."

Judge Landis quickly took care of the purging, and immediately advised the American League public that no player even remotely connected with the fix again would be received back in baseball. He issued the following statement: "Regardless of the verdict of juries, no player that throws a ball game, no player that entertains proposals or promises to throw a game, no player that sits in a conference with a bunch of crooked players and gamblers where the ways and means of throwing games are discussed, and does not promptly tell his club about it, will ever play professional baseball. Of course, I do not know that any of these men will apply for reinstatement, but if they do the above are at least a few of the rules that will be enforced. Just keep in mind that regardless of the verdict of juries, baseball is entirely competent to protect itself against the crooks both inside and outside the game."

If Landis, on the surface, was not as active as Johnson in prosecuting the Black Sox, there never was any leniency on the Judge's part toward the culprits in the many years that followed. Every now and then moves were afoot to obtain pardons for some of the players. They said Joe Jackson, a poor, illiterate South Carolina mill-hand when he first came into baseball, didn't know what he was doing, and had been badly led and advised by more worldly, cunning and avaricious fellow players. But the Judge was adamant.

The biggest case for a pardon was built up for Buck Weaver, and a request for the great infielder's reinstatement was signed by 12,000 Chicagoans. Weaver, who hit .324 in the Series, always claimed that, while he was in attendance at the meeting where it was agreed to throw the Series, he had no part of it, took no money, and always played to win. Landis met a committee of the petitioners, and said that Weaver's very presence at the meeting was sufficient to convict him.

Even bringing up the names of some of those expelled White Sox players annoyed him. Years after the White Sox scandal, the trial and acquittal, we ran a feature story in *The Sporting News* on Joe Jackson. It was in the late summer of 1942. Shoeless Joe was a partly toothless middle-aged man, who ran a liquor store down in South Carolina. In addition to some of his baseball pictures, we ran a picture of Joe in his store behind some of his liquid merchandise. It wasn't a boost for Jackson, nor a plea for reinstatement, but a human interest story on what became of a great star who had made one bad mistake. Jackson was one of the few players I got to know well and I always felt that he was unwittingly taken into the alleged Black Sox ring. And after all, this is a live and let live world, with little to be gained by further booting a guy who is down. But the Judge was reported to have hit the ceiling when he saw Jackson on our front page, and said the "judgment and tact of that man, Spink, in using such an article was deplorable."

Landis never cared for racing; and, it is said, he based his feeling on his experience as an attorney for the Pinkertons, following disclosures made of race fixing in the early 90's. "There are too many questionable characters around a track—gamblers, touts, racketeers, men who wouldn't know how to make an honest living," he once said. Though admitting that some of our very best people were race track patrons and attendants, he never mentioned "the Sport of Kings" without wrinkling up his nose as though he had smelled something quite offensive to his nostrils. He always felt that the Black Sox frame-up was engineered by racing habitues, men who in his own picturesque language "would sell out their mothers or the Virgin Mary."

Illustrating his point by the use of his extended fingers, he said: "These vermin no doubt got so double-crossed by other crooks on the track that it no longer was profitable, so they tried to entwine their slimy fingers around baseball. But, by God, so long as I have anything to do with this game, they'll never get another hold on it."

That was the reason for his almost fanatical attitude against anyone even remotely connected with racing having any financial interest in baseball, and his continual cracking down on umpires and players who liked to follow the ponies. Some fine people, it is said, including the popular song-bird, Bing Crosby, were kept out of baseball because the Judge detected the odor of a racing stable on their well-groomed clothes. However, Landis' successor, A. B. Chandler, took a more liberal view and permitted Crosby to buy into the Pittsburgh club in 1946.

Exasperated by the fact that some players and umpires felt he was interfering with their Constitutional and free inalienable rights, when he requested them to keep out of tracks during the winter off-season, the Judge exclaimed: "The God damn fools; don't they know I am doing this for their own protection?"

In his first season as Commissioner, 1921, Landis had an immediate racing problem in the family of his club owners. John J. McGraw, vice president and manager of the New York Giants, long had spent his winter vacations in Havana, Cuba, and since his playing days with the old Orioles, McGraw was an inveterate racing fan. Shortly after the war, he saw an opportunity to buy Oriental Park, the Havana race track, along with the Cuban-American Jockey Club with its valuable Casino gambling house concessions. It was in the lush post-war years, when American prohibition sent many well-to-do American play-boys and play-girls to Cuba for recreation, diversion and unadulterated liquor. It looked like a gold mine.

86

McGraw, of course, didn't have the money to swing it, but his wealthy baseball partner, Charles Stoneham, did. McGraw had good political connections in Cuba, and with Stoneham putting up most of the cash, they acquired the track, the Jockey Club and Casino in 1920. Stoneham even purchased the English language newspaper in Havana, the Havana *Post*.

No doubt, it didn't strike these men that they were doing anything detrimental to baseball, especially as they were purchasing their track in a foreign country. They saw a good chance to make money, and McGraw enjoyed his comparatively brief role as vice president of the Jockey Club. Baseball men frequently had had racing interests. Frank Farrell, the first owner of the New York Highlanders (now the Yankees), had a string of race horses, and once ran a gambling house in New York. Chris Von der Ahe, the owner of the original St. Louis Browns and later the St. Louis Nationals, had a race track as well as a ball club. Ruppert and Stoneham, the wealthy owners of the rival New York clubs, both owned racing stables before they came into baseball. Frank Navin of Detroit also had been interested in racing, and his wife owned a stable.

But Judge Landis soon called Stoneham and McGraw to Chicago, and advised them that in his administration racing and baseball would not mix. He didn't issue an ultimatum, but made it plain to the New Yorkers that it would have to be the New York ball club or the Havana race track. With McGraw, baseball was his business, and his entire life was wrapped around the Giants; it left him with no alternative. The Giant owners got rid of their Havana properties.

Stoneham was charged with another indiscretion the same season, 1921, that got very much under Landis' skin. I don't know who was more worked up, Landis or Ban Johnson. Ban almost exploded when he heard of it. On a summer afternoon, who should sun himself in Stoneham's private box at the Polo Grounds—right next to the Giant dugout—but the notorious Arnold Rothstein, who despite his denial of any guilt in the Black Sox business was associated in the public mind as the "brain" of the Big Fix.

Stoneham's explanation was that he had had business dealings with Rothstein; the latter had had a brokerage account with the Stoneham firm, and as I recall it the two men had owned some mining properties. Stoneham also said the Chicago Grand Jury had exonerated Rothstein. But Landis was considerably annoyed—and riled. I don't know what the Judge said to the father of the present Giant owner, but that was the last time Arnold Rothstein ever saw a game from Stoneham's box.

12: Landis Sets Some Precedents

In the season of 1921, Landis still was feeling his way, but he was setting precedents which were to stand during the remainder of his 23 years at the head of the game, and which Senator Chandler, his successor, said would remain in force unless he saw fit to change them. The Judge had many vexing problems, and also was looking into the cases of ball players who had been passed quietly out of the leagues, apparently dropped for the good of the game. "There will be no more of this," he said. "If a player is dropped from baseball, he will know all about it, and the public will know it; also why he no longer is wanted."

In his first decision as Commissioner, it is interesting to recall that Landis spanked Branch Rickey, present impresario of the Dodgers, who in 1920 was vice president-manager of the Cardinals, after being president from 1917 to 1919. Sam Breadon took over the Cardinal presidency in 1920, but still was more interested in his automobile business, and Rickey ran the club. It was the first of Branch's numerous appearances in the Judge's baseball court, and the charge usually was the same—covering up young ball players.

Both St. Louis clubs, the Cardinals and Browns, claimed a young first baseman, Phil Todt, a St. Louis boy, who later became regular first baseman on the Red Sox. Rickey apparently picked up the lad off the St. Louis sandlots when Phil was only seventeen years old. Todt was released unconditionally, first to the Sherman, Tex., club of the Western Association, and later to Houston of the Texas League. The evidence showed he signed no contract and played with neither club; nor did either club advise John Farrell, the minor league secretary, of the player's release. In the meantime, the St. Louis Browns signed the young player in the middle of the 1920 season, and both Mound City clubs wrangled for the services of the youngster. They appealed to what was left of the old National Commission, Presidents Heydler and Johnson, who couldn't agree, and the case was in the new Commissioner's lap as soon as he assumed office.

The Judge ruled against Branch, and in favor of Phil Ball, the

Brown's fire-eating owner, and the only club president who declined to sign the agreement with Landis. In his finding, he said that Rickey had had secret agreements with both the Sherman and Houston clubs, that "the various transfers to which player Todt had been subjected were simply colorable and therefore void; that Todt was made a free agent by the arrangement between Rickey and the Sherman club"; and that "Todt was a free agent when signed by the St. Louis American League club in whom clear title was invested."

One of the first players to feel the Commissioner's wrath was Benny Kauff, the Giant outfielder, and former "Ty Cobb of the Feds." Benny was a fair player, but never as good as he thought he was, nor as good as his Federal League averages made him look. Still he was good enough to play center field on McGraw's championship club of 1917, and he hit two home runs in one World's Series game that year. Benny was in the Army in 1918, and after the war he apparently started running around with the wrong kind of people.

Kauff's name appeared several times in the Chicago Grand Jury investigation; he testified in regard to gambling activities of two of his 1919 Giant teammates, Hal Chase and Heinie Zimmerman, and McGraw, in turn, testified that he believed Benny to be an honest player. Kauff, in the meantime, had gotten into a bad jam in his own town, New York, and was arrested on the charge that he had stolen an automobile and had received stolen goods (also cars) in December, 1919. Benny's play suffered in 1920, and he was optioned to Toronto for part of the season and then recalled.

Benny was out on bail, and was ready to accompany the Giants on their 1921 training trip, but word came to McGraw from Landis' office that, pending the outcome of the trial, Kauff wasn't to play with the New Yorks. The trial got under way in Bronx County Court, and on May 13, 1921, Benny was acquitted. He had been defended by Judge Emil F. Fuchs, later president of the Boston Braves, and it was generally believed that character testimony in Kauff's behalf by John K. Tener, former president of the National League, John McGraw and fellow Giant players had much to do with his acquittal.

Kauff, at the instigation of the New York club, applied immediately for reinstatement after the acquittal, but the Judge refused even after Benny made a personal appeal. He didn't say at the time why he was keeping Kauff out of baseball, but asked that all the papers in the stolen automobile case be sent to him. Landis later said to Fred Lieb of *The Sporting News* staff, but then with the *New York Evening Telegram:* "I read every line of that testimony, and the acquittal smells to high heaven. That acquittal was one of the worst miscarriages of justice that ever came under my observation."

Later in the year, Benny went into a New York court, and procured a temporary injunction restraining Judge Landis and John Heydler from preventing him from playing in the National League. If Kauff won the first round, he lost the second. The hearing to make the injunction permanent was postponed until November 22, when Judge Whittaker ended the case by refusing the injunction. Landis wasn't in the court, but he was ably represented by John Conway Toole, then National League attorney and president of the International League.

In the arguments before Judge Whittaker, Toole introduced a letter which Landis had written to Kauff, August 25, which among other things said "the evidence in the Bronx County case disclosed a state of affairs that more than seriously compromises your character and reputation.

"The reasonable and necessary result of this is that your mere presence in the line-up would inevitably burden patrons of the game with grave apprehension as to its integrity."

In his answer to Kauff's suit, Landis also said: "Kauff could not be restored to good standing without impairing the morale of the other players and without further injury to the good name of professional baseball."

The expulsion of Kauff was early evidence of the tremendous power which baseball had given to the new Commissioner, and his "life or death" authority over everyone in the game. There never were any charges brought against Kauff's ball playing. And regardless of what Landis thought of that Bronx jury, it had acquitted Benny, and as far as the law was concerned the little

91

center fielder was innocent. But Landis decided Kauff no longer was a fit companion of other players, and at the age of thirty-one, Benny's baseball career was blacked out.

The Giants seemed to be getting regularly into Landis' tousled white hair in his first season, or perhaps it would be more accurate to say that he got into the hair of Stoneham and McGraw. The Giants were getting terrific competition from their tenants, the Yankees, in the battle for Polo Grounds patronage. Babe Ruth, who had cracked out 54 home runs in 1920, was boosting it to new heights in 1921, and eventually finished with 59. And the Yanks were in a race which was to bring them their first pennant. The Giants, once the overlords of New York baseball, were falling well behind the Yankee upstarts in attendance and gate receipts.

McGraw was making every effort to strengthen his club. His club was running second in June, but Pittsburgh, the leader, was far ahead and threatened to make a runaway race of it. Heinie Groh, the great third baseman of the Cincinnati Reds, had been a determined holdout all through the training season, and after the playing season was launched the controversy between Groh and Garry Herrmann, the Cincinnati president, took on added heat and intensity. Early June passed, and Heinie still was unsigned. The Cincinnati board of directors held several meetings, expressed their general dissatisfaction with the entire business, and authorized Herrmann to dispose of Groh, if he could make an advantageous deal.

In the meantime, Groh broke into print with an ultimatum, saying he would sign with the Cincinnati club only on condition that he would be traded.

McGraw had had Groh as a young player in New York, before Heinie developed into stardom on the Reds. He called up Herrmann, and said: "Groh is doing you no good—sitting in his apartment. I can satisfy him, and I am willing to make a profitable deal with you."

A tentative Giant-Red deal then was agreed upon, and the newspapers at the time speculated that McGraw would give up $100,000, Goldie Rapp, his starting third baseman; Outfielder

Curt Walker and Catcher Mike Gonzalez, until 1947 Cardinal coach and now the operator of the Havana club in Cuba, for the return of Groh. As is often the case with such big deals, the story popped ahead of time—before the officials of the two clubs could confirm the deal.

Landis no doubt had been watching the case, but with the reporting of the proposed trade, he swung into action. He first called off the deal, and secondly, he ruled that for the balance of the season Heinie Groh could play for no other club than Cincinnati. He felt it was an "unhealthy situation if a dissatisfied player could dictate his transfer to a strong contender before he agreed to sign a contract."

Then he added: "However, this is not to be regarded as establishing a precedent for cases arising hereafter." But, it served as a precedent for the balance of his term—no holdout player has been permitted to dictate his transfer to a contending club.

After Landis nixed the first Groh deal, McGraw procured Johnny Rawlings, a stop-gap infielder, from the Phillies for Rapp, two outfielders, Lance Richbourg and Lee King, and $20,000, and at the end of the season, after Landis' ban on a Groh deal expired, the Giant manager obtained Heinie's services from the Reds for that $100,000 check, the popular outfielder, Georgie Burns, and Mike Gonzalez.

However, later in the 1921 season, the Judge found it necessary to scrutinize carefully another of McGraw's transactions, this one involving Emil "Irish" Meusel, the former slugging Philadelphia National outfielder. My Pittsburgh correspondent, Charles "Chilly" Doyle, still can work himself into a froth over that deal. Unquestionably, it cost the Pirates the 1921 National League pennant.

William F. Baker, the Philadelphia club owner, who always was selling his top-ranking players, said he reached a point where he "no longer could endure the sight of Meusel." With the Phillies in their usual cellar position, that apparently was all right with "Irish," the best batter on the club, who had seen one of his fellow stars, Shortstop Dave Bancroft, sold to the Giants the year before for $100,000. Being kicked upstairs from a chronic cellar-dweller to a club which almost invariably was in the money wasn't hard to take.

After being benched for a few days, Meusel was traded to the Giants for Outfielder Curt Walker, two players out on option—Catcher Butch Henline and Pitcher Jesse Winters—and $30,000. Not long after Emil Meusel joined New York, the Giants—with "Irish" blazing away with from both barrels—wrecked the Pirates at the Polo Grounds by cleaning them up in a five-game series. That whittled Pittsburgh's lead down from seven games to two, and New York went on to win the 1921 pennant and World's Series.

The Sporting News apparently didn't think so much of the deal, for in its issue of August 4, 1921, under the heading: "Reward for 'Indifference,'" we ran the following: "Mr. William Baker of the Phillies says Emil (Irish) Meusel acted so 'indifferent' concerning the success of the team that he couldn't endure the sight of him any longer, so last week, a few days before the time limit for making such deals, Baker traded his great hitter and capable outfielder to the New York Giants for a rookie bench warmer and a catcher who isn't even in the big leagues.

"Of course, nobody believes Mr. Baker when he says he had to rid the Phillies of Meusel for the team's good. If that really was the case he would be subject to severe censure for thus rewarding a bad actor. As it is, the only censure is that it aids John McGraw's Giants when they need aid so badly. As for Meusel, the innocent cause of the rumpus, it's all to his advantage any way you look at it. He goes from a club that any real ball player is ashamed to associate with to a possible contender. He is dead certain to land as high as third money. He's saying nothing in his own defense regarding Baker's charges against him—probably does not think any remarks are necessary."

Landis did not act immediately on the Meusel deal, though there were later repercussions that brought him strongly into the Philadelphia picture. He said later the Meusel deal never should have gone through. I feel in later years he never would have approved of it. It may be that having thrown Kauff out of baseball and nixed

94

the first Groh deal, he didn't want to appear in the role of persecuting the Giants and their owners.

Philadelphia fans, as well as the Quaker City sports writers, were pretty well worked up over the Meusel business, as it followed a series of other deals whereby Baker had sold the cream of his club to teams higher in the standing. Shortly after the deal, Baker let out his manager, the popular Smiling Bill Donovan, a native Philadelphian, with a legion of friends. Donovan had been called to Chicago as a witness in the Black Sox trial.

Before Baker officially fired Bill, the manager broke the story to Philadelphia writers in Buffalo, saying that Baker had relieved him because he knew gamblers and had been expected to testify at the White Sox trial concerning their operations.

The import of Donovan's remarks was that he wasn't any more acquainted with gamblers than any other man of sporting blood, and that Baker had used the fact that he had been called to Chicago to testify as an excuse to ease him out of the Philadelphia managerial picture. He pointed out that his contract with Baker was for one year, and that he had called on Judge Landis to see that his contractual rights were respected.

Landis always had been a great admirer of Donovan, both as a ball player and a man. He had seen him pitch his two-hit shutout against the White Sox in the final game of the 1908 season, when a Tiger pennant hinged on the outcome, and had seen him suffer some heart-breaking losses to his old favorites, the Cubs, in the 1907 and 1908 World's Series. He sent Leslie O'Connor to get Donovan's version of his break with Baker, also Bill's views of the Meusel deal.

The Judge learned that Donovan never suspended Meusel for indifferent play, nor had he reported such indifferent play to his club owner. There was a question of veracity between Baker and Donovan as to a meeting to which Bill had been called to discuss Meusel's status. The manager claimed he never had received a telegram asking him to attend such a meeting, saying "I never ran out on a meeting in my life." Press reports of the time said that both Landis and O'Connor were in Donovan's corner, and the Judge saw to it that Donovan was paid in full for the 1921 season. And Landis was as irked as Wild Bill when Baker made the announcement: "Donovan's activities with the Philadelphia National League club for the balance of the season will be limited to the endorsement of his pay check every two weeks—provided, however, that he does not break any rules of Organized Baseball."

The last line was especially in bad taste, for though Donovan had a Philadelphia reputation as a man about town, he was a teetotaler throughout his entire career as player and manager.

Landis was learning more about the men who had selected him to run their game. Baker, a former New York City Police Commissioner, was chairman of the temporary meeting in Chicago, November 12, 1920, when the club owners first decided to adopt the Lasker plan and offer Landis the Commissionership. However, Landis never liked Baker after the Meusel deal and the Donovan firing. Impressions stuck vividly in his active mind, and by nature he was a man who never forgot and rarely forgave.

Landis really had been coming into conflict with Baker all through that season. On March 21, a fortnight before the start of the season, he tossed the Phillies' first baseman, Eugene Paulette, out of the game for life. However, in justice to Baker, he approved of the Commissioner's action. Paulette had been with the Cardinals before a deal in July, 1919, sent him to the Phillies.

In announcing that Paulette had been placed on the dreaded ineligible list of baseball, the Judge said the player had "offered to betray his team, and had put himself in the vicious power of the alleged gamblers." Paulette's misconduct was in the early part of the 1919 season, before Rickey traded him to the Philadelphia club. He was accused of accepting gifts or loans from two St. Louis gamblers, Elmer Farrar and Carl Zork. The latter was one of the men who later went on trial with the Black Sox octet in Chicago. In giving Paulette the "death sentence"—as far as his baseball career was concerned—the Judge again castigated his old enemies, the gambling fraternity, saying: "My only regret is that the real culprits, the gamblers, cannot be reached by this office."

The Judge also ruled against Baker and the Phillies—and in favor of the Indianapolis Club, in a case that attracted wide attention—far more than the amount of money involved warranted. It was called the Leo Callahan case, and was important, as it set another Landis precedent. In 1920 the Indianapolis club purchased Callahan, a run-of-the-mine outfielder-pitcher, from the Phillies for $1,500. The player failed to report, and the Hoosiers asked for the return of their $1,500.

There were some interesting circumstances, and a pretty good sidelight on the Baker methods of running his club. The Indianapolis club testified that it offered Callahan a $300 bonus to sign, and offered him $500 a month, which was $100 a month more than his Philadelphia National salary. However, the player apparently had a grudge against Baker and refused to sign or report to Indianapolis unless Baker gave him $200 of the $1,500 purchase price. Baker refused to cough up, and the player stayed at home. One of Baker's arguments was that the National Agreement was not in force in 1920—after the break-up of the old National Commission. Landis ordered Baker to return the $1,500 to the Hoosiers.

During his time on the federal bench, it often was said of Landis that while he could be almost sentimentally lenient—as in the case of the freight car sugar thieves and the boy who stole $750,000 in Liberty bonds—he could be one of the toughest judges in all the United States courts. The Judge literally and figuratively threw the book at them.

I always thought he threw the book at Ray Fisher, the respected baseball coach at the University of Michigan, one of Branch Rickey's old jobs, and where Ray in 1946 put in his twenty-sixth season. And a decision by Landis in 1921 was largely responsible for Fisher's long tenure at Ann Arbor. A Middlebury College boy, Fisher was a successful pitcher with the New York Yankees before World War I; he was in the Army in 1918, and was released to the Reds after the war. He pitched on the 1919 Cincinnati World's Champions, the club which profited by the Black Sox sellout. However, Fisher getting into Landis' bad graces had nothing to do with this unhappy Series.

Fisher refused to report to the Reds in the Spring of 1921, taking the Michigan coaching job. Ray also had been dissatisfied with his terms, and there were some reports he would jump to an independent team in Franklin, Pa. When the college season was nearly over in May, Fisher applied to Landis for reinstatement. Garry Herrmann of the Reds then advised Landis that the Cincinnati club had offered Fisher an advance of $1,000 on his signed contract as a guarantee that he would not jump. The Commissioner then made the pitcher's ineligibility permanent, a drastic penalty for his offense. Fisher at the time was only thirty-three, with another seven or eight years of pitching ahead of him. In the same year, 1921, Landis also barred Pitcher Phil Weinert of the Philadelphia Nationals five years for contract jumping. Weinert, however, was reinstated the next season.

And Landis also cracked down hard on the old so-called "gentlemen's agreements," then very much in vogue in baseball, where one club owner released a player to one of his fellows, later expecting to have the player returned. He held these "gentlemen's agreements" were plainly in violation of the optional agreement rules, and made free agents of some of the lesser fry in baseball.

In his contact with the minors, he came out strongly in favor of the old draft system, and insisted it was a "strictly fair American system," and the only one that made sure players had their opportunity in baseball. During the chaotic situation in 1920, resulting from the abrogation of the old National Agreement, five of the minor leagues, the three AA's—the International and Pacific Coast Leagues and the American Association; the Class A Western League and the Class B Indiana-Illinois-Iowa League, refused to accept the draft. Jack Dunn, former player and owner-manager of the Baltimore Internationals, was the most vociferous fighter among the non-draft people. However, Landis left no doubt where his sympathies rested.

"A situation where a group of ball players can be boxed into a minor league, and can advance higher only at the whim of their employer, is intolerable and un-American," he said with his usual vehemence. "So long as I am in this job, I will fight for the full restoration of the draft."

From the start, Landis was a stout defender of the game which had honored him and made him its supreme dictator. A distinguished group of Federal judges threw a dinner for him at Fort

Worth not so long after he officially took over in baseball in 1921. And the Judge, who still was on the bench, let his colleagues know just what he thought of his new interest, and he contrasted it with other fields of human endeavor.

"Gentlemen, you all know the new activity that I have entered into," he said. "And, you doubtlessly have read some of the things about some of the persons in baseball. Much that you have read is correct. But, if you think that this was typical of baseball, I want to set you right. I've known and followed this game pretty intimately since I was a boy, and I looked into it very thoroughly before I accepted their offer. So, I would like to say this in behalf of ball players: Notwithstanding what recently has happened, I believe there is a higher degree of honesty in the profession of playing ball than there is in any other that I know. And I do not except the clergy or the judiciary."

In later relating the incident to baseball writers, the Judge said: "I don't believe all those fellows down there liked that. But, in our more intimate get-together after the formal dinner, no one challenged my statement or asked me to present any figures."

13 : Ruth Gets in the Judge's Hair

There has been a lot of comment by veteran sports writers as to who saved baseball after the great scandal broke in 1920. One school of thought always has contended that it was the white-haired jurist from Chicago; another has argued with equal vehemence that it was the former chubby urchin from the Baltimore waterfront, George Herman "Babe" Ruth. Knowing my baseball history from 'way back, and that the game has survived some critical periods, I always have felt it would have muddled through even this crisis. The game is pretty well entwined around the grass roots of the nation. At the same time I recognize that both the Judge and the Babe are entitled to generous assists for pulling baseball through this difficult period.

In the language of Hollywood, Babe Ruth was colossal, stupendous and super-duper in 1921. After almost doubling the home run record in 1920, advancing it from 29 to 54, Babe jacked it up by another five homers to 59 in the Commissioner's first year in office. He scored 177 runs, and drove in 170. He even pitched a few games and stole 17 bases. His mighty bat blasted the Yankees, pennantless waifs since Ban Johnson first put an American League club in New York in 1903, to their first championship. A Columbia professor, after giving Ruth some twenty tests in reactions, coordination, eye-sight, hearing, etc., called him one man out of a million.

The nation was Ruth-conscious from Maine to California, and from Key West to Seattle. Cowboys rode for miles to their nearest railroad station, "caught" the Babe for a day or two in Chicago or St. Louis, and returned happily to the ranch. Warren Harding was President, and Ruth's name appeared in American newspapers more often than that of any person other than the Chief Executive. Even while the Black Sox trial was on, Ruth's homers batted it almost off the sports pages. His name was on every tongue, from kiddies, aged six, to their grandfathers.

Eulogized, petted and pampered, Ruth, then 26, got a pretty exalted idea of his position in the game, and considered himself baseball's No. 1 man, the fellow who could do no wrong. Now, as

Judge Landis was most zealous of his prerogatives, during his years on the Federal bench and in his long sojourn in baseball, it isn't surprising that sooner or later, the Bam and the Judge should meet in a head-on collision. And, when they met, Ruth came out decidedly second best.

In 1921, the two New York clubs met in the first of the five so-called "subway World's Series." Both clubs then were still using the Polo Grounds, and the Series was for the best out of nine. Garry Herrmann had inaugurated the nine-game Series in 1919; it gave the players a cut in five games, instead of four, and if the Series ran to an eighth or ninth game, it provided a tidy sum for the Commission's treasury.

From his first World's Series in 1921, Landis took complete charge of this annual baseball classic. The new Commissioner felt that the league races were the particular provinces of the league heads, but that the World's Series was his show. The Advisory Council, made up of the two league presidents, had little weight with him. He made the Series arrangements, without any advice from the experienced league heads. That became another sore spot with Ban Johnson, who had been so conscious a factor in the pre-Landis World's Series. "I'm as important in this thing as the American League's office boy," said Ban bitterly. And though Landis was quite friendly with John Heydler, the National League head, he couldn't go to him for counsel, and then not consult with Johnson. So, he advised with neither, drew up his own schedule and made other arrangements.

I guess I was an early Landis World's Series casualty. I had served as one of the World's Series official scorers for 11 straight years, from 1910 to 1920, inclusive. In selecting scorers, the old National Commission had given recognition to the baseball weeklies, *The Sporting News*, and our Philadelphia rival, *Sporting Life*. When Landis came into office, I told Ban Johnson I did not wish to continue to serve on the scoring board. Later I learned that Johnson put in a bid for me, tried to battle in my behalf, but the new Commissioner rejected his recommendation.

The Series was one of the most dramatic and nerve-wracking of all World's Series history. The Yankees got off to an early

jump, with both Carl Mays and Waite Hoyt winning 3 to 0 shut-
outs. The Giants then tied it up by winning the third and fourth
games by scores of 13 to 5 and 4 to 2.

Fred Lieb, who was in charge of the New York World's Series
press arrangement, told me of an interesting development after
that fourth game. I give it to show how Landis was on the job
and was quick to look into anything which seemed even slightly
suspicious. For seven innings Mays had been unhittable, giving
up only two scattered singles, as his team had given him a
1 to 0 lead. In the eighth inning, he suddenly went to pieces, as
the Giants scored three runs on four hits, including Emil Meusel's
triple and a double by George Burns. He gave up another run
in the ninth, yielding seven hits in the last two frames. Of course,
that often happens to a pitcher; he bears down so hard for seven
innings that he hasn't enough left, and weakens or is knocked out
of the box in the closing frames.

However, as Lieb relates it, shortly before midnight, George
Perry, who worked with him on the Series in providing liquid
refreshment, brought an excited actor to press headquarters, who
had a wild story that the afternoon's game had been thrown. He
claimed a lot of money had been bet on the Giants, and that between the seventh and eighth innings, Mays had been given a sign
to stop bearing down. He claimed to have evidence to back up
his charges.

Failing to get Col. Ruppert, the Yankee president, on the phone,
Lieb got in touch with Lieut. Col. Huston, the other half owner,
and advised him of the actor's charges. The party made an early-
morning call on Landis, got him out of bed, and acquainted him
with the story. At that hour of the night, Landis got in touch with
a detective agency and by the time Mays got up next morning a
dick was shadowing him. He "remained' with Carl for the remainder of the Series. However, he found nothing wrong with the
off-the-field conduct of this often maligned player, nor with Mays'
associates. Neither could the actor produce any witnesses or
tangible evidence to substantiate his charges. The end of the Series
left Carl absolutely in the clear; in fact, few persons even knew he

was being investigated. But, as will be noted, Landis was quick to root out anything that wasn't strictly on the up and up.

After the Yankees lost this Mays game, Waite Hoyt put the American Leaguers ahead again, three games to two, by defeating Artie Nehf for a second time. But, from then on, National League forces were on the up-grade. Babe Ruth had been developing an abscess on his left elbow, and was unable to play after the fifth game, except for one appearance as a pinch-hitter in the last game. He had been only moderately successful in the Series. He came out with a batting average of .313, hit only one homer and frequently was struck out by McGraw's pitchers. With Ruth out of the line-up, the Yankees lost the last three games by scores of 8 to 5, 2 to 1 and 1 to 0.

The World's Series rules at that time prohibited players of the two contending teams from participating in any barnstorming tours after the Series. It was felt the players were well rewarded in the Series and that it cheapened their efforts to exploit them immediately afterwards in small tank towns for a few hundred dollars. I never entirely subscribed to that point of view, as the fans of the alleged "tank towns" are all part of the game, and it always was my opinion that they are deserving of consideration. However, there was a rule "agin it," and those who had contact with the Judge know that he enforced any rules to the letter.

As the 1921 Series neared its conclusion, reports began to circulate in New York that Ruth and several other Yankee players had signed contracts with a local promoter for a month's barnstorming trip to start immediately after the last Series game. In view of the fact that everyone knew of the rule against barnstorming, it generally was discounted. With Ruth sitting on the bench with his abscessed elbow, the question naturally was asked: "If he can't play in a World's Series, how could he play in an exhibition game?" But, the reports persisted.

After Ruth did go on this forbidden trip, it frequently was said that the Babe was ill advised and that if the club could have gotten to him in time, Ruppert and Huston would have prevented him from making this foolhardy move. However, I can say that

Ruth knew exactly what he was doing when he defied Landis in October, 1921; he was willing to back his own popularity and well known drawing powers against the Judge. Also, the Yankees knew of Ruth's intentions and did everything they could to stop him from making the trip.

Fred Lieb also provided me with the details of how this storm broke, and Landis' fury when Ruth challenged his authority. On the night of October 13, after the Yankees lost that 1 to 0 heart-breaker, their final rally being smothered on that historic double play, Rawlings to Kelly to Frisch, Lieb had occasion to see Landis in his Commodore suite in connection with some press matters which had come up during the Series. The telephone rang, and it was Ruth on the other end. Apparently Landis had been trying to get the Babe for some time, and was annoyed that Ruth hadn't telephoned before. Then he told Ruth to come to see him immediately, but the Babe pleaded an engagement. That further angered Landis. Then Ruth apparently told him that he was catching a midnight train for Buffalo, on the first lap of his barnstorming jaunt.

"Oh, you are; are you? That's just fine," snapped the Judge. "But, if you do, it will be the sorriest thing you've ever done in baseball." He hung up on Ruth, with such a bang that he nearly wrecked the instrument. He swore a blue streak, and trudged angrily up and down the room. "Who does that big monkey think he is?" he demanded, without really asking or waiting for any reply. Then he went on a fresh tirade. And "big monkey" was one of his milder terms. Calming a little, he said: "It seems I'll have to show somebody who is running this game."

Lieb again called on Col. Huston at his private headquarters at the Martinique. It wasn't late, but Huston apparently had tried to drown out the bitterness of those last three Giant defeats. He and Harry Frazee were both stretched over a bed, sound asleep, and snoring so loud you could hear them at Times Square.

With some difficulty, Fred awakened Huston, and told him: "Judge Landis is on the war path. He is awfully sore at Babe. Ruth and Bob Meusel are set for that exhibition trip, and intend to leave Grand Central at midnight. If you don't stop them, there is no telling the severity of the penalty Landis may inflict on them."

Huston got up, took a taxi to Grand Central, and contacted Ruth before he left on the midnight train. But Babe told him he could do nothing about it, saying: "We've signed contracts to make this trip, so we've got to go through with it."

On the trip were Ruth, Bob Meusel, the second leading hitter on the Yankees, and Bill Piercy, a third-string pitcher. Tom Sheehan, the former Brave coach, also was in the party. He had been with the Yankees most of the 1921 season, but had been released to St. Paul. The promoter had surrounded these four big leaguers with a cast of New York semi-pros. Not only did Ruth leave for Buffalo on the night of October 13, but played in Buffalo on the 14th.

The trip early turned out to be a fiasco. While it was to have lasted to the first week in November, it early ran into a siege of rain and cold weather. Games also were scheduled in parks belonging to clubs in Organized Baseball, and they called off the games, not wishing to get into Landis' bad graces. The expedition was called off before playing half of its schedule. Later development brought out that Mays and the crack Yankee catcher, Wally Schang, also were to have made the trip, but after the developments of the night of October 13 wisely decided to pass it up.

Landis waited until December to mete out his penalties. He early withheld the World's Series shares of Ruth, Meusel and Piercy. In his finding, he fined the three players the sums of their World's Series purses and suspended them until May 20, 1922. That made the three players ineligible for the first 39 days of the 1922 season. Inasmuch as Tom Sheehan was a member of the St. Paul club, and had not been one of the World's Series eligible players, he was not suspended. In view of the heavy punishment and loss of part of their 1922 salaries, Landis later paid the disciplined players their withheld Series shares.

Many efforts were made to have Landis ease the punishment. Ruppert and Huston, the New York owners, both contended that they were the parties punished, rather than Ruth and Meusel, and that by depriving the Yankees of the services of these valuable men in the important spring campaign of 1922, their investment was being jeopardized, when they had been guiltless of any rule infractions. They even sent their attorney to Chicago to try to prove to Landis that he had no right to punish the two colonels for a mistake by Ruth.

A fan petition, with thousands of signatures, also was sent to Landis, asking him to pardon Ruth, who was the pal of every small kid in the nation, and not make it appear that their hero was a culprit. Club owners also pointed out how much it would cost them not to have Ruth play for more than a fourth of the season. However, Landis was obdurate, and the long suspensions stuck.

When Landis first tried to stop the trip, the Babe said: "Aw, let the old guy jump into the lake."

Landis felt at the time that he had to be severe; he still was comparatively new in the game, and believed that he had to convince all players, great or small, that he was bigger than any star, even one who could pack a 50,000 stadium. The Yankees at the time frequently winked at some of Ruth's romps and frolics. "He gets away with a lot in the American League, but in this office, he's just another player," the Commissioner said.

Ruth and Meusel challenging the authority of Landis on the old rule prohibiting all barnstorming by World's Series eligible players did have some effects. Landis admitted the rule wasn't entirely fair. He later had it changed, so that Series players could participate in exhibitions up to October 31, provided they had his written consent, and that no more than three of the World's Series players appeared in the same game. The rule then later again was tightened so that these players could barnstorm only ten days after the end of the World's Series. Commissioner Chandler made a further extension in 1946 up to 30 days after the close of the season, which arrangement then was incorporated in the rules.

14: The Judge Tosses out Phil Douglas

Early in 1922—on February 18, 1922—Judge Landis finally resigned from his federal judgeship in Chicago, saying: "There aren't enough hours in the day for me to do all the things that I am obliged to do." He had been under considerable criticism in Congress for holding the two jobs. Some of his Congressional critics pointed out that it served as a poor precedent for a high federal judge to have such a remunerative sideline with a private business or industry. There were a few threats of impeachment, though they were not taken very seriously.

"The Judge really would have resigned earlier but for those Congressional critics," said Leslie O'Connor recently. "He waited until one of those Washington storms blew over—so that it wouldn't look that he quit under fire and then quietly resigned."

It again was an interesting and eventful season in baseball. That Black Sox business kept coming up again. Oscar Felsch, a Milwaukeean, and Joe Jackson, of the expelled White Sox, brought damage suits in Milwaukee against Charley Comiskey, the White Sox owner, charging "a conspiracy against them by the defendant and other unknown persons." One of these unknown persons was believed to be Landis. In another suit, Jackson sought to get $19,-000, allegedly due him in back pay under his contract, from the elder Comiskey, and his son, Louis. Swede Risberg filed a similar suit. The players were represented by Ray Cannon, a former Congressman from Milwaukee, who had been one of Landis' critics.

These Milwaukee cases, of course, brought Landis and Johnson in the same camp, as they advised with Comiskey's attorney on a course of action. Ban and Commy still weren't speaking and the same frigidity remained between the Judge and the American League president. Judge John L. Gregory at first ruled against Comiskey, but later the court ordered amended petitions filed in the cases of Felsch and Risberg to make more definite their charge that a conspiracy existed to keep them out of baseball. Various papers which were placed in the hands of the Sheriff of Vilas County, Wisconsin, never were served, as the two Comiskeys stayed out of Wisconsin jurisdiction, and the case dragged through the year.

Before the year was out, the Judge again turned down George "Buck" Weaver's strongly backed plea for reinstatement. Weaver told the Judge the only player who ever spoke to him about the sellout was Eddie Cicotte, that he scouted the idea, and then heard no more about it.

In rejecting the request, the Commissioner gave these reasons: "Indictments were returned against certain members of the Chicago team, including Weaver. On the trial of this case, a witness for the prosecution gave what he claimed was a detailed account of his meeting with the indicted men and arranging with them for the throwing of the World's Series games. The report showed that Weaver was present in Court during the testimony of this witness, who most specifically stated that Weaver was present at the conference, and yet the case went to the jury without any denial from Weaver from the witness stand. If the incriminating evidence was false, the baseball public had a right to Weaver's denial under oath. Of course, it is true that a verdict of not guilty was rendered in Weaver's favor. It was also likewise true that the same jury returned the same verdict in favor of Cicotte, Claude Williams and Joe Jackson, each of whom had confessed his guilt."

The Benny Kauff case was finally ended on September 11, 1922, when New York Supreme Court Justice Marsh signed an order dismissing the suit of the former "Ty Cobb of the Feds" to restrain Landis from enforcing his order barring Kauff from Organized Baseball. The dropping of the suit had been agreed upon by Senator George Wharton Pepper and John Conway Toole, representatives of Landis, and Judge Emil Fuchs, counsel for the unfortunate Benny.

Organized Baseball also got a wonderful break that year, when the United States Supreme Court finally ruled in the game's favor in the celebrated Baltimore Federal League suit. The Baltimore club had brought action under the Sherman anti-trust laws, and baseball once was faced with the prospects of paying $900,000 damages, plus heavy court costs. The Feds had scored heavily in some of the lower courts. The case had dragged for nearly seven years, ever since the old Federal League had made peace with the major leagues in December, 1915, while making no provision for its Baltimore club.

Baseball was most fortunate in having a good friend of the game as Chief Justice in former President William Howard Taft, a half-brother of Charles P. Taft, former owner of the Cubs. When the nation's highest tribunal finally acted on this case, it had to decide on questions which were before Landis when the full Federal League lodged its anti-trust case in the Judge's northern Illinois docket in January, 1915—whether the majors operated in restraint of trade, baseball "chattel slavery" with the reserve and ten-day clauses.

The Supreme Court ruled that baseball was a "peculiar business," that the games were played by personal effort, and therefore nothing is produced, that baseball is not a commodity, and therefore trust laws were not violated.

Because of having had the original Fed suit in his Chicago court, Landis had more or less kept himself in the background in this vital litigation, and Senator George Wharton Pepper led O.B.'s battery of lawyers. However, Landis was gratified with the decision. In his own mind, he always had been a little doubtful as to how some of baseball's practices would fare if scrutinized by the higher courts. The decision of the Supreme Court that baseball was a "peculiar business" met this situation, and the Judge felt that he now had not only baseball law, but the laws of the land behind him, in acting as supreme ruler of the game and in handling subsequent cases involving player contracts.

Most of the men on Landis' blacklist were the Black Sox and players accused in gambling cases before Kenesaw Mountain took hold of the game's reins. But if the first man he put out on his own was a Giant, Benny Kauff, so was the second player to feel his iron discipline—Phil Douglas, the big spitball pitcher, who had been a valuable member of McGraw's World's Championship team of 1921. "Shufflin' Phil," as he was called, was shuffled out of Organized Baseball's deck on August 16, 1922.

Phil Douglas, a big Alabaman with a big thirst, had been a difficult man to handle, and frequently had been disciplined in his former major league engagements with the White Sox, Reds, Dodgers and Cubs. Douglas, however, was one of the best pitchers in the game; and McGraw, who always was ready to take on the tough boys, procured him from Chicago in a deal for Dave Robertson. Douglas had frequent lapses in 1922, and his arm was not in good condition. McGraw employed several keepers for him, including the former great St. Louis outfielder and hitter, Jesse Burkett.

Through one of his clever wiles, Phil escaped from his keeper and went out on another toot, which still further infuriated McGraw. Shortly before the Giants left on a mid-August western trip, McGraw gave the husky pitcher a terrific tongue-lashing in the Giant clubhouse. And when McGraw boiled over, he could pour on the vitriol.

The player had a hangover at the time; there is no doubt his mind was muddled, and that he didn't know what he was doing. With McGraw's bitter tirade still burning his ears, Douglas sat down in the Giant clubhouse and penned a most damaging note to Leslie Mann, an outfielder on the St. Louis Cardinals, who had been a teammate of Douglas on the Cub 1918 National League Champions. At the time Phil wrote the letter, the Cardinals, managed by Branch Rickey, were running second to the Giants.

Phil Douglas' incriminating letter follows:

"Dear Les: I want to leave here. I don't want to see this guy (McGraw) win the pennant. You know that I can pitch and I am afraid that if I stay I will win the pennant for them. Talk this over with the boys, and if it is all right, send the goods to my house at night and I will go to the fishing camp. Let me know if you all want to do this and I will go home on the next train.

PHIL DOUGLAS."

Receiving such a letter put Mann on the spot. He is a graduate of the Springfield, Mass., Y.M.C.A. College, and has been close to "Y" activities all of his life. Sending the letter to a player with such a background was further evidence of Douglas' confused thinking. The story is that Mann, knowing Phil's erratic habits, didn't want to turn him in. But baseball had just gone through a turbulent period. If it was learned he had received such a letter, and Douglas dropped a number of games, he would be in the same boat with Douglas. He turned the letter over to Branch Rickey, and Branch promptly sent it to Judge Landis. Things after that began to move swiftly.

The Giants left New York on August 15, and when they arrived at Pittsburgh the next day, Judge Landis already was there, staying at the Schenley Hotel, where the New York team has put up for years. Douglas and McGraw had scarcely checked in, when they received word to report to Landis' room immediately.

After the two men were seated, Landis brought forth the letter written on Giant stationary and in Phil's handwriting.

"Did you write this, Mr. Douglas?" asked the Judge.

Phil reddened to the roots of his hair, and then slowly replied: "Yes, I did."

Landis then handed the note to McGraw to read.

"You know what this means," said the Judge. "Phil Douglas, you are permanently out of Organized Baseball."

Later in discussing the case with newspapermen with the Giants, Landis said: "I called Douglas in and asked him whether he had written that note. He confessed that he had. There was nothing else for me to do but put him on the permanent ineligible list."

Some ten years later, Zipp Newman, veteran Birmingham sports editor, tried to go to the front for Phil. Things were breaking pretty tough for the big pitcher, and his family. Douglas was well past his prime, and Zipp thought that if Landis reinstated him, it would do much for Phil's morale, perhaps even enable him to catch on with some minor league team. The Judge said he was sorry he couldn't reinstate Douglas, but he did send the pitcher a generous check from his private funds.

When a second Giant-Yankee World's Series rolled around, Landis again reduced this autumn classic to seven games. "That 1921 Series stretched out too long," he said. "This should be the greatest sports event of the year, but if it drags into two weeks, the public loses interest." The reaction to this move was good, as it generally was agreed that the nine-game Series was too long.

The 1922 Series saw the Yankees take another humiliating defeat. The great Ruth, who felt the Judge's wrath in the early part of the season, bagged only two hits, and batted a feeble .118, while the American champions failed to win a game. They did manage to get a 3–3 ten-inning tie out of the second game, a game which had the Judge in a tub of steaming hot water, though he was the innocent victim of an umpire's poor judgment. But the Judge got out of this predicament with one of those usual Landis precedent-breaking decisions. He gave away the entire receipts of the game to charity.

The game was played at the Polo Grounds on a pleasant sunny afternoon, October 5. The Giants had scored three runs in the first inning, but the Yankees, picking up runs one at a time, managed to tie it up by the eighth, and it was a fine pitching duel between Bob Shawkey and Jesse Barnes when George Hildebrand, the American Leaguer working behind the plate, called the game at the end of the tenth. The game started a little after 2 P.M.; the ten-inning fray lasted two hours and 41 minutes, so it was a quarter to five when the big explosion took place. The Judge, already wearing his battered hat, was leaning over his box rail, expecting to enjoy a few more innings, when Hildebrand spoke to him briefly, and then to the great surprise of the crowd announced: "Game called on account of darkness." At that time the sun still was well up in the heaven, and there was approximately 20 minutes of good sunlight. The early amazement of the crowd turned to incensed anger. There were loud boos and catcalls, and the wrath of the 36,514 spectators turned especially on Landis. Somehow, they got the idea that it was the new Commissioner who gave Hildebrand the office to call the game. They figured it was a cute little scheme to enrich baseball by the $120,000 gate.

As the Judge and Mrs. Landis left their box, accompanied by a British celebrity who was the Commissioner's guest, several hundred angry New Yorkers trailed Landis across the field. They yelled "Crook," "Robber," "You're trying to make yourself right with your bosses," along with other personalities which don't look good in print. The Britisher didn't make the Commissioner feel any better, when he remarked, "My word, Judge, but they are giving you the bird!"

Landis was burned up when he got to his hotel downtown, and said, "I never saw such a damned thing in my life. And those darned fools thinking I called that game to make a little more money for the club owners. As for that blankety-blank umpire, what was he thinking about? I may not be the smartest person in the world, but I've got sense enough not to call a ball game on account of darkness in the middle of the afternoon."

In justice to Hildebrand, who took the rap for calling the game, the fellow really responsible was my good friend, Bill Klem. And Bill certainly meant to do the right thing. Before the Yankees went to bat in their half of the tenth, Klem, the umpire at third, came to the plate and engaged Hildebrand in a lengthy conversation. He told him of a 14-inning game between the Red Sox and Brooklyn in Boston in the 1916 Series. "It still was light before that fourteenth inning started, but before it was over, it was so dark it was difficult to follow the ball," said Bill. I recall that Boston game well, for as one of the scorers we could scarcely distinguish the players when Del Gainer scored the Red Sox' winning run. Klem didn't want Hildebrand to run into such a situation. All umpires respected his views and judgments; Klem was umpiring in his eleventh Series, Hildebrand was in his second. So "Hildy" took Bill's bad but well-intended tip, and called the game.

Crowds which milled around Times Square and the Grand Central district around dinner time still were griping about the "outrage." Then the Judge acted. Without consulting either Johnson or Heydler of the Advisory board, or Ruppert and Stoneham, the rival club presidents, Landis announced that all of the receipts of the game would be given to worthy New York charities.

The decision was better received by the general public than by the persons most concerned. I believe most of the fans thought the Judge did a wise and smart thing. However, the reaction among the club owners was not overly favorable. Some of them thought that Landis at least should have consulted with the league heads and rival club presidents, before giving away the entire gate receipts. "I didn't want a lot of talking about it," said the Judge, "and arguing whether it should or should not have been done. I just did it."

Of course, Ban Johnson again was on the other side from Landis. He resented again that an important decision affecting his league was made without him being called into consultation. Ban always was one to back up his umpires, and he felt Landis had put Hildebrand in a bad light. He felt that Landis' action in giving away the $120,000 gate gave the public an idea that Hildebrand had done something reprehensible, and that the umpire had some ulterior motive for calling the game. He felt a better solution for the problem would have been to take the public into full confidence, to have explained Klem's fears that if an eleventh inning had been started, it might have brought about a repetition of the Boston game of six years before, which was almost finished in darkness.

One of the consequences of the called game was that Landis took the authority for calling any subsequent World's Series games from the head umpire and assumed it himself. He also had the starting time for World's Series games moved forward to 1.30 P.M., to reduce the possibility of future Series tie games to a minimum. Where the 1922 contest was the third Series tie game, there have been none since that date.

Baseball men, especially the writers, were getting to know Landis better, and to enjoy his confidence and friendship. They also learned that Landis was a different sort of person when he shook off the cares of his office. He not only could be a congenial and delightful playfellow, but he liked to play. The New York writers learned that at a dinner for Bill Donovan, the former Yankee and Philly manager, in New Haven a few weeks after the close of the 1922 World's Series.

After leaving the Phillies in 1921, under circumstances investigated by Landis, Bill Donovan went to work for George Weiss, the present Yankee farm superintendent and then owner of the New Haven Eastern League team. Weiss handed Smiling Bill a particularly strong team in 1922; it had such strong players as Jimmy Wilson, Bill Hargrave, Johnnie Cooney, Sterling Stryker and others. It not only won its own pennant easily in the class A Eastern League, but defeated the strong Baltimore Orioles, champions of the Class AA International League, in a post-season series. Weiss and the New Haven fans thought it appropriate that a big party be thrown to celebrate such success. Judge Landis was invited and, as he was a great admirer of Donovan, he readily accepted. Weiss also invited a carload of the New York baseball writers.

The party was held during the height of the prohibition period. At the main dinner, held in the hotel's banquet hall, the diners followed the old prohibition procedure. Fans brought along their own, and such bottles as Weiss provided for his guests were kept under the tables, until one surreptitiously poured his own or his neighbor's drink. Landis made a nice talk, extolling Bill; it was a pleasant party, but the real fun didn't begin until Weiss and some of New Haven's leading lights, including bankers and doctors, invited the special guests to a private little affair in one of the smaller dining rooms.

In this room, cocktails and highballs were freely distributed and bottled goods were on display on the table. Yet there was an air of apprehension. It was only a little over a half year since Landis had resigned from the Federal bench, and as I said in an earlier chapter, he was one of the toughest "prohibition judges" in the country. Weiss even asked a few of the New York writers whether they thought it wise to have the Judge attend the private party.

When the Judge entered the room he sensed that there was a feeling that he might put a chill on the affair, even might publicly express his disapproval. Shortly after the guests were seated, he stood up with the cocktail which had been at his chair in his upraised right hand. "Gentlemen, before we begin, I want to propose a toast," he said. "I want to drink a toast to the Eighteenth Amendment."

He said it with a tone of seriousness, but with a mischievous smile playing around his mouth. Everybody laughed; the Commissioner swallowed his drink, and joined in the laugh. That let down the bars and lifted the tension, and from then on everyone present voted it one of the best parties ever held in baseball.

The Judge never was in a better mood, and he proved the life of the party. His story of being caught in a Minnesota lumber yard by an irate Scandinavian, when he had to get off an inter-urban train bound for Duluth because it lacked proper conveniences, had everybody in the aisles, convulsed with laughter. One old gaffer tried to recite, "The Shooting of Dan McGrew." He would forget his lines, and Landis was his prompter. But the Judge would give him the wrong word. Then, the reciter would start again from the beginning, only to have Landis throw him off again.

There naturally were quite a few references at the party to Judge Landis. One of the inebriated guests, who didn't know his baseball too well, got it mixed up, and thought the remarks were addressed to George Landis. At regular intervals, he would get up, hold up his hands for attention, and then would remark, "That George Landis is all right," or "Here's to George Landis."

For years thereafter, there was a standing joke between the Judge and the late Sid Mercer, Bill Slocum, Fred Lieb and other New York writers who attended the New Haven party. They would greet him with: "How are you, George?" or "How's good old George Landis?"

The Judge always laughed and never resented it. He would grin from ear to ear, and say: "Wasn't that a great party in New Haven?"

The season of 1922 also saw one of the Judge's most famous cases in minor league baseball—Commissioner Landis' effort to boot William H. "Bill" Klepper, the president of the Portland Beavers, out of baseball, or at least declare him out of bounds for three years. Klepper retired in 1924 after a stormy controversy, but returned as general manager of Portland in 1943 to remain until 1946.

The Landis decision of May 24, 1922, making Klepper a baseball outcast, became known as the Bill Kenworthy case, as Kenworthy had started out to be the 1922 manager of the Beavers and also was heavily penalized. The case went back to 1920, when Klepper was president of the Seattle club, James R. Brewster secretary, and William (Duke) Kenworthy the second baseman—

playing manager. In 1921, Bill became just one of Seattle's leading stockholders, and Brewster moved up to the presidency, with the Duke still serving as playing manager. The latter had a fine season, too, finishing fourth in a tight Pacific Coast League race, only three and a half games from the top, while his .343 batting average gave him fourth place among over-100-game players.

During the season, James Boldt, owner of a string of Seattle restaurants, bought the Seattle ball club, and in the fall of the year Klepper and Brewster acquired the Portland franchise, which had become run down after several seasons of tailend baseball. Klepper became Beaver president and Brewster vice president in the new set-up, and presently Bill pulled somewhat of a sensation when he said Kenworthy, his old Seattle manager, would be associated with him in Portland. The allegation was that when Kenworthy signed with Seattle he was given a letter by Klepper, then president, that if the player and the Seattle club could not agree on terms, Duke would be made a free agent. Just a letter was produced.

In the meantime, Boldt, the new Seattle owner, yelled his indignation to the high heavens. He figured Kenworthy as a player and manager one of Seattle's best assets when he purchased the club. The decision went to the National Association and eventually went to Landis. While the matter was before the Judge, and hearing Landis was pretty hot over it, a deal was hastily arranged by which Marty Krug, later a Detroit and Phillies scout, was sent by Portland to Seattle. Seattle subsequently sold Krug to the Chicago Cubs for $7,500.

Landis' decision in the Klepper case was one of his well known bombshells, which no doubt would have blown a less sturdy citizen than Klepper right out of the baseball picture. Its essence was:

1. William H. Klepper, Portland president (and Seattle president in 1920), was placed on baseball's ineligible list until January 1, 1925; and James R. Brewster, Portland vice president (and Seattle president in 1920), was made ineligible until January 1, 1924.

2. In Landis' words: "During these periods of ineligibility, they

will not be recognized as representing any baseball club by any player, official, agent or employe of the National Association, or by any major or minor league or clubs."

3. William Kenworthy (who had been ineligible since the preceding February, pending Landis' investigation) was continued on the ineligible list until August 1, 1922, and after that he was not eligible to play with or manage any Coast League club until the beginning of the 1924 season. Kenworthy's contract was made the property of the Pacific Coast League.

4. Player Marty Krug, the ex-Portland second baseman, "traded" to Seattle, was declared the rightful property of the latter club, and Seattle was permitted to keep the $7,500 it obtained from the Cubs for his release.

Landis made his finding on the charge that the arrangement between Klepper and Kenworthy, based on Kenworthy's alleged free agency, was fraudulent, and that the letter presented as evidence of such an agreement was post-written, after the fact.

In a special meeting of the Pacific Coast, June 6, the league requested Landis to consider an appeal by the Portland men, on new evidence promised, but said the league would stand by the Commissioner's decision in the case if it was not modified. It looked as though the jig was up for Bill, but he continued to fight—and, despite the ukase from the Commissioner, to run his club.

On July 15, Judge Landis refused a petition by Klepper's attorneys for a rehearing. They cited Sec. 3 of the existing major-minor league agreement which specified: "Punitive action by the Commissioner may take the form of a public reprimand and in the case of a player a declaration of temporary or permanent ineligibility," as limiting his powers with respect to throwing out owners. The Judge ruled that his action wasn't "punitive," but "preventive"— and added, "In this instance, it will at least prevent further misconduct during the period of ineligibility."

On August 2, 1922, the Judge backed down on a part of his order with what on the Coast became known as the famous "internal affairs" ruling. Klepper's attorney, the late Gus C. Moser, wired Landis for an interpretation of that part of his order "relating the ineligibility of Klepper and Brewster, as to whether it was to be construed as meaning that Klepper must go out as president of the Portland club, an Oregon corporation, provided he had no official dealings with the Coast League, with other leagues or club owners or with ballplayers."

The Judge answered on August 2, 1922, with his interpretation of his own decision:

"May 24 decision dealt with baseball matters as distinguished from purely internal corporate administrative affairs. It prohibits all players, officials, agents and employes of all leagues and clubs from recognizing Klepper and dealing with him in respect to such baseball matters, and in this respect it applies to officials, agents and employes of Portland and to players on the Portland team. Therefore Pacific Coast League is not required to cease relations with Portland if Klepper's activities as president are limited to purely internal corporate administrative affairs."

This liberalized interpretation forestalled threatened action by the Portland club in Federal Court. It also was a body blow to Klepper's enemies in the Coast League, who after the June 6 meeting split into two four-club factions. The faction out to get Klepper had presented a resolution requiring the Portland directors immediately to oust Klepper as president on pain of a $250 fine "for every day of delay."

When Landis ruled that Klepper could handle "internal affairs" of his club, the result was that technically the Judge saved face and his decision prevailed, but for all practical purposes Klepper ran his club as before the decision. He sold about $200,000 worth of ball players that very year on trips east, contacting all the big league people himself, and the following year personally sold the Portland club to Tom Shibe and associates on the Athletics for $325,000. The purchase was made partly to enable the Philadelphia club to get Mickey Cochrane, the Portland catcher. The way Bill Klepper went around peddling ball players to people who weren't supposed to have any dealings with him, and said: "The Portland club will do this or that" brought many amusing smiles and grins at the time.

Just in closing up this Klepper decision, the Pacific Coast League washed its hands of the case by declaring Bill Kenworthy a free agent after Landis had awarded him to the league. The Duke played for Columbus in 1923 and was back with Portland as manager in 1924.

15: Rube Benton Gets a Favorable Nod

The season of 1923, Landis' third in office, passed fairly peace-fully. There still were repercussions of the gambling cases. The Commissioner was subject to some criticism, but most of it came in the press, as baseball people were standing by their pledge to back Landis to the limit and to make no public criticism of him or his conduct of baseball's affairs.

Landis made a decision against John Heydler, one of his orig-inal boosters, in the case of Rube Benton, capable but undepend-able National League lefthander, which was a touchy subject with genial John for some time. Heydler felt the Judge had left him dangling out on a limb, but the Judge's decision was sound. John Calhoun Benton, a South Carolinian now deceased, was no white lily; he frequently was disciplined by his managers for beering up, and by 1922 the majority of National League club owners wanted no more of him. They were, however, perfectly willing to let him fade out in the American Association. But Landis ruled if the pitcher was eligible to pitch for St. Paul, he was eligible to pitch for Cincinnati.

The Benton case was an aftermath of the messy business which infested baseball in the Federal League and World War I periods. Rube originally came up with the Reds in 1910, and McGraw pro-cured him for the Giants five years later. Benton was in the Army in 1918, and then returned to the New York club after the war. In 1920, Benton told Frank Graham, then the *New York Sun* baseball writer, that Charley Herzog, former Giant infielder but by this time on the Cubs, had attempted to bribe him to throw games. The offer supposedly was made in a Chicago saloon. Frankie reported the matter to Joe Vila, his sports editor, and Vila told him to repeat Benton's story to John Heydler.

Heydler took Benton with him to Chicago; the pair got into a taxicab, and made a tour of Chicago's bar-rooms, dives and speak-easies. But nowhere could Benton recognize the place where he claimed Herzog made his offer, nor find a bartender who might help him to support his story.

In the meantime, Herzog made counter-charges against Benton

that he had had guilty knowledge of the 1919 crooked World's Series, that he had profited by betting on Cincinnati on a tip by Bill Burns, one of the fixers. Herzog backed his assertions with affidavits from Art Wilson, the former Giant and Cub catcher, and Norman Boeckel, a Pittsburgh infielder.

Benton was released to the St. Paul club by the Giants in 1921, the National League having found him an "undesirable player." The American League also took action that Benton was unwanted in that circuit. However, for that matter Ban Johnson always disproved of his league engaging National League discards. In the meantime, Rube had quite a year with St. Paul in 1922, and in February, 1923, Garry Herrmann, Benton's original big league employer, regained the lefthander in a deal with St. Paul for Cliff Markle, a pitcher, and cash. Ever since Heydler's old fight against Garry on the old National Commission, the Cincinnatian rather enjoyed needling the league head. Heydler was furious; he held up the deal, and advised Herrmann that Benton could not pitch for the Cincinnati club because of the player's "undesirability" and "irresponsibility."

The National League's February meeting was held in New York shortly afterwards, and Herrmann came to the conclave to make a fight for his pitcher, claiming that if Benton was an undesirable player for the majors he should have been equally undesirable for the minors for the last year and a' half. By a majority vote, the National League supported Heydler's stand, and then by a unanimous vote agreed to leave the final disposition of the case up to League President Heydler.

The National League head then said he would take no final action on the Benton case until Judge Landis had ruled on the charges that Benton had guilty knowledge of the Black Sox sellout. He felt if Landis ruled against Benton, he would go automatically on the game's permanent blacklist; if on the other hand Landis absolved Rube of the more serious charge, Heydler felt the Commissioner would respect the league's wishes not to have any more of Benton.

I know that Heydler felt sure he would get a favorable verdict from the Judge, and was stunned when the Commissioner not only ruled that the Rube could pitch for the Reds, but bore down pretty heavily on those he thought were taking the bread and butter right out of the South Carolinian's mouth. In his decisions in the U.S. Court, the Judge often was unpredictable, and this time he was as solicitous of Rube Benton's welfare as he had been severe on Benton's former New York teammate, Benny Kauff.

The Commissioner severely criticized persons who brought charges against Benton nearly two years after these alleged irregularities occurred; he approved the transfer of Benton from St. Paul to Cincinnati, and upheld Garry Herrmann's contention that if Benton could pitch in the American Association he could pitch anywhere in baseball. On that ground he contended that after Benton had been permitted to play a season and a half for the New York club and a similar length of time in the American Association, he should not now "be deprived of his livelihood" on belated charges of alleged misconduct dating back to 1919.

He completely ignored all of John Heydler's private investigation of Benton, also the affidavit presented by two players against whom there never was the slightest breath of scandal, Art Wilson and Norman Boeckel. Those who criticized Landis' decision said his Benton finding was a complete refutal of his own decisions in the cases of Joe Gedeon, Benny Kauff, Gene Paulette, and to a lesser degree Buck Weaver. Gedeon was tossed out for no wrongdoing of his own, but for guilty knowledge of the 1919 frame-up; Kauff, acquitted by a Bronx County jury, was ruled not a fit person for other big leaguers to associate with; and Paulette, though not accused of throwing games, was on the outside for accepting gifts or a loan from St. Louis gamblers.

For the only time in John Heydler's baseball career, he staged a little rebellion against Landis' authority. He was in California enjoying a March vacation after a tough winter, when he got word of Landis' decision. He was stunned, and then he wired Herrmann that, despite the Commissioner's finding on Benton, he (Heydler) would stand by his guns. He had no objection to Benton remaining in Organized Baseball, but years before the National League had decided on determining for itself who should or should not play in the league. He had decided that Benton was not the type or character of player wanted by the league and that he never would sanction Rube's return to any of his clubs.

The revolt was of short duration. Landis requested Heydler to call on him on his way east, when he returned from the Coast. Just what passed between the pair at a lengthy conference in the Judge's office never was known, but after it was over Heydler saw the Benton matter from a different light. He said that as far as he was concerned Judge Landis' decision in the Benton case was final, that the Benton case was closed, and that Rube would pitch in 1923 for the Cincinnati club.

Garry Herrmann was flayed for his action in bringing Benton back into the league, putting his league president in an awkward and humiliating position, and giving Landis a chance to blast the National League's rule of deciding for itself on the fitness and desirability of its players. Benton, on his part, showed his appreciation to Herrmann, also that he still possessed big league skill, when he helped pitch the 1923 Reds into second place by winning 14 games out of 24.

This 1923 National League race developed a new gambling controversy, which proved another vexation for Landis and Heydler. In a series in Cincinnati, running from August 4 to 7, inclusive, the Giants, the eventual champion, greatly increased their lead by defeating the strong Reds in five straight games. Shortly after the series, *Collyer's Eye*, a Chicago sports weekly dealing largely with racing, ran a story that gamblers again were active in baseball, and that prior to the August Giant-Red series, Second Baseman Sam Bohne and Left Fielder Pat Duncan of the Cincinnati club had been approached by gamblers with an offer of $15,000 each to throw the series to the Giants.

Heydler immediately got in touch with Landis, and also acted on his own, with the Judge being willing that John should make the preliminary investigation. The Reds were in the east when the charge was made, and Heydler summoned Bohne and Duncan, as well as the Cincinnati baseball writers, to his New York headquarters. Under oath, the players testified they never had been approached by any gambler and to the best of their knowledge the story was without foundation.

124

The Cincinnati writers, Jack Ryder, Tom Swope, Bill Phelon and Bob Newhall, testified that they had seen nothing about the play of Bohne and Duncan to indicate they weren't doing their best all through the series. In fact, Duncan hit .350 and played errorless ball in the five games. Bohne hit .286 in four games, and made two errors. The only thing even slightly suspicious was that after Bohne was guilty of an error in the first game of an August 6 double-header, Pat Moran benched him in the second game and played Lew Fonseca at second. But Sammy was back at his position in the fifth game.

Following Heydler's investigation, in which he was in constant communication with Landis, he advised the players to bring both civil and criminal action against the Chicago publication. This the players did, both Duncan and Bohne filing $50,000 damage suits, September 7, against *Collyer's Eye* in the United States District Court in Chicago, Judge Landis' old jurisdiction. The players sued for defamation of character in the allegations that they had been approached by gamblers.

In a statement to all the newspapers, Bert E. Collyer, publisher of *Collyer's Eye*, asserted that he did not charge Bohne and Duncan with throwing games, but had merely recorded that they had been "approached by gamblers." He sent Commissioner Landis a public telegram, in which he insisted that gambling cliques still were operating in baseball circles. He said that President Heydler "ought to—and probably does—know all about these charges," and requested that Landis start an immediate and thorough inquiry, to which end Collyer offered his "sincere and tireless co-operation."

Landis never replied to the telegram. The baseball people had no high opinion of Collyer or his sheet. Only Ban Johnson of the American League was inclined to accept any help from him. Ban knew that baseball gambling still was rampant, and felt that Collyer, with his knowledge of big gamblers who tried to corrupt and fix racing, also knew some of the persons who had done baseball so much harm in the five previous years.

The cases of Duncan and Bohne vs. *Collyer's Eye* were settled out of court, when Collyer said he was unable to subpoena witnesses to Chicago who would have substantiated his story. It always was difficult to get members of the gambling fraternity into court, and they had their little ways of staying out of a court's jurisdiction. Collyer settled for $100 and court costs. Landis said the size of this modest sum was of little importance. By Collyer's agreeing to pay damages, he felt baseball had scored an emphatic victory. "Both the game, and players Bohne and Duncan, have been vindicated before the American public," he said.

Judge Landis also won a partial victory in his fight, waged ever since he came into office, for the complete restoration of the draft to all minor leagues. Big league club owners had slapped back at the non-draft leagues by refusing to send them optional players and few on outright releases. The majors, backed by Landis, offered a compromise plan to the non-draft leagues whereby they again would get optional players and others on outright release if they recognized the principle of the draft and permitted a certain class of players to be drafted. It was called the "modified draft plan." The Western and Three-I Leagues, which found it difficult to operate without big league aid, quickly accepted. The three AA leagues at first rejected the plan, but before the year was out, the American Association and Pacific Coast League also came in, leaving only the International as a non-draft circuit. Landis had a number of verbal clashes on the subject with his attorney of the Kauff case, John Conway Toole, then president of the "Ints."

The Judge was not entirely pleased with the gains made. Despite the new order, only sixteen players were drafted by nine major league clubs in 1923, a decrease of five from the preceding year. He held that players who could escape from Baltimore and other International League teams "only by the purchase route were in virtual peonage," and said the draft principle alone assured the player of "advancement in his profession."

The Yankees and Giants met in their third straight World's Series that fall. By this time Yankee Stadium was completed, and half of the 1923 games were played at the new American League park. Judge Landis had a lot of fun, but he asked: "Isn't this World's Series job ever going to get me out of New York? It looks as though I can keep in a standing hotel reservation there at World's Series time."

Friction developed between the two New York clubs before the Series was played, and Landis had to rule in favor of McGraw, and against Ruppert, the doughty Colonel of the Yankees. Wally Pipp, regular first basemen of the American League Champions, broke several ribs in a September game. Yankee Manager Huggins finished the season with a sturdy New York lad at first base who returned to the club after he had finished the Eastern League season with Hartford. It was old Biscuit Pants himself, young Lou Gehrig. And he was hotter than a firecracker; in 13 games with the Yankees he hit .423.

Under World's Series rules, only players who are with the championship clubs on September 1 are eligible for the Series. Lou returned to the Yankees after that date, but in view of Pipp's injury, Ruppert asked Landis' permission to permit Huggins to play Gehrig. He felt there was precedent for making such a request in the 1920 Series between Cleveland and Brooklyn, the year of the Ray Chapman tragedy. Brooklyn had waived the rule, and permitted Cleveland to play the young shortstop, Joe Sewell, and then after Dodger third baseman Jimmy Johnston had met with an injury, Cleveland permitted Manager Robinson to play Tommy Sheehan, a young infielder, who joined the Brooklyns in latter September.

Landis put it up to McGraw. He said if McGraw agreed to waive the rule, he was agreeable to let Gehrig play in the Series. But he pointed out that the rule was there, and if McGraw wished it enforced, he would have to stay within the letter of the law. McGraw refused to consent, and Lou had to wait until 1926 to get into his first World's Series. The Yankees trussed up Pipp; he really played a fine Series, and the New York American Leaguers won their first title, four games to two.

However, the refusal of McGraw to permit Gehrig to play rankled with Ruppert and Huggins. Home runs by Casey Stengel decided both of the games won by the Giants. In the third game, Casey's homer into the right field bleachers at the Stadium was the only score of a 1 to 0 pitchers' duel between Sam Jones and Art Nehf. As the good-natured Stengel, always the clown, trudged happily around the bases, he kept his thumb at his nose and pointed in the general direction of the Yankee dugout.

Not only did Ruppert feel none too good about losing that 1 to 0 game, but Stengel's conduct offended his fastidious taste. Meeting Judge Landis in the Commodore Hotel, Ruppert said: "I don't think Stengel's actions were any credit to baseball." Billy Fleischman, his assistant, broke in: "It was an insult to all our fans."

However, when Landis later was asked whether he was going to do anything to Stengel, he grinned and said: "No, I don't think I will. A fellow who wins two games with home runs may feel a little playful, especially if he's a Stengel."

During the Series, Jimmy Carroll, brother of Earl Carroll, the theatrical producer, got up a party of baseball celebrities to attend one of the early editions of "Carroll's Vanities"—I believe it was the third. The Judge and Mrs. Landis accepted invitations. Ruppert, Fleischman and a few baseball writers were in the party. Joe Cook, the comedian of the show, was especially funny, putting on a special baseball act in which he kidded Landis, especially about the umpire who called the game with the sun high in the heavens the year before.

Nudity in the best theaters wasn't as common in 1923 as it is today. The baseball party had "ringside seats"—right up in front. Earl had some big-breasted babes whirling around on a miniature merry-go-round, with only a cotton gauze sheet between them and the ringsiders. The most daring feature of this third edition was a nude lass draped around the swinging pendulum of a big stage clock in one of the show's biggest scenes.

After the show, Mrs. Landis was asked by one of the party how she enjoyed it. "Well, Joe Cook certainly was very funny," replied the Squire's lady, "but I must say I would have preferred if the young ladies had worn more underwear."

When the Judge was asked how he enjoyed it, he replied: "Bully! Bully! Wouldn't have missed it for anything." And then in an aside whisper, he added: "They had on enough clothes for me."

16: That O'Connell-Dolan Business

If 1923 was a comparative romp for Landis, he had another difficult, heart-rending year in 1924. Whenever he thought he had gambling scotched, it raised its evil head again. New York had monopolized three straight World's Series, and the entire country—outside of New York—was rooting for somebody else to get in on this big October sports show. The Commissioner, of course, had to be neutral on the surface, but he knew that baseball was suffering from New Yorkitis, and secretly was pulling for some other clubs to get into the Series. We in the baseball publication business felt the same way about it.

For quite a while, however, it looked as though the Yankees and Giants would put on their familiar October act, but in a tight finish, the Washington club, led by Bucky Harris—then the boy manager—beat out the Yankees in the American League by a mere two games. It was Washington's first championship, and one of the most popular pennants ever won by a big league club.

In the National League, the Giants also were having a difficult time making it four straight. The Pirates battled the McGraw team all season, and the Brooklyn Dodgers, aided by a terrific September campaign, pushed ahead of the Pirates and fought the Giants right down to the wire. But as the two Greater New York clubs reached the final week-end of the season, the odds were all with New York. The Giants had single Saturday, Sunday and Monday games with the seventh place Phillies and the Dodgers had two games with the tailend Braves. But McGraw had a game and a half edge on his former Oriole associate, Wilbert Robinson. The Giants had won 92 games and lost 59; Brooklyn had a 91–61 record. The only way New York could blow the pennant was to lose two to the Phillies, while the Dodgers twice were defeating the Braves. Even in that eventuality, the Giants would finish no worse than tied for the lead.

Though McGraw held most of the winning cards and he seemed reasonably certain of a fourth straight pennant, a new National League record, there were persons who wanted to make it even "safer" for the Giants to win. Before the Saturday game of September 27, Jimmy O'Connell, the Giants $75,000 outfielder and extra first baseman, walked over to Heinie Sand, Philadelphia shortstop, and said in an undertone: "It will be worth $500 to you if you don't bear down too hard against us today."

According to his later statement, Sand said he replied to O'Connell: "Get away from me. You must be crazy. And don't ever say anything like that again to me, or to anyone else."

At first Sand's inclination was to let the matter rest there, but the fate of players even remotely connected with the Black Sox scandal, those who had guilty knowledge, flashed into his mind. He repeated the remarks to his manager, Arthur Fletcher, at one time McGraw's crack shortstop on the Giants and later a Yankee coach.

Fletcher told the player: "Go out and play your best, but I am glad you told me this. It puts you out in the clear, and now I can protect you. I don't know what's behind this, but I mean to find out."

The National League race ended that day, as the Giants, with Lefthander Jack Bentley opposing Jimmy Ring, defeated the Phillies, 5 to 1. Sand handled his three fielding chances without a flaw; he made no hits. The stupidity of the O'Connell "proposition" was made further evident by the fact that Boston, with Johnny Cooney pitching, defeated Brooklyn on the same afternoon, 3 to 2. Even had the Giants lost that day, they still could have done no worse than tie for the pennant.

The glory of the Giants winning their fourth straight flag was of short duration. There were quick and ugly repercussions. Fletcher telephoned League President Heydler at the latter's Long Island home that Saturday night, saying: "I've got something important to tell you, but I do not wish to discuss it on the telephone. Where can I meet you?"

Heydler made an engagement to have breakfast with Fletcher on Sunday morning at the hotel where the Phillies were quartered. Arthur asked Sand to join the breakfast party, and then said to his shortstop: "I want you to repeat to Mr. Heydler exactly what you told me just before yesterday's game."

Sand repeated O'Connell's remarks, and shortly afterwards Heydler had Landis on the long distance telephone and gave him the story. The Judge, Mrs. Landis and Leslie O'Connor already were preparing to leave Chicago for Washington, where the first game of the World's Series was scheduled for October 4. Instead, the Commissioner and his secretary quickly jumped a fast train for New York, and arrived on Monday morning.

After conferring briefly with Heydler, Landis summoned Sand to his room. The Phillies had a final unimportant game with the Giants scheduled for that day, but it was called off on account of rain.

Landis immediately popped the question: "Were any other Philadelphia players approached—as far as you know?"

"I did not hear of any, Judge," replied the player.

"Why do you think O'Connell approached you, the only Philadelphia player, with such a proposition?" continued the Judge.

"I can't say. I have no idea," said Sand.

"Is he a friend of yours?"

"No, not particularly, though I've known him for some time. We were in the Pacific Coast League together, O'Connell with San Francisco and I with Salt Lake City. But, we never were on the same team."

The Judge then told O'Connor to have Stoneham and McGraw call on him immediately. Up to the time that they received this call, neither of the Giant executives knew anything about the matter. They didn't even know Landis was in town.

Heydler was with Landis when Stoneham and McGraw called. After Landis advised them of O'Connell's attempt to reach Sand, McGraw's first reaction was against Heydler.

"Why didn't you advise us of this matter before?" he demanded irately.

"It is something that I felt concerned the Commissioner," replied Heydler.

"Well, he's our ball player, isn't he? And it is our player who is being accused. We had the right to know," continued McGraw.

"That isn't getting anywhere," interrupted Landis. "I am here to make an investigation."

"Well, how do you know that Sand is speaking the truth?" snapped McGraw.

"I don't know, but it is my business to know. I want you to get hold of O'Connell as soon as you can and bring him here. Then I want to talk to him alone."

Strangely enough O'Connell made no attempt to deny that he had offered Sand the $500 bribe. He readily admitted it. In fact he was almost naive in his answers to the Judge's questions. He said Cozy Dolan, the New York coach, put him up to it. He had no idea where Cozy was to get the money to pay Sand, that apparently was Dolan's business; O'Connell merely forwarded the message.

But more important than involving a non-playing coach, O'Connell mentioned three of the big Giant stars, Second Baseman Frank Frisch, Right Fielder Ross Youngs and First Baseman George Kelly.

"Kelly spoke to me at the batting cage, asking me what Sand had said, and Frisch and Youngs also spoke to me about it," said the naive O'Connell. None of them had mentioned the matter to him before, but he seemed to think this trio, as well as most of the team, knew all about it.

Landis took his own notes of all that O'Connell said. Poking a finger in the young ball player's face, he said: "Do you understand, O'Connell, that as the result of what you are telling me, you will be expelled from baseball?"

"Yes, Judge; I know that," said Jimmy, then only 23, and at the threshold of his career.

Landis immediately summoned Dolan, Frisch, Youngs and Kelly. Dolan proved an unsatisfactory, exasperating witness. To all of Landis' questions, he had one stock answer: "I don't remember" or "I can't remember." Apparently he had been coached by some lawyer on these answers. He couldn't remember whether he had spoken to O'Connell about the Sand proposition; he couldn't recall whether anyone else had suggested the bribe to him.

Landis was furious with Dolan. He knew how to cow witnesses and to make them talk, but he could get nothing out of Dolan.

LANDIS AS FEDERAL JUDGE

LANDIS AFTER MAKING PEACE WITH BABE RUTH AND BOB MEUSEL

"Damn you, Dolan; don't you remember anything?" he shouted at McGraw's coach.

"I don't remember anything," said Dolan.

Frisch, Youngs and Kelly were examined and questioned separately and again with O'Connell in the room. Except for Frisch's famous remark at the time, that there "always is a lot of kidding going on on every bench," the three stars denied they knew anything of the attempted bribe or that they had questioned O'Connell about it.

Landis was in an awkward spot. The opening of the World's Series was getting nearer, the whole country was steamed up over Washington's first appearance in a World's Series, and the Giants were the National League contender. He had to make a quick decision. He ruled that O'Connell, having confessed to attempting to bribe a fellow National League player, was placed on baseball's permanent ineligible list, and that Dolan, because of having such a poor memory and being such a poor witness, would join him on the blacklist. Frisch, Kelly and Youngs were given clean bills of health.

The story did not break until Wednesday, October 1, three days before the opening of the World's Series. There were rumors in New York that something big was on, but no one knew exactly what. Landis' finding was given out just as he left New York for Washington. He never was much to grant interviews, and when he reached Washington he wasn't prepared for his newspaper reception. Almost one hundred sports writers, many of them already in Washington for the Series, crowded outside of his door at the Willard, and wouldn't go away until he gave them some kind of an interview. They especially wanted to know whether the thing went deeper, who was behind Dolan, and what further investigations he would undertake. He said his New York finding told the story, but that he would re-open the case, if additional evidence warranted it.

Coming almost on the eve of the World's Series, the story was almost as much of a sensation to the country as the White Sox scandal which broke in the late season of 1920. Ban Johnson and

Barney Dreyfuss, who had fought each other for years over the Garry Herrmann issue, both immediately got into Kenesaw Mountain's hair with barbed-wire newspaper statements. Johnson again was peeved that he had been ignored as a member of the Advisory Council, and what made him even more perturbed was the fact that he knew nothing of the incident until he had read of it in the newspapers. He also had hated McGraw ever since the Giant manager left the Baltimore Americans in midseason, 1902, and cast his lot with the Giants, taking a parcel of valuable Oriole players with him. Ban now offered the suggestion that in view of the attempted bribe, Brooklyn should play the Washingtons in the World's Series instead of the Giants. "And if Brooklyn isn't permitted to play, there should be no World's Series at all," said Ban. Despite the fact that Judge Landis had been voted supreme power by the major league club owners on November 12, 1920, to handle all such matters, Johnson called for a Federal investigation of the case and announced that he had dispatched the American League attorney to Washington to see what steps could be taken to get such an investigation under way. Naturally that irritated Landis, and made the feud between the pair still more bitter.

Johnson got some support, when Representative Sol Bloom of New York, former chairman of the House's Foreign Affairs Committee, came out with a declaration that baseball should be regulated by federal act. Early in the Washington-Giant Series, Congressman Bloom made this statement:

"The nation-wide interest in the World's Series now in progress, combined with national chagrin that one of the participating teams is involved in a scandal, convinces me that the time has come when the Federal Government should take a supervisory interest in baseball.

"Baseball is a matter of inter-state commerce. The two major leagues, and most of the minor leagues, are inter-state affairs. Congress has power to regulate the inter-state operation of railroads and the inter-state movement of foodstuffs, medicines, etc.

"If Congress can do this, it can regulate inter-state baseball. The sport is a national pastime and it has taken such a hold on our public that the government should provide some sort of regulation for the good of the sport itself, as well as the protection of the public. Baseball club owners recognized the demand for some sort of super-regulation when Judge Landis was chosen as czar, but the game is too big for one man to control. When Congress reconvenes I shall introduce a regulatory bill, and I believe it will be enacted into a law."

This is just what Landis and most of his supporters among the club owners did not want, as a Federal regulatory board or commission would have taken away much of Landis' great power, and reduced him to a subordinate position, just as the Judge's elevation to the supreme Commissionership in 1920 reduced Ban Johnson, baseball's former strong man, to a mere league president. Ban Johnson would have welcomed the law, but it never came to pass, being buried in committee.

Barney Dreyfuss, the scrappy little Pittsburgh leader, joined Johnson in asking that the 1924 World's Series be called off, after Landis had paid no attention to Johnson's suggestion to substitute Brooklyn for the Giants. Barney's club finished only three games out of the lead, and he said if there were shenanigans in the last fortnight of the race, his club might well have been unfairly deprived of its chance at the pennant. Following a wire from Dreyfuss urging that he call off the Series, Landis publicly admonished Dreyfuss by telling him "to keep his shirt on."

Dreyfuss refused to attend the Series, but while the games were in Washington, he took a train to the Capital, not to see any of the games, but to call on Landis. He said he could give the Commissioner some additional evidence on the Dolan-O'Connell case. When Dreyfuss called at Landis' hotel, the Judge personally sent out word: "The Commissioner is not in."

The pair later met in the Willard Hotel elevator. Failing to get an interview some thought Dreyfuss had jockeyed the meeting in this way. He was accompanied by his manager, Bill McKechnie, now coach of the Indians. "When can I talk to you, Judge?" asked Dreyfuss. "I came all the way from Pittsburgh to see you."

"I will not be in," snapped Landis abruptly.

Annoyed by the brush-off which Landis was giving his employer, McKechnie asked: "Why won't you be in?"

In a flash, the Judge turned on McKechnie. Leaning over until his angry face almost touched Bill's, he yelled: "Who are you? I have nothing to do with you."

When the elevator reached the street, Landis stormed out of it, giving the two Pittsburghers no further recognition. Dreyfuss returned to Pittsburgh with no chance to tell his story and burned up.

Later Landis got to "know" Bill McKechnie, and I believe he was one of the sincere Pennsylvania Scot's admirers. Certainly he congratulated Bill most warmly when McKechnie's Reds won the 1940 World's Series from the Detroit Tigers. Yet, I never could get Landis' attitude at that time. He was scrupulously honest, and certainly no one wanted to get behind the O'Connell-Dolan business more than he did. When the club owner and manager of one of the leading contenders came to see him, supposedly with evidence, there is no reason why Landis should not have heard them. But he was vain, autocratic and easily offended. Dreyfuss had offended him by requesting that he call off the Series, so he would have nothing to do with Barney.

Before leaving this incident I probably should mention a letter which appeared in a New York newspaper at the time, supposedly written by a gambler. It attracted a lot of attention. The letter said a certain group had wagered $100,000 that New York would win the National League flag by two games (they won by a game and a half) and that $5,000 had been paid to a Giant player in the bribe effort. The crippling of the team late in the season "worried" the gamblers, and they were concerned about those final games with Philadelphia. The letter concluded with the statement that O'Connell was only the goat.

Landis probably thought so himself, but he couldn't catch the higher-ups. Some years later, during another World's Series, the door to his Pullman drawing room was open as the late Damon Runyon and Sid Mercer were making their way to the dining car. "Let's stop in a minute and see the Judge," said Runyon.

"You know I've always thought that O'Connell was just a poor tool for others in that 1924 business," began Runyon. "I don't think he ever knew exactly what he was doing. I've just returned from California, Judge, and things aren't going very well with

Jimmy. He is working now on the San Francisco docks. He should be right in his baseball prime. Don't you think this boy has been punished enough, Judge? I believe the public would be with you if you reinstate him."

"Damon, I'm just as sorry for that young fellow as you are," said Landis. "But, what can I do? O'Connell confessed his guilt, namely that he tried to bribe another player to throw a game. I couldn't let him back. You know that. Every ball player we expelled would be in my office seeking reinstatement. As for the great bulk of other players, what would they think? They know now that any action seeking to throw, or otherwise tamper with a game, means expulsion. And it has to stay that way. Damon, no, I can't do it."

The Washington-Giant World's Series proved one of the most thrilling ever played, and fully vindicated Landis' judgment in playing it. No Series prior to that ever attracted such nation-wide interest, and no World's Series contender ever had so many well-wishers as that 1924 Washington team. For one thing, the country was rooting for Walter Johnson, who finally got into the blue ribbon games in his eighteenth big league season. The Series stretched out to the full seven games, with President Coolidge, and his gracious lady, attending three of the four games in Washington. The Senators eventually won the Series when they were victorious, 4 to 3, in a wild 12-inning seventh game, in which most everything happened. The Giant catcher, Hank Gowdy, caught his foot in his mask while going after an easy foul, and Washington's winning run came over when a ground ball by Earl McNeely hit smack at Freddy Lindstrom, substitute Giant third baseman, struck a pebble or chunk of hard dirt, and hopped over Freddy's head. Walter Johnson, defeated in both of his starting assignments, was credited with winning the seventh game, going in as Washington's fourth pitcher of the day.

The Washington team's victory set off the wildest baseball demonstration seen anywhere up to that time. In Washington's long history in the nineteenth century National League and the early American League, the baseball fate of the Capital City fans usually had been a succession of second division teams. Often they were at the very bottom. But the 1924 Senators not only had won in their own league, but now were proud champions of the universe. And the city really removed the lid! From shortly after the game until early next morning, joy-crazed Washington fans of both sexes, from dignified bureaucrats to Capitol bootblacks, snake-danced down Pennsylvania Avenue, blowing horns, beating dishpans, whistling, singing, shouting. They carried improvised signs and banners, praising their heroes and belittling McGraw's powerful team from New York.

Fred Lieb, who was chief scorer at that Series, had occasion to call on the Commissioner that night. He found him on a little balcony, outside of his hotel window, staring intently on the milling thousands down below. The Judge was visibly affected by this delirium of the Washington rooters.

Placing his hand on Lieb's shoulder, he said seriously: "I wonder whether we are looking at the high tide of this thing we love [meaning baseball]. Greece and Rome had their sports; they must have reached a peak, and then receded. Are we looking at such a peak tonight?"

After the Series the repercussions of the Dolan-O'Connell incident continued in the press. When the sports writers had written themselves out about Johnson's pitching, Griffith's strategy, etc., they went back to the National League finish and demanded that Landis come out in the open, and give the full details of his hearing with everyone involved, including Sand, Heydler, Fletcher, McGraw, Dolan, O'Connell, Frisch, Kelly and Youngs.

Cozy supplied some of the details himself. He engaged William J. Fallon, then one of New York's top criminal lawyers and personal attorney to Charles A. Stoneham, Giant president, as his attorney to bring suit against Landis for barring him from baseball.

Cozy even held open house at Fallon's New York office, inviting the New York writers to hear his side of the story. Dolan's account of the Judge and himself almost coming to blows, at Cozy's second hearing, bears repetition, as the 130-pound Judge, then nearly 58, apparently was willing to take on McGraw's burly coach.

"When I replied to the Judge's questions, and said: 'I don't remember,' I really meant to say, 'No,'" said Cozy. "I always use that expression. O'Connell told a pack of lies to Landis in his confession to the Judge, who I thought would believe me to be innocent.

"When I read in the newspapers the next day that I was barred from baseball for life, I was stunned. I asked Landis for another hearing and my request was granted.

"After we exchanged some words, I said to him: 'Judge, you know damned well that I am not guilty.'"

"At that, he rushed at me, almost poked his finger in my eye, and yelled: 'Dolan, you ARE guilty!'

"Then we exchanged a lot of ugly words, until the Judge finally cried: 'I am an old man, Dolan, but I still can take care of myself.'

"To this I replied: 'Judge, I didn't come here to fight, but to clear my name. You are taking the bread and butter right out of my mouth.' At that, he ordered me from his room."

At the time, there was considerable discussion in New York, also elsewhere in baseball, how Dolan, the expelled coach, whose bread and butter had been taken out of his mouth according to Cozy's own admission, could engage the highest-priced criminal lawyer in New York. Joe Vila, the *Sun*'s sports editor and *The Sporting News*' enterprising New York correspondent, kept hammering away at the question: "Who sent Cozy Dolan to William J. Fallon? And who is meeting the legal bill?"

Fallon called up Vila and asked him to have luncheon with him. "I'll answer you, if you stop demanding to know who sent Dolan to Fallon," said the attorney. "It was John McGraw."

When Vila wanted to know why, Fallon asked in turn: "If you had a man working for you for years, and he had been faithful to you, and then got into a jam, would you try to help him, or would you run out on him?"

Fallon drew up the necessary papers to bring action against Landis. There even was talk in the New York papers that Cozy would sue for $1,000,000 damages for libel and defamation of character. But suddenly the expelled coach grew lukewarm in his suit, told Fallon to go easy, as he heard that Landis was going to relent and reinstate him. Fallon later said he would have enjoyed going on with the case. He had no interest in baseball, or for the rules necessary for its good conduct, but said: "I would have liked to have had some fun with the Judge on the witness stand. I was in court one day when he got awfully tough with a bootlegger, and sentenced him to two years in the penitentiary."

Judge Landis was perturbed when word came to him that McGraw, or the Giants, were footing Fallon's legal costs. Some hot telegrams and letters were exchanged between the Commissioner and the Giants' office at 42nd Street and Sixth Avenue. The Judge was blistering mad and didn't try to hide it. It was around that time that Dolan grew cool in his suit, and returned to his home in Oshkosh. Had Cozy, backed by the Giants, gone through with it, I believe the Commissioner would have ripped the game wide open.

On January 10, 1925, Landis gave out complete stenographic reports of his conversations with Dolan, O'Connell, Frisch, Kelly and Youngs. Judge Landis said he did it at the insistence of sports writers, some of whom seemed to think he was hiding something. It contained 20,000 words of questions and answers, and several of the New York newspapers printed the testimony in full.

However, George Kelly, the Giant first baseman, helped bring the matter to the fore again, when it developed that he and Jimmy O'Connell were members of the same California professional basketball team, the Adam and Eves of San Francisco. Sammy Bohne of the Reds, mentioned in the 1923 *Collyer's Eye* story, was a member of the same team. This story broke in early January, and started a new furore in baseball.

John Heydler, the National League president, got more excited about it, at least in the press, than Landis. In an A.P. statement, which follows, he was severe on George Kelly, and suggested possible suspension.

"George Kelly was one of the men who was charged with complicity in the O'Connell affair. He should be the last one to have any dealings with this man, and it is hard to believe such is the case. If the story is proved untrue, all well and good. If not, it will go hard with the players involved. Judge Landis is not the man to accept the implied flout of his authority and the stigma to baseball's good name without adequate reply."

Garry Herrmann immediately announced that Bohne had not asked permission to play in the league, and he wired him, forbidding him to take part in any of the contests. Dan P. Maher, president of the league in which Kelly, O'Connell and Bohne were signed, first said that Kelly would play only home games with the Adam and Eve team, while O'Connell would appear only in the road contests. He felt that would keep the players apart, and "meet with Mr. Heydler's objections." Apparently, he didn't know his baseball people, for shortly afterward he announced that O'Connell had been dropped from the league. This happened on January 6, and started a new wave of pro-O'Connell feeling throughout the country. People said he again was being made the goat. That no doubt smoked out the Judge, for four days later he released everything he had on the O'Connell-Dolan case for the press, the public and all the world to see.

One of the sequels of this last phase of this celebrated case was still stricter baseball contracts, whereby the club owner took absolute control of the player's athletic activities for the full 12 months of the year.

Landis not only was nettled at Ban Johnson for his conduct at the time of the 1924 World's Series, but for Ban's action in hiring detectives to investigate gambling and alleged approaches made by gamblers to players of the Pacific Coast League. Johnson learned that a big ring of gamblers, betting thousands of dollars daily, operated out of Los Angeles, and he gave the inference that neither Harry Williams, the new Pacific Coast president, nor Landis was sufficiently active in seeking to correct the situation.

In defense of his conduct, Johnson said: "I am not so much interested in Coast League gambling in itself, but these gamblers are so strongly entrenched and have so much money, they can reach their slimy fingers right into the American League." Five years before, two former American League players, Bill Rumler and Harl Maggert, and Gene Dale, a former Cardinal and Cincinnati pitcher, then with the Salt Lake City club of the Coast League, were all expelled for allegedly conspiring to throw games.

Landis did not deny that there was heavy gambling on the Coast, centering in Los Angles (which then had no racing), but

141

Johnson again was stepping on his toes and poaching on his game preserve. Landis was the game's policeman, and if there was any sleuthing to do in the Far West, he would do it through his own operatives. William Wrigley, Jr., the chewing gum millionaire, who then was building a new ball park in Los Angeles, took a blast at Johnson. Wrigley, who also owned the Chicago Cubs, always was believed to be the man behind Lasker in the Lasker plan and in Lasker's early campaign for Landis as Commissioner.

At the annual meeting of the minor leagues at Hartford, Conn., December 22-3-4, which preceded the major league meetings in Chicago and New York, Coast League president Williams and Bill Lane, owner of the Salt Lake City club, lashed out at Johnson, and an effort was made to put the entire National Association on record as opposing Ban.

Landis did not attend the Hartford meeting, owing to the death of a sister-in-law and the fact that Mrs. Landis had to go to the Mayo Clinic for a jaw condition, but he was bristling with anger and ready for a showdown struggle with Johnson when he arrived in New York for the joint major league meetings a week later. A committee of American Leaguers, headed by the Yankee, Ruppert, and including Ernest Barnard of Cleveland and Tom Shibe of the Athletics, had been selected by American League club owners at a previous meeting in Chicago to see whether they could patch up the feud between their president and the Judge.

Ruppert was optimistic enough to give out a statement: "The quarrel between Judge Landis and Ban Johnson should be patched up. Both are big men and have accomplished much good in base-ball. They should work in harmony, instead of pulling in opposite directions, and I feel sure that when spring arrives there will be no further trouble."

Poor well-meaning Jake! His statement merely added fuel to the flames. It intimated that there was a lack of harmony on both sides, and that if Big Ban pulled one way, the "Mountain" didn't help matters any by throwing his weight in the opposite direction.

The American League's conciliatory committee found an irate, uncompromising Landis when they called on the Commissioner at his suite at the Commodore. "Ruppert, you people have got to make up your minds whether you want me or Ban Johnson," he said. "I've stood all that I intend to stand. You've promised me repeatedly that you would control Johnson, but this year he has been more impossible than ever."

When Ruppert, Barnard and Shibe reported back to their fellow club owners, the result was a public censure of Johnson which was one of the most humiliating rebukes in the entire history of baseball. Johnson was removed from the game's Advisory Council, and given to understand that he was only being retained on sufferance, and subject to his good behavior. Though the expression was given out as the unanimous action of the league, that doughty ex-Federal Leaguer from St. Louis, Phil Ball, alone declined to sign it. The statement, as given to Landis, and released to the press, follows:

"We recognize that conditions have arisen that are gravely harmful to baseball and that must be intolerable to you and that these conditions have been created by the activities of the president of the American League.

"While you were dealing promptly and efficiently with a most deplorable exception to baseball's honorable record, our president sought to discredit your action and to cast suspicion upon the 1924 World's Series.

"One year ago you made known to us, in his presence, various of his activities, and that it was our expectation and hope that the unanimous action then taken certainly would operate as a corrective, but in this expectation and hope we have been disappointed.

"We do not extenuate these things or question their harmful effect on baseball. However, he has been president of our league since its inception and we ask you again to overlook his conduct and accept from us these guarantees:

"1. That his misconduct will cease or his immediate removal from office will follow.

"2. That legislation will be adopted that will limit his activity to the internal affairs of the American League.

"3. That any and all measures which you may deem advisable to the above will be adopted.

"As expressing our attitude toward your administration of the Commissioner's office, we tender you herewith a copy of the resolution unanimously adopted at its annual meeting in New York, December 10, 1924.

   (signed)   THOMAS S. SHIBE, Philadelphia
                CLARK C. GRIFFITH, Washington
                ROBERT QUINN, Boston
                CHARLES A. COMISKEY, Chicago
                E. S. BARNARD, Cleveland
                JACOB RUPPERT, New York
                FRANK J. NAVIN, Detroit"

I do not know whether Landis dictated this resolution, but I always have felt that he told Ruppert exactly what he wanted in it, and in no unmistakable terms. Though Johnson no doubt was much to blame, after twenty odd years I cannot help but feel that this rebuke was cruel and far more than Ban deserved. Landis left the meeting the victor, with banners flying; Johnson was heartsick, disconsolate and suffering a mental torture. His only statement, and public reply to the rebuke, was: "I am sorry that the American League club owners could not conceive their faithful and exact duty to the public. I have no criticism to make."

During the year, Landis saw the International League, the lone non-draft league left after 1923, come into the fold, completing the Commissioner's fight for the removal of the "un-American wall," which he claimed had blocked the paths of certain players to advance in accordance with their natural ability. However, the system of the baseball chains, or farm club organizations, inaugurated by Branch Rickey, vice president of the Cardinals in St. Louis, already was starting to irk him. He considered it another method to hold players in the minors, and opposed any innovation whereby the old style minor league owner—the town editor, undertaker or haberdasher—would fade from the baseball picture.

And, among his many duties the Judge found time to attend the first annual dinner of the New York Baseball Writers in that tumultuous year of 1924. It was a small affair at the Commodore, compared with the big dinners which followed, but it was an intimate affair and some 250 guests and "the Mountain" had a gay evening. Bob Kelley, then of the *New York Times* sports staff, was the first "Landis" in a New York sports skit, and Frank Barnett, the fresh professional waiter, insulted the Judge, Ruppert, Walter Camp, Sam Crane and others until they were blue in the face. From the start, the Judge was smart enough to suspect it was a rib. And, when he was called on for some remarks, Landis said: "I've had just such a wonderful evening that I'll make you fellows a promise. If you repeat this performance in subsequent years, I'll promise to attend no matter what part of the earth I will happen to be on, if the condition of my physical being permits." And, until Landis' health interfered in later years, or he wintered in Phoenix, Arizona, he always lived up to that promise.

17: Ban and Ken Get Raises

Following the tempestuous year of 1924, the season of 1925 was calm in contrast, perhaps the quietest of the Judge's first term in office. The Judge and his lady took a late winter vacation to Cuba and Panama, and when he returned he learned that the New York District Attorney's office had come practically to the same conclusion that he did in the celebrated O'Connell-Dolan case.

In view of the fact that some of the Metropolitan newspapers still were demanding that the real culprits be brought to light, J. H. Banton, the District Attorney for New York County, requested one of his assistants, George N. Brothers, to make a full investigation and ascertain whether a crime had been committed. Most of the principals were interrogated. Heydler volunteered to testify, but was not called. Leslie O'Connor was present in behalf of Landis, and brought statements from two players, Bill Cunningham of the Braves and Emil Yde of the Pirates, denying that they knew anything worth while about the business.

In his report to Banton, Assistant District Attorney Brothers intimated that O'Connell was the "goat," and while there was no legal evidence against Dolan, he must be regarded with suspicion. Kelly, Frisch and Youngs were cleared as strong as Brothers could make it, saying: "Kelly, Youngs and Frisch are completely exonerated. There is no evidence whatsoever in connecting them with the case. Considering their straight-forward replies and their clean reputations as players, there is no doubt of their innocence."

Brothers further said that on Landis' return from the Caribbean, he would confer with the Commissioner on the advisability of indicting O'Connell for having committed a felony in New York County by offering the bribe to Sand at the Polo Grounds. Landis advised against it, feeling the Californian already had been punished enough.

Ban Johnson, slapped severely by his league the preceding December, was on his good behavior. At least, he avoided any public criticism of the Commissioner, and that was difficult for Ban to do. When he felt something was wrong with the conduct of baseball, he never pulled his punches.

With Landis miles away, Johnson put on something of a come-back in his own league, when he had his club owners pass a resolution barring all exhibition games between the American League champions and the National League pennant winners, otherwise the World's Series clubs, for a full year. It was generally taken as a slap against Griffith and Johnson's old enemy, John McGraw. Relations between Ban and Griff were strained as the result of Johnson's comment on the 1924 World's Series and his part in drawing up the rebuke of December 10. The Giants and Washingtons had 13 spring games scheduled for 1925, but they were exempted from the resolution. The rule remained in effect only a few years.

Even though the American League promised that Johnson would confine his activities to the affairs of his own league, I now can reveal that Johnson continued to hire detectives on the Coast all through the Pacific Coast League season of 1925, especially before and during the 1925 Washington-Pittsburgh World's Series. Whether Landis knew that Johnson kept his sleuths at work, I do not know, but he probably did. There was little that got past him in his quarter of a century in office.

I have seen some of these private 1925 reports to Johnson, and actually millions of dollars were bet on the Series of that year. Los Angeles apparently was the clearing house, and the big syndicate operating from there was on the Pirates. And, from L.A. they would send their money to representatives all over the country, to be placed in Chicago, Detroit, Kansas City, even smaller cities like Fargo and Scranton. Most of the little fellows, or the so-called "sucker" money, was on Washington.

The Series saw the Pirates put on one of the gamest uphill fights in the history of World's Series play. Trailing three games to one, McKechnie's fighting team pulled out the event by winning the last three games. After Walter Johnson had held Pittsburgh to eleven hits and one run in eighteen innings while winning the first and fourth games, the Washington ace was called on to pitch the seventh and final game in the rain and mud of Forbes Field, October 15. Walter couldn't get his footing on the mound or his stuff on the wet slippery ball; he blew an early 4 to 0 lead and eventually lost a heart-breaker, 9 to 7. Staking all on his Big Train, Bucky Harris, the Washington manager, kept Johnson in to the finish, while McKechnie employed four Pirate pitchers. Walter was tagged for fifteen rain-bespattered hits. Because of the continued feeling between Ban and Griffith, Johnson did not attend the Series, but after Ban got the news of that distressing seventh game, he wired Harris: "You sacrificed a World's Championship for the American League through your display of sentiment," referring to Harris' failure to lift Johnson, even though his early formidable lead was slipping away. Washington led until a three-run Pirate rally in the eighth shot Pittsburgh out in front. Landis made no public comment on Johnson's action in sending such a telegram, but privately his comment was: "That was a lousy thing for Johnson to do."

The unfortunate "goat" of the Series was Roger Peckinpaugh, the great Washington shortstop, and now the General Manager of the Buffalo club in the International League. Peck, a big factor in the Washington club's American League success, was voted the American League's most valuable player for 1925 on the eve of the Series, and then proceeded to make eight errors, a World's Series record. Many came in what ball players call "the clutch."

There never was a more honest, conscientious player than Peck-inpaugh; he fretted over his early blunders, and the harder he tried, the worse he got. His fingers were all thumbs. The story during the Series was that Landis had Peck shadowed after the early games, not that he believed the great shortstop wasn't trying; but he knew, as did Ban Johnson, of the great sums which the professionals had wagered on Pittsburgh. And, if there was to be any unpleasant aftermath, or any innuendo against Peckinpaugh, he wanted to be in a position to clear the great shortstop.

During the 1925 World's Series, the former great pitcher of the New York Giants, Christy Mathewson, the twirler Judge Landis had rooted against in Matty's memorable duels with Mordecai Brown, died at Saranac Lake, N.Y. John Heydler, John McGraw and other baseball men left the Series to attend the funeral; Mathewson at the time of his death was president of the Boston Braves. Landis could not leave the Series, but he was deeply touched. "Why should God wish to take a thoroughbred like Matty so soon, and leave some others down here that could well be spared?" he asked.

There were a few minor league incidents that year which had Landis peering under the surface of things in this part of his realm. In New Orleans, one of the newspapers made the charge that several of the Pelican players were "playing crooked baseball" in an effort to get away from the New Orleans club. Judge John D. Martin, president of the Southern Association, officially brought the charge to the attention of Commissioner Landis. The Judge made a thorough and rigorous investigation, after which he absolved the accused Pelicans of any wrongdoing. Judge Martin, incidentally, also became a Federal judge, of the Court of Appeals in Cincinnati.

In the Blue Ridge League, President J. V. Jamison, Jr. gathered evidence that the conduct of some of his league's players was open to suspicion, and Jamison felt they were subject to the influence of professional gamblers. Jamison was a great admirer of Ban Johnson and an intimate of the American League chief. Even though Johnson had been dropped from the Advisory Council the preceding winter, Jamison brought his first suspicions and evidence to Ban's attention. That probably was no way for Jamison to go about it; Landis' interest in the case was cursory, and nothing came of Jamison's investigation and intimations of improper conduct.

The Judge again gave Cozy Dolan an emphatic "No" to the former Giant coach's last plea for reinstatement. Dolan again wrote: "You know, Judge, there is no evidence that I did anything wrong," but Landis shot back: "Nothing has happened to change my opinion as to your status in baseball."

In the American League's annual meeting in December, 1925, the club owners gave Landis something to think about when they did an "about face" in their conduct toward their chief. No doubt penitent over the manner in which they had publicly humiliated Johnson a year before, the American League owners gave Ban a $10,000 raise in salary—increasing his stipend to $40,000—and offered him a new contract, extending his term to 1935.

In *The Sporting News* issue of December 17, 1925, an unnamed American League club owner was quoted as saying: "We wronged Ban Johnson and the league a year ago, but we did not give Johnson the new contract wholly as a balm to assuage injured feelings. We did that because the organizer and life-long head of our organization was entitled to it."

Already there was speculation in the nation's newspapers as to how Ban's comeback would affect future relations with Landis. Landis' contract would expire in January, 1928, and there was talk that after that date baseball would go back to more "self-determination in the affairs of individual leagues," and that while Landis no doubt could have another term, he would have to share some of his great power with the major league heads.

The joint meeting of the majors in New York, December 10, 1925, exactly one year after Ban's spanking, saw another interesting development—Landis tossing in his lot with the American League in a schedule dispute with the National League. Up to this point, a number of American League owners, though publicly giving Landis lip-service, privately considered him a "National Leaguer." "They (the N.L.) put him in," was another remark one heard, even though Landis was elected by the unanimous vote of all the sixteen clubs. It was unfair, of course, but perhaps because of the antipathy between the Judge and Ban, these American League people felt the jurist leaned toward the senior league. It, therefore, was occasion for much surprise to see Landis rule against his National League friends.

The matter was of no great importance, but it engendered considerable heat. For years, the National League was a late-closing league, and twice at the instigation of the late Charley Ebbets of Brooklyn had the schedule dragged out to include Columbus Day, October 12. However, since Landis came in, the leagues agreed to open and close on the same day. The American League voted to close the 1926 season, September 26, a full week earlier than the end of the 1925 season. The National League, seeing its schedule gradually pushed out of October by football, voted for an October 3 closing. Landis voted for the earlier closing.

There was an echo of the 1919 White Sox sellout late in 1925.

Ever since this scandal broke late in the season of 1920, the major league presidents and later Judge Landis withheld $4,800.53 in 1920 second place money from the eight Chicago American players who had been placed on baseball's ineligible list. Receiving word that Happy Felsch and Joe Jackson had lost suits in Milwaukee for their shares of this money, Landis decided to divide the entire sum among the unaccused members of the 1920 White Sox team, including players who had been sent to the minors or traded to other clubs.

The season of 1926 was another one which was fairly easy on the Commissioner's nerves. Most of his cases were of a routine nature. It was a most eventful season, in which the fan Commissioner had a bully time. The St. Louis Cardinals, under the leadership of the aggressive Rogers Hornsby, who later took a permanent lease on the Commissioner's doghouse, won their first National League flag, and in the American League, the Yankees, a seventh-placer in 1925, made the remarkable leap back into Pennantland. The World's Series between the two clubs was one of the most dramatic ever held, and the receipts, $1,207,864, have been exceeded only three times since then.

The Commissioner was strictly neutral at all Series games, but who can guess what thoughts ran through that tousled head, as crouched over his box at Yankee Stadium, in that never-to-be-forgotten seventh game, he first saw Tony Lazzeri whistle one of relief pitcher Grover Alexander's fast ones down the left field foul line—a ball which was foul by inches—before Alex struck out Tony on the next pitch, leaving the bases full of Yankees. Was the Judge rooting for the old master of the mound, by that time thirty-nine, or for the lusty young Italian from the Golden Gate?

As the fall of 1926 wore on, and the early winter rolled around, there was a lot of politics played under the surface as the major leagues approached their December annual meetings. For a time it augured for a happier situation between those old baseball enemies, Landis and Johnson, but it was only a brief lull before the final storm.

At the annual meeting of the American League held in Chicago, December 14, 1926, a committee of Colonel Jacob Ruppert of the

Yankees, Phil Ball of the Browns and Ernest S. Barnard of the Cleveland Indians was appointed to wait on Landis and ascertain whether the organization could work in greater harmony with him for the general good of baseball. They also were instructed to tell the Commissioner, as gently as possible, that the original agreement with him provided that he should have two advisers from the ranks of baseball. They felt that the American League was handicapped by not having its league president on the Advisory Council. Johnson now had been kept off the Council for two years, and Landis was not vengeful. He was conciliatory and intimated that if the committee would vouch for Ban's good behavior, he would not oppose his return. The committee, along with a National League delegation, also sounded out Landis on his willingness to accept a new term.

When the committee reported back to the league, Clark Griffith, who had resumed his early friendly feelings for Johnson, made the motion that Ban be restored to the Advisory Council, and seven affirmative votes were cast. Only Charley Comiskey of Chicago, Ban's erstwhile crony but now implacable enemy, declined to vote.

This action had an interesting sequel, as Phil Ball, who had fought with Johnson against Landis and alone, among the club presidents, refused to sign the original 1921 agreement with the Commissioner, offered the resolution that Kenesaw Mountain Landis be elected to a new seven-year term after his first term ran out on November 12, 1927.

Two days later, December 16, at the joint meeting of two majors, the same spirit of good will prevailed. Landis not only was given a new seven year contract, but his salary was boosted from $50,000 to $65,000. And Santa Claus also came to Leslie O'Connor, the Judge's secretary, as his annual stipend was upped from $10,000 to $12,500. Peace! It was wonderful!

The story at the time was that the $10,000 raise given to Johnson a year before was directly responsible for Landis' increase of $15,000. Some of the club owners, especially National Leaguers, felt that when the American League rewarded Johnson with a tidy raise, putting him only $10,000 under Landis, it was an indirect

152

slap at the Judge. They feared an effort was being made to build up Johnson to his former prominence in the game. So, they widened the gap between the Judge and Ban to $25,000.

Even at that time, the Judge was opposed to that man Rickey's farm idea. It had been a factor in the Cardinals' pennant of 1926. During the debate on the subject, one unidentified club owner was reported as saying: "Unless some steps are taken to bring about a mutual understanding on the price to be paid for players, the practice of creating farms probably will be more extensively adopted. It would be hard to restrict the owners to a maximum price to be paid for minor leaguers, but this matter of bidding for stars has got to be a cut-throat proposition and it is difficult to tell what it will lead to."

That the "farm system," despite Landis' dislike, would be more extensively adopted proved a good prophecy.

18: The Affair of Ty and Tris

The American League's wish for more harmonious relations between the Commissioner and Johnson, expressed at their own December, 1926, meeting and carried into the joint session with Landis, no doubt was inspired by a new sore which was festering under the surface of the American League. It also explains the league's urgent wish to have Johnson restored to the Advisory Council, and in part for Landis' acquiescence.

I would rather that this chapter could be omitted as it involves two of the greatest names in baseball, Ty Cobb and Tris Speaker, both of them men for whom I hold a high regard and whose friendship I have enjoyed and appreciated through the years. Yet, one could no more write the story of Landis and omit his vindication of these stars in 1927 than to write a life of Babe Ruth and pass over his 60 home runs. The Cobb-Speaker case, plus some further hanging of soiled Black Sox on baseball's clothes line, again brought the Landis-Ban Johnson feud into the open in all its bitterness. It became practically war to the death between these Titans of baseball, as Johnson, in ill health—beaten and disillusioned—was forced to resign from the league he founded, leaving Landis in absolute control of America's national game.

Ty Cobb and Tris Speaker were two of the famous player-managers of baseball in 1926. Cobb, by this time thirty-nine, had spent his entire baseball career in Detroit, the last six years as manager. There still is some question as to how good a manager Cobb was; some people felt he failed when he had a manager's chance. Ty never thought so; in his six years, he had one second place club, two thirds, one fourth and two sixths. He finished sixth in 1926, but still was a good ball player, hitting .339.

Speaker was thirty-eight; after a great career with the Boston Red Sox, he was transferred to Cleveland in 1916. He was appointed manager of the Indians in 1919, and won Cleveland's lone major league pennant and the World's Championship in 1920. After dropping back several years, he had a fighting team in 1926, which fought the Yankees right down to the wire before losing the pennant by three games. In eight seasons in Cleveland as manager, Tris had six first division clubs, won once and was the runner-up three times. It was a far better showing than any Cleveland manager before him. He played 150 games for his team that season, hit .304, and still was at the height of his popularity in Cleveland.

During the early fall, rumors began to circulate in baseball circles that Cobb and Speaker might not be back with their respective clubs in 1927, in fact, might not even be in baseball. It didn't make sense, as these outstanding stars were part of the very fabric of baseball.

However, that it was more than a rumor became evident November 2, when Ty Cobb announced his resignation as manager of the Detroit Club. Frank Navin, the Tiger owner, further gave out that George Moriarty, the American League umpire and former Detroit third baseman, would be the new Tiger manager, and that Cobb, the greatest player of all time, had been released. Just like that!

As a result, Detroit seethed with baseball gossip and sensation for several weeks. Exactly a month later, December 2, the Cleveland fans were thrown into consternation by the announcement that the great "Spoke" had resigned as manager and had been replaced by an obscure coach, Jack McCallister. Speaker also had been released. In way of an explanation, the Cleveland club announced that "Speaker is retiring from baseball to go into private business."

Now, there might have been some justification in Cobb's release, in view of his sixth place finish, but none after Speaker's great 1926 showing. By cutting a Yankee ten-game lead to almost nothing, Tris made a five-game September series played between the Bronx Bombers and the Indians a madhouse and the "richest" series played in Cleveland up to that time. Speaker not only finished a good second, but made a barrel of money for his club.

During the December annual meetings, in which Landis got his $15,000 raise and Ban was restored to the Advisory Council, the resignations of Cobb and Speaker were continually in the foreground. Why did these great stars resign? Why were they leaving baseball? Ugly rumors began to circulate that the American League had something on them. Being in Ban Johnson's confidence, I knew the story, and it was a whale of a story, but I couldn't print it. The American League felt it had damaging evidence against both players, but felt because of their great reputations, they should be allowed to resign and "enter other business."

However, newspaper pressure became so great that Judge Landis finally broke the story, December 21, when he released two letters which Hubert "Dutch" Leonard, former Red Sox and Detroit pitcher, had received from Ty Cobb and Joe Wood, a former Red Sox pitching associate but in 1919 an outfielder on the Cleveland club, seven years before. The letters involved betting on a questionable game between Cleveland and Detroit late in the season of 1919. Disgruntled over some alleged grievances, Leonard sent the letters to Ban Johnson, who, after an investigation, turned them over to Commissioner Landis. Leonard's position as informant in the case subjected him to considerable criticism. His peeve against Cobb was that as Tiger manager, Ty had released him to the old Vernon club of the Pacific Coast League in 1925, and against Speaker, a former teammate on the Red Sox, that he hadn't claimed him when the Detroit club asked for waivers.

The game in question was played in Detroit, September 25, 1919; the Tigers won it by a score of 9 to 5. The American League race already had been decided, as Chicago had won the pennant and Cleveland had clinched second place. However, there still was a fight between the Tigers and the Yankees for third money. It was the year the Yankees bought Carl Mays, related in an earlier chapter.

In giving out details of the story, Landis told the press that the matter had not been made public before "because none of the men involved is now associated with Organized Baseball." Cobb and Speaker both had been released, and Joe Wood had been baseball coach at Yale for three years.

Landis' report, released to the press, ran into 100 typewritten pages, and included much of the evidence turned over to him by Ban Johnson, including Leonard's statement. It alleged in part that between the games of September 24 and 25, 1919, Cobb, Leonard,

Speaker and Wood happened to gather under the Detroit stands and talk of baseball, and according to Dutch, "we (Cobb and himself) wanted to finish third." (There then was no fourth place money; the season ended September 28.)

Speaker then was quoted in the statement as saying: "Don't worry about tomorrow's game. We have second place cinched, and you will win tomorrow."

Leonard then added in his statement: "And everybody then agreed that if it was going to be a set-up we might as well get some money out of it.

"Then we talked about getting the money down on the game, that is, how to get up the dough and how much we would put up, and Cobb said he would send Fred West (a Detroit club employe, who ran errands for the players) down to us.

"I (Leonard) was to put up $1,500 and as I remember it Cobb $2,000, and Wood and Speaker $1,000 each. I had pitched that day and was through for the season and so I gave my check for $1,500 to Wood at the ball park and went to the hotel, packed my things and left that night for Independence, Mo.

"Several days later, I received the Wood letter at Independence, with a check for $1,630. He wrote that West was only able to get up part of the money and that my share of the winnings was only $130."

As so much of the testimony, and the Commissioner's subsequent verdict, concerned the Wood and Cobb letters, both of which were printed in the nation's press, December 21 and 22, 1926, they are reprinted:

The WOOD *Letter*

Cleveland, O., Friday.
Enclosed please find certified check for sixteen hundred and thirty dollars ($1,630).
Dear Friend "Dutch":
The only bet West could get up was $600 against $420 (10 to 7). Cobb did not get up a cent. He told us that and I believe him.

157

Could have put some at 5 to 2 on Detroit, but did not, as that would make us put up $1,000 to win $400.

We won the $420. I gave West $30, leaving $390, or $130 for each of us. Would not have cashed your check at all, but West thought he could get it up to 10–7, and I was going to put it all up at those odds. We would have won $1,750 for the $2,500 if we could have placed it.

If we ever have another chance like this we will know enough to try to get down early.

Let me hear from you, "Dutch."

With all good wishes to yourself and Mrs. Leonard, I am, always
JOE WOOD.

The COBB Letter
Augusta, Ga., Oct. 23, '19.

Dear Dutch:

Well, old boy, guess you are out in old California by this time and enjoying life.

I arrived home and found Mrs. Cobb only fair, but the baby girl was fine, and at this time Mrs. Cobb is very well, but I have been very busy getting acquainted with my family and have not tried to do any correspondence, hence my delay.

Wood and myself are considerably disappointed in our business proposition, as we had $2,000 to put into it and the other side quoted us $1,400, and when we finally secured that much money it was about 2 o'clock and they refused to deal with us, as they had men in Chicago to take the matter up with and they had no time, so we completely fell down and of course we felt badly over it.

Everything was open to Wood and he can tell you about it when we get together. It was quite a responsibility and I don't care for it again, I can assure you.

Well, I hope you found everything in fine shape at home and all your troubles will be little ones. I made a this year's winner's share of World's Series on cotton since I came home, and expect to make more.

I thought the White Sox should have won, but am satisfied they were too confident. Well, old scout, drop me a line when you can.

158

*We have had fine weather here, in fact, quite warm, and have had
some dandy fishing since I arrived home.*

With kindest regards to Mrs. Leonard, I remain, sincerely

                                                          TY

Landis' report then showed that he had Cobb and Speaker before him for lengthy questioning, November 29, and there were
pages of Questions and Answers. Though out of baseball, Leonard
also was summoned to the Commissioner's office, but he declined
to attend. Much of the testimony concerned Wood, who had been
Speaker's roommate for 15 years.

Cobb admitted writing the letter, but denied he ever bet on
ball games, or on this game in particular, and stressed that he never
had committed any act harmful to baseball.

In the course of the interrogation, Landis said: "Mr. Cobb, I
hand you a document, dated Augusta, Ga., October 23, 1919,
addressed to 'Dear Dutch' and signed 'Sincerely Ty,' which will be
marked Exhibit 1, and I ask you to look at that document and tell
me if you know who wrote that letter."

A. It is my letter.

Q. I call your attention to the letter which you have just identified as having been written by you and ask you if you recall the
occasion of having written that letter.

A. Yes, I wrote the letter.

Q. And what was it about?

A. It was in response to a request by Leonard that I ascertain
from Wood (Joe Wood) the amount of money that was wagered
on this game in question.

Q. The amount of money that was wagered on what?

A. On the game in question.

Q. That is the game of September 25, 1919?

A. Yes, sir. He stated—you want me to relate what he said?

Q. Yes.

A. He stated he was leaving and wanted to check up on the
amount that had been wagered.

Q. Do you recall where you were and where Leonard was at
the time he made that request to you?

A. On the ball field.

Q. When was it that he made this request to you, as you say, with respect to the playing of that game—before or after the game?

A. If my memory serves me right, it was the day of the game.

Q. Well, before the game was played or after?

A. Yes sir, before.

Q. Give the conversation, as near as you can remember it, just what was said.

A. Well, he was leaving, could not be there after the game, and he wanted to find out as quickly as possible—he wanted me to ascertain from Wood the amount that was paid. That is to the best of my knowledge.

Q. When did you first hear that a bet was to be put on the ball game?

A. Leonard came to me and wanted to know who would be a man they could trust, and that is where I figured that the—

Q. What was your answer to him?

A. I told him I would get a man for him.

Q. And what did you do along that line?

A. I pointed out West, a man that was employed around at the park.

Q. Where was West at the time you pointed him out to Leonard?

A. Well, to the best of my knowledge, he was either close to the edge of the playing field or was inside the field.

Q. At all events, this conversation between Leonard and you, and your pointing West out, was inside the ball park?

A. Yes, sir.

Q. How long before the game started?

A. Well, I imagine it was around 1 o'clock.

Q. What did you understand Leonard to mean when he asked you the name of somebody he could trust, or you could trust, whichever it was?

A. Well, I figured he wanted to bet on the ball game.

Q. What made you think so?

A. That is the only inference that I could gather from what he said.

Q. Had you any conversation with him before, about betting on ball games?

A. No, sir.

Q. Or, about anything else.

A. No, sir.

Both Cobb and Speaker were in Chicago when Landis gave out the sensational details. Both stars strongly protested their innocence, and Cobb called attention to the brevity of the conversation under the grandstand, saying: "If such a frame-up was true, why should we stop for a few minutes under the stands and arrange such an important matter?"

Ty also stressed that he had admitted in the letter to Leonard that it was a responsibility (helping Dutch to get his bet down) and that he didn't want that responsibility again.

"I have been in baseball 22 years," Cobb said. "I have played the game as hard and square and clean as any man ever did. All I have thought of was to win, every year, every month, every day, every hour. My conscience is clear. I have had very high ideals in this game of baseball and I have carried them out from the beginning of my career until the end. I will rest my case with the American fans."

Cobb also made the interesting declaration that he understood that the American League had paid Leonard $20,000 for the two letters.

Speaker called himself the "goat" of the game, declaring that he was not mentioned in either of the Leonard letters. "I know nothing of any wagers being made in this contest or any fixing. The only thing they have against me is the word of a man behind this flare-up, Leonard. I have requested repeatedly that Leonard be brought in to face me, but he has positively refused to come into the meeting."

Maintaining that he had been told of a threat by Leonard to get him after the latter had been waived out of the American League, Speaker said he had hoped the former pitcher would appear before Landis and clear his name. "The testimony on file with the Commissioner, together with the explanations given him by Cobb and Wood, proves beyond doubt that there was no

161

thought of wrongdoing on the part of either man, and there is absolutely nothing to show that the ball game was fixed."

Hughie Jennings still was manager of the Tigers in 1919, at the time of the questioned game. He was taking a tuberculosis cure in 1926 at Mount Tocona, Pa., where he issued a formal statement: "This is the first information I have had of any such deal. My reputation in baseball has been beyond question and if I had known of anything of this sort you can bet your life I would have gone the limit to oust the guilty parties. It is a great surprise to me that anything like that was carried out."

Donie Bush, Detroit shortstop in 1919, was manager of the Pittsburgh Pirates by this time. "I can recall the game distinctly, but the news that anything was wrong is a big surprise to me," said Donie. He led off that day for Detroit, made three hits and scored two runs. However, it developed that after Speaker was released by the Cleveland club, the Pittsburgh club wanted to sign him as coach and assistant manager, but was tipped off not to continue the negotiations by someone high up in baseball. Our Pittsburgh correspondent surmised it was Landis; I rather believe it was Ban Johnson.

In the meantime, thousands of Cobb and Speaker fans from all over the country rallied to their defense. Among the leaders was Senator Hoke Smith of Georgia, who said in Washington he would see to it that his famous fellow Cracker would get justice. Both players engaged legal counsel, and there were threats of big suits against baseball if their names were not cleared.

Ban Johnson, however, seemed to feel that the evidence he presented to Landis was sufficient to convict these shining lights of his league. While he made no formal statement, he was quoted as saying: "I feel deeply sorry for the families of Cobb and Speaker. It is a terrible blow to them. Cobb and Speaker evidently saw the crash coming and stepped out before the scandal became a by-word.

"While it shocked me beyond expression, it simply goes to show that ball players cannot bet on ball games and escape the results that are bound to come. This thing of betting on games was a common condition previous to the 1919 World's Series scandal.

The type of player who bets has been virtually cleaned out of our league and every player should know by this time that we will not countenance wagering if we know about it. The club owners are with me on this."

After giving out his pages of testimony, Commissioner Landis said he would withhold his decision, but that it would come later in the winter. Some said he sweat blood before he decided on his verdict. It was to be one of his toughest during his quarter of a century in baseball. He understood all the implications. He knew what a terrific blow it would be to baseball, if, on top of the Black Sox business, such men as Ty and Tris should be declared ineligible. He had a fan's high regard for both Cobb and Speaker; he not only admired both men as great players, but he liked them personally. Happily and properly, the names of these great stars and sportsmen eventually were to be cleared.

The Commissioner was about to earn that new $65,000 salary, as a new series of problems tumbled into his lap.

19: Swede Risberg Makes New Charges

The Christmas-New Year season of 1926–1927 was a hectic time for baseball and a poor holiday for Kenesaw Mountain Landis. "Won't these God damn things that happened before I came into baseball ever stop coming up?" he exclaimed. If the Cobb-Speaker case wasn't hot enough, Charles "Swede" Risberg, 1919 White Sox shortstop and one of the expelled Chicago players, brought up new charges, namely that in 1917, when the Chicago team was battling the Red Sox for the pennant, the Detroit Tigers "sloughed off" a September series to the White Sox, and were repaid with two games in 1919, after the White Sox had clinched that pennant and Detroit was in a third place fight with the Yankees.

Risberg also alleged that the 1917 White Sox were assessed approximately $45 a man to make up a purse for the Tigers, particularly their pitchers, for their play in late season games against the Red Sox.

The 1917 games, which the Tigers were supposed to have sloughed off, were in a four game series of two successive doubleheaders in Chicago on Sunday, September 2, and Monday, September 3 (Labor Day). The White Sox won the four games by scores of 7 to 2, 6 to 5, 7 to 5, and 14 to 8. The Chicago players stole 12 bases in the Labor Day double-header, and the four victories put Chicago five and a half games ahead of the second place Red Sox. On Labor Day, Boston lost twice to the New York Yankees.

The Cobb-Speaker affair really brought the other matter to light. Risberg was living on a small farm near Rochester, Minn., and he broke into print with the statement he could divulge something that wasn't "quite as silly as the thing Cobb and Speaker were accused of participating in." He intimated it was real dynamite. The *Chicago Tribune* hopped on the story December 30, and promptly called it to the attention of Landis.

Among other things, Risberg was quoted as saying: "I can give baseball's bosses information that will implicate twenty big leaguers who never before have been mentioned in connection with crookedness. Landis will never ask me to tell him what I know. The facts are there, but they don't want to know them."

LANDIS EXAMINING A WITNESS

ONE OF LANDIS' LAST PORTRAITS

With him three months before his death are, from left to right, Charles McManus (Yankees), Sam Breadon (Cardinals), Jack Zeller (Tigers), Will Harridge (President of the American League), William De Witt (Browns) and Donald Barnes (Browns).

Landis wanted to know, and to know quickly. He didn't even take time out on New Year's Day. Two days after Risberg's innuendoes appeared in the Chicago press, the Commissioner had Swede in his Michigan Boulevard office, January 1, asking the shortstop for full information on what he knew or thought he knew. The Judge then summoned Risberg and thirty-five of the Chicago and Detroit players of 1917 to an open hearing at his Chicago offices before representatives of the press. The first hearing was held on January 5, and the second, at which Arnold (Chick) Gandil, the blacklisted Chicago first baseman, tried to back up Risberg's story, followed two days later. So many newspapermen crowded into Landis' office to hear the testimony that they wrecked several chairs and almost ruined his carpet. He had to send the rug out for a cleaning after the hearing was over.

And the Judge was getting nettled, peeved and his patience was running out. Before he gave out his verdict on the Cobb-Speaker and Risberg cases, a sports writer got him on the telephone to ask whether it was true that he had privately investigated the 1922 World's Series, the one in which the Yankees had failed to win a game and Hildebrand got the Judge in bad by calling the second game in daylight.

"There's absolutely nothing to it," exploded the white-haired jurist. "These stories are now being cooked up by the newspapers. They print the story in one edition, and deny it in the next. I'm getting damn sick and tired spending all my time making denials to these silly stories. Some of these reporters get themselves filled with stale beer, mince pie, and oh well—"

At the open hearing of January 5, Risberg early brought the name of Clarence Rowland, 1917 White Sox manager, into this new case, Rowland at this time was an American League umpire; he now is president of the Pacific Coast League and a man of unquestionable integrity. Risberg testified that before the first game of the September 2, 1917 double-header, Rowland had said to him that "everything is fixed." "Then we proceeded to win the four games," Swede added.

Risberg then said: "About two weeks later, in the Ansonia Hotel, New York, Chick Gandil and I collected $45 apiece from the boys for the Detroit team. Rowland gave us permission to go to Philadelphia, and there we gave the money we had collected to Bill James."

Later Risberg testified that Detroit pitchers fed up deliveries with nothing on the ball, and to the Judge's inquiry: "Did it look off?" Risberg replied: "It seemed they were getting an awful big lead before Oscar (Stanage) let go of the ball."

Referring to the two games that Chicago supposedly paid back to Detroit in 1919, Risberg said: "We paid Detroit by sloughing off two games to the Tigers. I know I played out of position, and Jackson, Gandil and Felsch also played out of position."

The score in the testimony was thirty-five to two, with only Chick Gandil siding with Risberg, while the entire strength of the Detroit club and such White Sox as were not enmeshed in the 1919 Black Sox scandal was unanimous in branding the Swede's charges false. Some of the greatest names then in baseball paraded past Landis' witness stand—Rowland, Ty Cobb, Eddie Collins, Ray Schalk, Kid Gleason, Ed Walsh, Harry Heilmann, Donie Bush, Oscar Stanage, Nemo Leibold, Bill James, Howard Ehmke, George Dauss, Bernie Boland and many others. Frequently the Judge scowled when something a player said displeased him, and reporters edged expectantly on their seats as Landis fired questions at these greats of the game.

When Landis asked Clarence Rowland: "What do you say of Risberg's testimony?" the former Chicago manager raised his voice and said heatedly, "It's a damned lie. I made no such remark to Risberg as 'It's all fixed.'"

To Landis' observation, "Risberg says he and Gandil went to Philadelphia to give this money to Detroit," Rowland replied: "Gandil came to me and asked if he could go to Philadelphia and I said, 'All right.' But no one asked me to contribute anything to any pool."

To Landis' point-blank question: "Did you see anything wrong in these Chicago-Detroit games?" Rowland said emphatically: "There was nothing wrong in those games. There was no talk about any 'sloughing' of ball games. We were two games ahead before that series, with twenty games to go, and that is considered safe.

166

If I said anything at all to Risberg, it was: 'Get in there and win that ball game.' "

After Rowland had satisfactorily answered a number of other questions, Landis turned to Risberg and asked: "Do you want to ask Rowland any questions?" and the accusing player replied: "No, sir."

"What Risberg said, I don't believe," said Ray Schalk, who had just succeeded Eddie Collins as White Sox manager.

When Landis said to Eddie, "Risberg says those four Detroit-Chicago games were 'sloughed' to the Sox; is that true?" Collins replied in a clear concise voice: "I don't believe it. I played in those games and saw nothing wrong about them."

Collins did admit that he contributed $45 to the Gandil fund to reward Detroit players, but not until the White Sox-Giant World's Series was under way in October and after Eddie had been assured such a fund had been raised. At the time, it was a common practice in baseball for a contending team to reward another for bearing down particularly hard against a pennant rival in late season games.

Much of the testimony revolved around that fund, with players of both sides testifying it was a reward for the Tigers making a special effort against Boston. Pitcher George Dauss admitted he was the recipient of $180, and that it had been paid him by Bill James. Landis then turned sharply on the pitcher, and asked: "What did James say when he gave you the money?" Dauss replied:

"James didn't say anything. It was understood that any pitcher that beat Boston would get $200. I got that idea from Bill James. He said that Chick Gandil told him that any pitcher that beat Boston would get the $200. The catcher who caught the Boston series was to get the other $20. I got $180. I think Stanage got $60."

"Those games were not sloughed," insisted Howard Ehmke, one of the defeated pitchers in the Labor Day series. "The only thing I can recall about that game [the one he pitched] is through the box-score. The Sox got six hits off me in six innings." When the Commissioner asked, "Did you ever get anything of the Sox pool?" Howard answered, "I never heard anything about that money until it came out in the papers the other day. I never got a cent out of it and know nothing about it."

During his testimony, Ty Cobb said, "There never has been a baseball game in my life that I played in that I knew was fixed." While Cobb was being questioned, Landis continued firing questions on a Detroit-St. Louis game on which Ty already had made a denial.

"I have already denied making this statement," said Cobb, and then he got one of the few laughs of the hearing when he asked, "Do you want to swear me in?"

The interrogation of Oscar Stanage about the many Chicago stolen bases in the series was one of the most interesting features of the hearing. When Landis called the hefty Oscar to the stand, the Commissioner had in his hand the box-scores of the 1917 Chicago-Detroit games, in which Stanage caught three of the games and appeared as a pinch-hitter in the fourth.

"If there was anything wrong about that series," said Stanage, "I didn't know it. Nobody approached me, and I didn't see any wrong plays."

Landis then read the list of Chicago stolen bases, two in the first game, six in the second, seven in the third and five in the fourth. "That's quite a crop of stolen bases," said the Commissioner.

"It's happened to me lots of times," said Stanage amid laughter. But Oscar became serious and added: "If there were Detroit players 'sloughing' those games, I didn't see it or hear anything about it. Neither did I see anything about those two 1919 games that was out of the ordinary."

"When did you first hear of the money raised by the Sox?" asked Landis.

"Bill James came to me in the dining room of the Aldine Hotel in Philadelphia, after the Boston series. Dauss said I got $60. I think it was $75. James said: 'Here's a present from the White Sox. Buy yourself a suit of clothes or something.' "

Donie Bush, the Pirate manager and former Tiger shortstop, testified: "All I know was that the games went along the same as any others. As far as I know they were on the square. I heard no talk about these four games being 'sloughed.' "

The only time when it looked as though one of the players might take a punch at Risberg right in Landis' court was when Bernie Boland, the Tiger pitcher, who was knocked out in the fourth game, was on the stand.

"As far as I know those 1917 games were on the square," said Bernie. "I don't believe this story that they were 'sloughed.'"

As Boland was speaking, Risberg leaned over towards Landis and whispered for the second time that Donie Bush was nodding to the witness. A sharp exchange followed between Boland, Bush and Risberg. Boland turned in his chair, and thrusting his chin to within a few inches of Risberg's face, he said bitterly: "You're still a pig!"

"I am not a pig," called back Risberg, while Bush hotly resented Risberg's accusations. He moved over to take a seat a few feet from Risberg and behind the witness chair.

Much of the second day's hearing, January 7, was given to taking testimony from Chick Gandil, who wasn't there the first day, further interrogation of Bill James and other players on the $1,000 "reward pool" for 1917 Detroit players, and the two games which Chicago supposedly "gave" Detroit as a belated reward late in 1919.

Gandil backed up the story and assertions of Risberg, but questioning of the first baseman wound up with the Commissioner wanting to know about his expenses and Chick demanding to know why he was on baseball's blacklist.

"Have you received any money for coming here, other than that I promised, for expenses?" asked Landis.

"The *Chicago Tribune* gave me $500 for expenses. It didn't take all that for my expenses. I promised to pay them back. I want to ask you, Mr. Landis, why, after I was dragged through a court trial and acquitted in the 1919 Series, is it that I was blacklisted?" said Gandil.

"Do you want to be reinstated?" snapped the Judge.

"No, I don't, but I want to know why I was blacklisted," shot back the player.

"I couldn't pass on that unless I could ask you some questions about the 1919 World's Series," said Landis.

"I don't want to go back to that Series," Gandil replied.

"Well, if you want an answer right now," said the Judge, "you have just testified that you played out of position in two games in 1919. That would cause you to be placed on the ineligible list."

There also was a dramatic moment when Buck Weaver, another of the ineligible players of the 1919 World's Series, used his presence on the witness stand as an opportunity to make a personal plea to Landis to get back into baseball's good graces. Buck had testified that he wasn't with the White Sox at the time of the so-called "sloughed series," being out of action with a broken finger, and that he had refused Gandil and Risberg when they asked him to contribute his $45 to the Detroit pool.

Then, as Weaver arose from the witness stand, he looked straight at Landis, and said: "Judge, I don't feel that I owe baseball anything, but baseball does owe me something. I ask you now for reinstatement."

The question caught Landis entirely by surprise, and the room was so quiet one could hear a pin drop. The Judge hesitated nearly a full minute before replying, his eyes looking straight at the great infielder. "Drop me a line about that, Buck, and I'll take the matter up," he said at length.

Judge Landis went over this testimony for about a week, and then completely absolved the Detroit and Chicago players of 1917 and 1919 of any wrongdoing. In a lengthy prepared statement, he reviewed the entire case from the time Risberg's remarks first were published in Chicago, December 30, his New Year's Day conference with Risberg, to the two-day hearing at his office.

"To some it may seem inexplicable that Risberg and Gandil should implicate themselves in these alleged corrupt practices," said Landis, in his finding. "Obviously the implication may have been conceived upon the theory that they have been incriminated themselves, so it must be true. However, being already on the ineligible list, it would not affect them, and it might blacken the lily whites.

"It is the finding of the Commissioner that the fund raised by the Chicago players about September 28, 1917, was not collected or paid the Detroit players for 'sloughing' the Chicago games of

September 2 and 3, 1917, but was paid because of Detroit's beating Boston; and there was no 'sloughing' of the September 2 and 3, 1917 games, nor of the September 26, 27, 28, 1919 games, except possibly by Risberg and Gandil."

Landis called further attention to the alleged conversation they said they had with former Manager Clarence Rowland, Eddie Collins and others regarding the alleged fixed games and the pool, and said it was obvious that those men, and not Gandil and Risberg, were telling the truth.

The hardest words used by Landis towards the players named were in this paragraph: "If the Risberg-Gandil version be correct, it was an act of criminality. If the other versions be true, it was an act of impropriety, reprehensible and censurable, but not corrupt."

However, he was aware of the danger of players getting up pools for other teams to "bear down harder" on a pennant rival, and said testimony of Gandil and Risberg showed $1,100 had been collected, while Bill James admitted to have divided $850 Chicago money among Detroit players. This had been an old baseball custom, which he held to be unsalutary, harmful to baseball, and called on baseball to abolish it, with necessary penalties.

In fact, in giving his decision, Commissioner Landis introduced four new suggestions to the club owners, which he recommended be made part of the moral code of the game. They were adopted in principle and are part of baseball's law of today. The four suggestions follow:

1. A statute of limitations with respect to alleged baseball offenses, as in our state and national statutes with regard to criminal offenses.

2. Ineligibility for one year for offering or giving any gift or reward by the players or management of one club to the players or management of another club for services rendered or supposed to be, or have been rendered, in defeating a competing club.

3. Ineligibility for one year for betting any sum whatsoever upon any ball game in connection with which the better had no duty to perform.

4. Permanent ineligibility for betting any sum whatsoever upon

any ball game in connection with which the better has any duty to perform.

Of most importance was the proposed new statute of limitations under which ball players could not be tried for offenses going back more than a specified number of years. Under that statute, neither the Cobb-Speaker case, seven years old, nor the Risberg-Gandil charges, which brought up a matter which supposedly had happened nine years before, ever would have reached the Commissioner's court.

20: Ken Finally KO's Ban

Landis had no more than cleared his desk of the Risberg-Gandil thing when he plunged into his last fight with his arch foe in baseball, Ban Johnson, and this time Ken was to score a knockout. The shaking hands by the two at Ban's return to the Advisory Council at the joint meeting in Chicago less than a month before was merely the hand clasp before the last round.

Ban again popped off, and this time the Judge was determined to give no quarter; he decided he couldn't live in peace while the doughty Johnson had any position of authority in baseball.

The last showdown came over the Cobb-Speaker controversy. I already have said that Ban believed he had a strong case against these star players, and took it for granted that they were out of baseball, at least out of his league. He seemed to think that when the evidence was turned over to Landis, the Commissioner quickly would support him and declare the players ineligible. When Landis showed no intention of making an immediate decision, indicating he was not satisfied with the evidence submitted, Ban again spoke out of turn. I loved Ban Johnson, but he never did know that there were times when silence is golden.

Maybe some of Johnson's Chicago friends also were a little lacking in judgment, as a strong newspaper blast against Landis, in which the Commissioner was accused of "making a mess of the Cobb-Speaker case," was attributed to "One of Organized Baseball's leaders."

"Speaker and Cobb never again will play in the American League, notwithstanding what action Landis may eventually take in this matter," said this leader. He also intimated that the public was not given all the evidence in the case.

Well, it wasn't difficult for Landis to know what "Organized Baseball leader" was talking out of turn. The Judge struck back by calling a special meeting of the American League in Chicago, January 24, "for the purpose of ascertaining what basis, if any, there was for the story to be printed." In his announcement to the press calling the meeting, the Judge lunged out at Ban with a verbal sock for being quoted anonymously. J. O. Murfin, attorney for

Cobb, and W. H. Boyd, counsel for Speaker, were invited to attend the meeting.

Johnson then popped off some more, and this time he permitted the reporters to quote Ban Johnson. "The American League is a business," he said. "When our directors found two employes who they didn't think were serving them right, they had to let them go. Now isn't that enough? As long as I'm president of the American League neither one of them will manage or play on our teams."

He went into his private investigation of the Cobb-Speaker matter and revealed that as early as September 9, the board of directors of the American League decided that the playing managers of the Detroit and Cleveland clubs be persona non grata with the league at the expiration of the 1926 season.

"I called a meeting of the directors of my league," continued Johnson's statement. "We met September 9 in a prominent Chicago club and we met secretly. We wanted secrecy, not because it meant anything to us, but because we felt we should protect Cobb and Speaker as much as we could.

"They had done a lot for baseball. We had to let them out, but we saw no reason for bringing embarrassment upon their families. We wanted to be decent about it.

"The directors voted to turn the results of the Leonard investigation over to Landis. We did that in compliment to him, not to pass the buck. We acted, but we thought he ought to know about it.

"When Landis released that testimony and those letters, I was amazed. I couldn't fathom his motive. The only thing I could see behind that move was a desire for personal publicity.

"The American League is a business. It is a semipublic business to be sure, and we try to keep faith with our public. Certainly we had the right to let two employes go if we felt that they had violated a trust. But Landis had no right to release the Leonard charges.

"He had taken no part in the ousting of the two men. It was merely a league, not an interleague matter, and there was nothing to be gained by telling the world that we felt Cobb and Speaker had made mistakes which made them unwelcome employes.

"When I take the stand Monday [at Landis' specially called meeting] I may tell the whole story of my relationship with the

174

Judge. If he wants to know when I lost faith with him, I'll tell him this: When the Black Sox scandal broke, the American League voted to prosecute the crooked players. Landis was given the job. After several months had passed, I asked him what he was doing and he said 'nothing.'

"I took the case away from him, prosecuted it with the funds of the American League, and never asked him for help. I decided he didn't want to co-operate.

"My second break with Landis came over a financial matter. I do not care to discuss it now, but I will tell about it Monday, if he wants me to."

Ban Johnson never faced Landis at the January 24th meeting. His club owners put the skids under him the Sunday night before. It was more or less a repetition of Johnson's rebuke after his remarks at the time of the Dolan-O'Connell business, but this time it was a real showdown. And though Ban lingered to the end of the 1927 season, Landis' challenge to the American League: "You've got to take Ban Johnson or me," was met with the elimination of Ban.

Johnson was an ill man at the time; I feel his many clashes with Landis, his humiliation in 1924, bitterness and disappointment with his own people—whom he thought let him down—all contributed to his illness. But, even if Ban had been an absolutely well man in 1927, he was doomed after his last tirade against Landis. The Judge practically demanded it.

The American League club owners gathered at the Blackstone Hotel in Chicago, January 23, a day before the Judge's called meeting. The air still was rife with the Risberg-Gandil business, and the entire nation awaited the Judge's decision on Cobb and Speaker. The club owners were in no mood again to try to patch things up. Landis was boiling mad, and told some of the club owners to their faces that they had failed to make good their pledge of December 10, 1924, and that Johnson's misconduct would cease or his immediate removal from office would follow.

Two meetings were held, but for some reason, Charley Comiskey, the worst Johnson hater in the league, was excluded from the first. Johnson also was not invited, though he submitted a written statement. The other men probably felt Commie would be so violently bitter as to prevent a calm discussion of the league's new problem with its turbulent executive. The meeting decided that Johnson should continue as president of the league in name only, draw his salary under his contract, but that he would have no further part in shaping the policy of the league, and that his voice would be stilled. Frank J. Navin, president of the Detroit club, and vice president of the league, would serve as acting president.

The club owners then called Comiskey into their second meeting, in order to make the league's action on a new punitive Johnson resolution unanimous. A committee then waited on Landis and asked him whether he would attend the meeting. Landis came and Navin read him the resolution.

"This time do you gentlemen really mean this?" asked Landis stiffly. "I believe I recall hearing such language before."

"Ban will give you no further trouble, Judge," said Ruppert, which was echoed by Navin, Shibe, Barnard and others. Landis then agreed to postpone indefinitely the meeting called for the following day.

The league then gave out a formal statement of its new policy to the press: "A meeting of the eight club owners of the American League was held Sunday (January 23) at the Blackstone Hotel, Chicago.

"The members of the league unanimously repudiated any and all criticism appearing in the public press as emanating from Mr. Johnson, reflecting in any way upon Judge Landis or his handling of his several investigations concerning the integrity of ball players in the American League, and commended Judge Landis for his efforts in clearing baseball of any insinuation of dishonesty.

"Mr. Johnson submitted to the meeting a formal written statement in which he announced that all evidence involved in the matter of Cobb and Speaker investigations had been submitted to the Commissioner and had been by him published.

"Dr. Robert B. Drury, Mr. Johnson's personal attending physician, certified to the meeting that Mr. Johnson's health was such that he should immediately take a much-needed rest.

"Thereupon the duties of the president were intrusted for the time being to Mr. Frank J. Navin of Detroit, vice president of the league.

"At our request, Judge Landis indefinitely postponed the meeting of the American League called for tomorrow (Monday)."

The general idea at the time was that Ban Johnson, after a reasonable period of time, would tender his resignation, saying his health would not permit his return to the game. I felt that way, for in February 3 issue of *The Sporting News*, we published nearly a page of observations from the nation's top sports writers on the passing of baseball's former strong man, under a heading: "Comment from the Nation's Press on 'Retirement' of Ban Johnson." Even our New York correspondent, Joe Vila, seemed to think the jig was up. He quoted Frank Farrell, the first owner of the New York American League club, as saying: "I fear Ban is losing his grip. The American League men are not standing by him as they used to. His heart will be broken and he can't stand that thing very long. I wish I was in there to fight for him."

But Johnson, as an American League president, had as many lives as a cat. He went down to Excelsior Springs, Mo., for the remainder of the winter, and seemed to thrive under the treatments. I visited him there in the early spring and found him in good spirits, with an agile step and effusing much of his old-time energy. Even though he had been "retired," I learned he had kept in close contact with the affairs of his league and had even visited his Chicago offices for a few days to make arrangements for the opening of the season.

And, to the surprise of a great many persons, among them Judge Landis, Johnson was on the job and took over control of the league from Navin at the start of the season. But not for very long! I've already said the chutes had been greased for him at that showdown winter meeting at the Blackstone. Perhaps, it would have been better had he resigned then and there.

I don't want to get ahead of my story, but Ty Cobb started that season with the Philadelphia Athletics. As Farrell had intimated, Johnson no longer could enforce his old authority. Umpire Emmet Ormsby called an unfortunate decision against the Athletics at Shibe Park; it precipitated a riot, and resulted in Ban suspending indefinitely Cobb and Al Simmons. Ray Schalk, the new manager of the White Sox, also drew several suspensions. Comiskey, of course, had long been anti-Johnson, but now even the mild-mannered Connie Mack was on his neck. Johnson also had made more remarks, privately, on matters of the previous winter, and he could be expressive. They may have been carried to the Judge. And, it may be that with Johnson living on borrowed time, his club owners had expected his resignation before this.

However, even though Landis had an element of cruelty in his nature, he was too much of a man to get a kick out of the circumstances under which Johnson eventually resigned. It was pretty sordid, and ill fitting for a man who had done so much for baseball. Ban was requested to call a special meeting in New York, July 8, by an unnamed club owner, supposedly to consider an amendment to the constitution. But Ban knew it was a smoke screen, and suspected it was "the works."

After arriving in New York, Johnson engaged a hotel suite, and locked his door. He was alone with his secretary, Will Harridge, now president of the American League. The club owners of his league met in a room on the same floor, and talked things over for three hours. Eventually a committee made up of Col. Ruppert of New York, Clark Griffith of Washington and Bob Quinn of Boston came out and knocked at Ban's door. They were denied admittance.

Harridge then passed out word that Johnson would see only Walter Fritsch, vice president of the St. Louis club, the Browns being the club that had stuck most loyally to him.

In less than five minutes, the door was partly opened; Johnson stuck his hand through, and handed his resignation scribbled in lead pencil to Col. Ruppert. And so the long battle between Ken Landis and Ban Johnson ended in this pathetic fashion!

While Johnson's resignation was dated July 8, it was to take effect at the end of the 1927 season. As Johnson had an ironclad contract, running to 1935 at $40,000, he could have collected a good part of $320,000 when the league requested his resignation, but he notified his owners he wanted no compensation after the 1927 season was over.

I saw much of Johnson in the remaining three and a half years of his life, as he took treatment at St. Louis' famed Barnes Hospital for diabetes, and from a St. Louis eye specialist. He was a man broken in spirit, as well as in body. He felt especially hurt at what he believed to be the ingratitude of some of the men he had helped to gain high places in baseball. Frequently he talked over the events of the preceding dramatic chapters. He mellowed somewhat at the end, but—I think—not much in his feeling for Judge Landis.

He died in St. Louis, March 28, 1931, at St. John's Hospital, where he had been removed when he was failing fast, to be under the close observation of Dr. Robert Hyland of the staff of St. John's. By a peculiar coincidence he outlived Ernest Sargent Barnard, who succeeded him to the American League presidency, by one day. Barnard died, March 27, 1931, at Chicago. Incidentally, August Herrmann, the old National Commission chairman, died four weeks later, April 25.

Both Judge Landis and Ban Johnson now have tablets to their memory at Baseball's Hall of Fame at Cooperstown. They were without a doubt baseball's two greatest executives. What a pity they couldn't have worked in better harmony! But dear old Ban; it was so difficult for him to play second fiddle.

21: The Judge Acquits Two Aces

The Sunday meeting at the Blackstone, January 23, at which the chutes had been greased for the exit of Johnson from baseball, preceded Landis' verdict on the Cobb-Speaker case by four days. The Judge gave the nation his answer on this *cause célèbre*, which almost had become a national issue, on the subsequent Thursday, January 27. What a month that January was for the Hot Stove League! There never was another like it in baseball history.

After the American League passed its resolution, repudiating Johnson and extolling Landis and his conduct of the investigation, there was a general belief in newspaper circles that Cobb and Speaker would be acquitted. That surmise proved correct, and Landis' decision, giving both players complete bills of health, was received favorably by the great majority of fans. Many felt the players had been foolhardy, but only a minority wanted to see the names of these great diamond heroes tarnished.

When Judge Landis cleared Ty and Tris, he did it in no half-hearted manner. After reviewing the entire case, the Commissioner summed it up in his last two paragraphs: "This is the Cobb-Speaker case. These players have not been, nor are they now, found guilty of fixing a ball game. By no decent system of justice could such finding be made. Therefore, they were not placed on the ineligible list.

"As they desire to rescind their withdrawal from baseball, the releases which the Detroit and Cleveland clubs granted at their requests, in the circumstances detailed above, are cancelled and the players' names are restored to the reserve lists of those clubs."

At the very start of his finding, Landis explained that he had acted on the case not because Johnson or the American League had turned its evidence over to him, but because the accused players had requested him to define their baseball status. He also took occasion to explain why he had not acted before, saying: "Messrs. Tyrus R. Cobb and Tris Speaker have asked that their baseball status be defined. This request is in contemplation of possible future service and is in accordance with the Commissioner's statement of December 21, 1926, as follows:

" 'These men being out of baseball, no decision will be made unless changed conditions in the future require it.'

"Preceding that announcement, both players had been released, that action following a resolution of September 9, 1926, by the American League's Board of Directors."

Landis then permitted it to be known that it was with his knowledge and acquiescence that Cobb and Speaker first expressed their desire to retire from the game in the fall of 1926, rather than to permit their illustrious names to be dragged into a scandal. His finding also revealed that he had gone into the case long before his hearing with Cobb and Speaker, November 29.

Through his entire report on the case, Landis showed his displeasure and resentment with Hubert (Dutch) Leonard, the former Red Sox and Tiger pitcher, for failing to come East and face the men he accused. As a result, he paid little attention to the Leonard letters, which Ban Johnson had considered so important when he placed them before his league's board of directors.

"Cobb, Speaker and Wood were available," said Landis in his finding, "but Leonard, a retired player, residing in California, declined to attend a hearing. Therefore, his statement was taken in California and in substance was that this game (September 25, 1919) had been fixed. Cobb, Speaker and Wood branded this charge as false. A wager had been made, but they vigorously denied that the game had been fixed and they insisted upon an opportunity to face their accuser. Leonard, however, persisted in his refusal to come, and despite the fact that his attendance could not be forced, the hearing was finally set for November 29, and all parties, including Leonard and the American league president and directors, duly notified. Leonard replied that he would not be present.

"Cobb and Speaker appeared on November 27 and were informed of Leonard's attitude, whereupon they canvassed the whole situation with the Commissioner and reached the conclusion that they would rather quit baseball than have a hearing with their accuser absent. Their reason was: The mere announcement of charges of this character, whatever the personality or motives of the accuser, or the scarcity or even absence of evidence supporting the charges, would be harmful to the accused persons, experience having shown that a vindication by baseball authority, based upon a manifest insufficiency or even a total failure of supporting proof, has been labelled a 'whitewash.' While they insisted they had no doubt of their ability to answer the charges, they were concerned about the possible effect upon themselves and others in whom they were deeply interested. They appeared to be particularly disturbed respecting the situation of Joe Wood.

"These considerations, as Cobb and Speaker represented the matter to me, brought about their desire to quit baseball, despite their appreciation of the fact that such action might be misconstrued.

"Inasmuch, therefore, as Leonard's attendance could neither be induced nor enforced, the Commissioner consented that the hearing be put over indefinitely, and it was understood that would be the end of the matter, unless conditions thereafter should so change as to require a different course. It was pointed out at the time that a number of people knew or had heard of the Leonard charges and of the Cobb and Wood letters and the likelihood of suspicion and rumor resulting from a retirement in these circumstances of two players of such prominence was discussed. And it was definitely understood that the interests of all concerned might thereafter require a public statement setting forth the charges and answers.

"The American League directors were informed of the status of affairs and that Cobb and Speaker desired to leave baseball for the reasons stated. Accordingly, the Detroit and Cleveland clubs granted releases and the American League directors rescinded their resolution calling for a hearing, with the same understanding that this ended the matter unless subsequent developments should necessitate a hearing and publication.

"Shortly thereafter, gossip and rumor got busy. As usually transpires when these two kindly, sympathetic agencies are at work, they left in their wake a variety of progeny infinitely more harmful to the individuals concerned than the truth could possibly be. Many press associations and scores of newspapers were persistently demanding the facts. Therefore, Cobb, Speaker and Wood were called to Chicago and the situation laid before them.

They all realized that untrue, distorted and garbled accounts were being innuendoed and agreed that a hearing had become desirable, even with Leonard persisting in staying away.

"Accordingly a final effort was made to induce Leonard to attend, but again he refused. The hearing was held, and the Commissioner at once issued the record for publication, in accordance with his definite understanding with Cobb, Speaker and Wood." The paragraphs vindicating the players and ordering them returned to the reserve lists of the Tigers and Indians followed.

The Commissioner seemed most unfair in the paragraph in his finding castigating the nation's press, the great daily newspapers and the powerful news associations, for spreading "gossip and rumor." As Landis said himself in the finding, "Players of such prominence as Cobb and Speaker don't just drop out of baseball without the nation's fans and the country's sports writers demanding to know the reason." Landis' long experience with the press, gained in Washington, his years on the Federal bench and in his job as Commissioner, should have taught him that such a story could not be suppressed, or played down.

In fact, both stars owe a debt of gratitude to the writers of 1926–1927, who refused to permit the matter to be hushed up. The Judge, in his finding, admitted he was willing to take this way out. Landis spoke scornfully and with his well known irony of those "two kindly sympathetic agencies, gossip and rumor." Without them there would have been no final decisions, no vindication, and fans and writers always would have known that the careers of Cobb and Speaker ended abruptly with the 1926 season under suspicious circumstances.

Both players played two more years in the American League, despite Johnson's former insistence that such a thing wouldn't happen. While the players, on Landis' order, were returned to their former clubs, Detroit and Cleveland, both Navin and Barnard gave the men permission to dicker for their services with other American League clubs. Landis had passed the word around that he didn't want either star to play in the National League, though McGraw, the showman vice president-manager of the Giants, was one of the first to express a wish to have Cobb on his team.

But, the Judge didn't want it to look as though Johnson had scored even a partial victory, and that these players no longer were wanted in the American League.

However, the hint was unnecessary, as all of the six other American League clubs promptly put in bids for the two stars. Cobb eventually went to the Athletics, and Clark Griffith landed Speaker for Washington. In 1928, "Spoke" joined Ty on the Athletics. Cobb made $70,000 from the Athletics in 1927 in salary, bonus for signing and another bonus on the size of the Athletics' gate. Though Ty was 42 in December, 1928, he could have gone on a while longer as a valuable player, but Connie Mack no longer could pay him his big salary. That Cobb and Speaker were far from being washed up as players when they "resigned" at the end of the 1926 season is apparent from their batting averages of 1927 and 1928. Ty, a .300-hitter to the end, hit .357 and .323 and Speaker closed his career with .327 and .267.

After giving his decision on Cobb and Speaker, Landis said wearily, "That cleans up the cases in my docket."

Other famous cases were to reach Landis' court in the next 17 years, but there were no others in which a player, either in the majors or minors, was charged with throwing, or attempting to throw, a game. Most of the cases in which Landis figured so prominently were inherited from an earlier era in baseball, especially during the late rule of the old National Commission, with 1919 being an especially unhappy season in that respect.

There is no doubt that Landis put the fear of God, and the fear of Commissioner Landis, into the ball players. The great mass of players always have been inherently honest, but if there were any likely to stray the very fact that they knew the white-haired Landis sat in the Commissioner's seat kept them on the path of righteousness.

Yet, even the Risberg-Gandil and Cobb-Speaker cases had their purpose. They brought about a general strengthening of the base-ball rules, with the Judge's anti-betting edicts and the cast iron rule making it an offense to reward one club for beating a contender's rival being important additions to the code. All of those things were most salutary, and one has no hesitancy in saying that baseball under Landis' administration was the cleanest during any time in the game's history.

As a result of these early cases which were heard in Landis' baseball court, he came to hate professional gamblers, or bookmakers, with a hatred which amounted almost to an obsession. This feeling went to the entire racing world, because of the close association of the "bookies" and the "sure thing boys" to the "Sport of Kings." At times his attitude toward racing people, even some of the country's finest citizens who supported this sport, bordered on the ridiculous. But he felt his reasoning for his attitude was sound. "Those wormy, crawly creatures [the professional gamblers] once befouled and almost ruined this great game we all love," he said with a depth of feeling. "They thrive and live at race tracks. And I will have no truck with those who consort with them."

Following his trying winter, Landis and his lady went down to Belleair—near Clearwater, Fla.,—for rest, relaxation and some badly needed recreation. If Johnson was near a breakdown at Excelsior Springs, Mo., Landis' nerves were pretty well frayed when he first arrived at Belleair. But a fortnight of golf and Florida sun rested him, and put him back in good humor. He could let out his inhibitions on a golf course, especially while talking to his golf ball. Once Harry Nash, former *New York Post* sports writer and then publicity director of the hotel in Belleair, was the Judge's partner in a foursome. A pretty fair golfer, Harry dubbed an important shot. He took his vengeance out on the little ivory-painted pellet. "You lousy, blankety-blank of a blank," Nash said to his golf ball.

Landis roared with laughter, even though his partner's dubbed shot had cost his side the hole. "That's no way to talk to a golf ball, and expect it to obey you, Harry," he said. "None of that mild lousy, blankety-blank kind of stuff. If you really want to get that ball mad, and to respect you in the future, you've got to call it a blankety, blank blank, blankety, blank son of a blank."

The Judge had taken up golf when he was on the Federal bench in Chicago, and he dearly loved the game. It was even quite a rival for baseball, as there were times when it was pretty hard to decide whether to play golf on a Sunday or see the Cubs or White Sox. The Judge worked out a compromise between his two favorite sports. He got up a little earlier on Sunday so he could play golf in the morning, and then attended Cub or White Sox games in the afternoon.

Ken Landis was a fair golfer for a man of his years, and quite proud of his game. He hadn't much of a drive—little over 150 yards, but he could keep it straight as a string and he had a pretty good game around the greens. Nothing tickled him more than to win a hole with a good approach and putt from a man who had been 250 yards off the tee. And he was a keen student of golf, and golfers. "Do you know, after I've played one game of golf with a man I know more about him than if he had come into my court every day for a year?" With his little cackly laugh, he used to derive great fun out of fellow golfers who threw their clubs or otherwise expressed their displeasure over a bad game. "Isn't old 'Sloke' mad?" he once said with much relish as the late Bill Slocum, former New York sports writer, tossed a club on a Tampa Bay course and it stuck in a palm tree.

And, when the Judge played golf, he was like the U.S. mail man, neither rain, snow, storms nor hurricane could deter him. In the early spring following the dramatic doings of January, 1927, the Judge was host to the New York scribes, then with the Yankees party at St. Petersburg, at his Belleair winter headquarters. A golf game was tossed in. The Judge, playing with John Orr, a former 275-pound minority stockholder in the Cincinnati Reds, played and defeated Fred Lieb of our staff, then of the *New York Telegram*, and George W. Daley, former baseball writer on the old *New York Morning World*. Daley and Lieb challenged the Judge and Orr to a return match at their "home course," the Jungle Club at St. Petersburg.

It was a bleak, gray March morning, and rain was in the air. The Judge called up and asked: "How's the weather over there?" He was told, "It isn't raining yet." "Well, if it isn't raining I'll be over," he said, without permitting any further discussion.

It wasn't raining when the foursome teed off about an hour later, but by the time the players reached the third hole, the downpour started. By the fifth hole, it became one of those torrential Florida rainstorms, with a stiff wind blowing in from Boca Cega Bay. After fighting the storm and rain for another hole, Orr and Lieb voted to call the match off; the Judge and Daley voted to carry on. Finally Landis said, "All right, if you sissies can't take a little rain, we'll go back."

The foursome and their relieved Negro caddies started the trek back to the clubhouse. As they did so, out of the storm emerged a pair of Amazons, playing through the wind and rain. "You goldarned tenderfeet, you're not going to let these women run us off the course and have it all to themselves, are you?" asked the Judge, with his fine irony.

So the foursome turned around again, and played the remaining 12 holes in as rainy a rain as Florida ever turned loose. The foursome eventually reached the clubhouse as wet as though all had been fished out of the gulf. The rain had slicked the Judge's white mane around his eyes, ears and face, and the flashing brown orbs shining through made him look like a bird dog.

Turning to Orr and Lieb, the two sissies, the Judge said: "Now, I think you fellows really have earned a little drink."

22: Landis' New Safeguards
Are Adopted

The Judge had smooth sailing during the 1927 season, especially after his old enemy, Johnson, had been stripped of his remaining power in July. The Yankees won the American League pennant in a breeze with what perhaps was baseball's greatest team of all time, while the Pirates, led by Donie Bush, the former Tiger shortstop, won a close race in the National League. It was the last pennant won by Barney Dreyfuss, the man Landis told to keep his shirt on three years before and whom he had snubbed in the Washington hotel. Landis passed up the honor of tossing out the first ball at the World's Series in Forbes Field to Governor Fisher of Pennsylvania, and the Judge had such a pleasant time in Pittsburgh that he remarked: "That Barney Dreyfuss isn't such a bad fellow after all."

It was an unhappy Series, however, for Barney, as the great Yankee juggernaut flattened his Pirates in four straight games. Dreyfuss said bitterly after it was over: "No major league champion is good enough to win four straight games from the championship team of the other major league." But, he didn't know how good those Yankees were, nor did he ask Landis to make any investigation. The Judge went into the Yankees' dressing room, after Earl Combs sped home on John Miljus' wild pitch at Yankee Stadium for the final play of the Series, and remarked to little Miller Huggins, the New York manager: "Well, you fellows didn't keep this thing going very long. Congratulations, Miller; I'm glad I didn't have to manage a National League club against you. You surely have a ball team."

It was the final World's Series played during Johnson's league presidency, but Ban didn't even attend. His health rapidly was worsening, and coming into close contact with Landis no doubt would have proved too embarrassing. However, old Ban got a tremendous kick out of the emphatic Yankee victory, and showed that he still regarded the National League as his enemy in his congratulatory telegram to Col. Jake Ruppert: "Hearty congratulations to you, Miller Huggins and the players. We like to destroy the enemy in that means. The four straight victory will have a wholesome effect upon the public mind and strengthen the position of professional baseball."

Sending that telegram was just about Ban Johnson's last piece of official American League business. The once stormy petrel quietly faded out of the baseball picture with the close of the season, and on November 2, Ernest Barnard, former Cleveland president and a man with whom Landis could work amiably, was elected president of the American League. Probably wishing to atone slightly for the kicks they had given Ban in the ribs in the way of former resolutions, the league passed a final one, thanking Johnson, the outgoing president, for his years of faithful service and praising him as a gallant, constructive figure in American baseball. Vengeful and holding his hate to the end, Comiskey, Johnson's former crony, alone refused to vote for it.

With a friendly, cooperative American Leaguer on the Advisory Council, Landis concentrated his energies on having the four suggestions he made at the time of the Risberg finding incorporated in baseball's fundamental law. As time went on, and he turned the Risberg-Gandil and Cobb-Speaker cases over and over in his mind, the need for even stronger teeth in recommended antigambling legislation became an absolute "must" on his calendar.

Before the major league meetings in New York in December, 1927, the two presidents appointed what was termed the game's "Steering Committee" to work with Landis in eradicating abuses and throwing new safeguards around the game. The National League representatives were made up of league chief Heydler, and club presidents Bill Veeck of the Cubs, Barney Dreyfuss of the Pirates and William Baker of the Phillies. On the American League side was the new executive, Barnard, Frank Navin, the league's vice president and Tiger owner, Col. Ruppert of the Yankees and fiery Phil Ball of the Browns. We ran a picture of the Steering Committee in *The Sporting News* at the time; Landis and Dreyfuss alone were seated at a table; the others stood up around them. Barney, though sitting down, was in better standing.

"Gentlemen, you know what I was up against last winter,"

Landis told the other members of the committee. "I feel some of these players got into these difficulties because there were no specific rules covering such conduct. But, we learn as we go on, and from now on there can be no more 'gifts' in baseball, or bonuses for 'bearing down' or 'making it easy for us.' That's got to stop, and stop now."

The Commissioner didn't need to sell the Steering Committee on his program. Landis' original suggestion of making a player ineligible for a year "for offering or accepting any present or reward" was increased to three years. It covered players, league and club officials, and now appears under Rule 21 of the Major League Rules, under the heading: "Conduct Detrimental to Baseball."

Any person seeking to influence an umpire's decision with a reward or gift also was to be permanently barred from baseball, as was an umpire accepting or soliciting such a gift. But, the Judge always had a wholesome respect for the "men in blue." "What a grand bunch of fellows they have been, and what a record for honesty and integrity they have made through the years!" he used to say with admiration. No major league umpire ever had been involved in any scandal in which he was accused of trying to influence a game with his decisions.

Not only players, but all officials of a club were to be barred for life if they were caught making a bet on a game in which they had a duty to perform. This rule caught up with William D. Cox, president of the Philadelphia Nationals, 16 years later. Officials or players betting on a game in which they had no duty to perform were to be suspended for a year. The Judge thought the latter rule should be even more stringent, and once thought of asking that the rule give him power to toss anyone out for making any bet on a baseball game, but this was never done.

At the subsequent joint meeting of December 15, 1927, all of Landis' and the Steering Committee's suggestions were passed, while still more stringent legislation was adopted. Any player or manager was prohibited from owning stock in any club other than the one in which he was engaged, while another amendment provided that "no employe, umpire, president, treasurer, secretary or other official of a major league shall, directly or indirectly, have any interest in a club." It prevented an old custom of having umpires scout players, especially those they might see while umpiring in college games. By this time they had set up Landis with as many rules and safeguards as he and the legalistic minds of baseball could think of.

Although Landis had been raised to $65,000 the previous year, and the 1927 World's Series ran only four games, money had been coming into the Commissioner's office so fast that his annual "cut" from the Series was reduced from 15 to 10 percent.

As Ban Johnson had retired from baseball at the end of the 1927 season, Garry Herrmann, the old chairman of the National Commission, followed him out of the game a few months later. In place of good-natured old Garry, president of the Reds since 1902, a new man, C. J. McDiarmid, represented the Cincinnati club at the 1927 meetings. Yes, the old order had changed, and Landis was supreme.

Landis brought up the subject of big league clubs operating minor league farms at the 1927 meeting, and again let the club owners know, in rather concise language, that he didn't favor the practice; in fact, he was very much "agin it." Some of the minor league club owners also were restless about it, and were threatening not to renew their agreement with Landis and the majors when the major-minor league agreement expired in January, 1928, at the end of the Judge's first seven years in office. However, there was other urgent business and the Judge did not press the matter.

The minors didn't go on their own, as they frequently have threatened to do, but a year later, at the joint meeting of the majors in Chicago, December 13, 1928, the Judge swung back to his new pet aversion, the then so-called "baseball chain gang." He called it one of the new dangers with which baseball was confronted.

Near the close of the meeting, Landis said: "I will have Secretary O'Connor call the roll, and I want each club president to tell me how many minor league clubs he owns, and if he doesn't own any, then I want to know how many he is interested in."

After Landis held his poll, he learned that National League

clubs had 12 farms, and those of the American League only six, a surprising few compared with later years when the St. Louis Cardinals at one time controlled 33 minor league clubs and some 600 players.

There was an interesting bit of repartee between the Commissioner and hard-boiled old Phil Ball of the Browns when O'Connor called the name of the St. Louis American League club.

"None," said Phil, meaning the Browns owned no minor league club.

Landis stared at the man who in the late American League fighting had been Ban Johnson's lone ally. "All right then," he said at some length. "Then maybe you will tell me how many farms the owner of the St. Louis Browns owns."

Ball couldn't dodge that one and admitted that Tulsa and Muskogee were his personal property. "But, I'm going to get rid of Muskogee just as quickly as I can," Ball added.

By this time, Branch Rickey, vice president of the Cardinals, had acquired Fort Smith, Joplin, Houston and had shifted his International League farm to Rochester. From the start, the Commissioner regarded him as the colored boy in the baseball farm's wood pile, even though Rickey's acumen and ability as an organizer had converted a lowly second division team into one of the top clubs of the National League, and which by that time already had won two pennants. I think I tell no secret, either in baseball or outside of the game, when I say that Landis had little love for Rickey and his methods, and dislike grew in intensity with the passing of the years. In fact, Branch almost took the place of Ban Johnson as the No. 1 Boy in Ken's "Bad Boy Book."

At the 1928 meetings the Commissioner just missed casting the deciding vote on a measure which would radically have changed the playing of baseball, not only in the majors, but all the way down the line. National League president John Heydler, usually a conservative gentleman, proposed a radical change in the rules whereby a tenth player could be used by a manager to bat in place of the pitcher throughout the game. If the manager had a hitting pitcher, he could, of course, have permitted him to hit, but under the suggested rule most managers would have carried an extra player whose sole duty would have been to bat. It would have been a paradise for the "good hit, no field" guys.

The National League generally favored the innovation. The American League was opposed. In those days, it was a usual procedure for each league to oppose anything, no matter how commendable, which emanated from its rival. It looked as though it would be up to Landis to break the deadlock, and I heard at the time he would have supported the Heydler idea. When he had been a Chicago fan, he had suffered too often when some weak-hitting Cub or White Sox hurler spoiled a rally by smacking into a double play. However, just before the joint meeting, the National League withdrew the "tenth player" suggestion, and the public never did get to know whether Landis would have voted "yes" or "no."

After a pennantless famine of 11 years, the Judge's old pets, the Cubs, crashed through to victory in the 1929 National League race under the leadership of the then "bush league" manager, Joe McCarthy. In the 1929 World's Series, played just before the Wall Street crash of middle October, the Cubs played the Athletics. Old Connie Mack, aged 66, had made a remarkable comeback, winning his seventh championship after a dreary uphill climb since 1915. In 1910, when Mack's young Athletics smeared Landis' old favorite, Frank Chance's famous Cubs, four games out of five, the Judge had had a most unhappy time. He was miserable and heart-broken when the Athletics pinned the great Brown's ears back for their final victory on a Sunday at old West Side Park. But this time, after 19 years, Landis had to be strictly neutral.

Connie Mack and Joe McCarthy have been noted for the sportsmanship of their respective teams, but in the 1929 Series both the Athletics and Cubs got out of hand. The A's blamed it on such Chicago jockeys as Pat Malone, Gabby Hartnett, Hack Wilson, Guy Bush, Charley Grimm and Charley Root. But the Athletics had such fellows as Jimmy Dykes, Eddie Rommel, Mule Haas, Mickey Cochrane and Al Simmons, who weren't exactly tongue-tied. In fact, Mack said to Haas on one occasion: "You can stop now, Mule, you have the championship."

193

Landis' ears weren't overly sensitive, and the Judge knew a lot of pretty good cuss-words himself. But, even he decided the players were getting too rough. He called the rival managers, Mack and McCarthy, to his hotel room in Philadelphia, and said: "I have stood for all of this monkey business that I intend to. The boys have been going entirely too far. From now on, any player guilty of offensive language will be fined a full share. Often it is difficult to tell exactly which player is yelling some of these objectionable things. In that case, I will fine the manager."

Both managers held meetings with their players, telling them the jockeying had to stop, or there would be serious trouble.

Just before the fifth and last game of the Series in Philadelphia, with President Herbert Hoover in the stands, Mickey Cochrane yelled at the gagged Cubs, "After the game, we'll serve tea in the clubhouse."

Mack was afraid the Commissioner heard it, and called Cochrane over to the bench. "Do you want this to cost you, and the rest of us, money?" he asked.

The Athletics won the game with a sensational three-run ninth inning rally, giving them the Series, four games to one, as in 1910. When it was over, Landis rushed into the Athletic clubhouse to congratulate the victors, especially lovable old Connie Mack.

Then Landis threw his arms around Cochrane, and said: "Now, Mickey, let us have that tea."

The major league meetings in New York in December, 1929, saw the old Judge crack the whip without any one even letting out a snarl. During meeting week, Landis tried his role as a peacemaker in the bitter internal feud which almost tore apart the Brooklyn club. Charley Ebbets, the old Flatbush Squire, died in 1925, and Ed McKeever, the vice president, caught cold at Charley's funeral, and died a fortnight later. At first they elevated Wilbert Robinson, the rotund manager, to the presidency, but Robbie soon engaged in a bitter personal quarrel with the surviving McKeever, Steve. The Ebbets and McKeever heirs were as friendly as a bunch of Kilkenny cats.

John Heydler tried to bring about some kind of a truce in the feud, but was unsuccessful, so Landis took a try at it. His role as a dove of peace was not one of his outstanding successes. He was invited into a room at New York's Hotel Roosevelt, where the rival factions sat glaring at each other. Joe Gilleaudeau, old Ebbets' son-in-law, and Robbie, represented the Ebbets interests, and "Judge" Steve McKeever and Frank York the McKeever interests.

After some blistering language could be heard from behind the closed door, the Judge, hatless and well nigh breathless, bolted through it, yelling: "Let me out of here! Let me out of this! I never heard anything like this in all my life."

Shortly before the meetings, Judge Emil Fuchs, the president of the Boston Braves, announced that he also would take over the management of his club. Fuchs, a former New York City magistrate, was Benny Kauff's lawyer in his action against Landis some years before, but the two judges always liked each other. Putting his hands on Fuchs' sturdy shoulders, Landis said: "You're a braver man than I am, Judge Fuchs."

At the joint meetings, December 12, Sam Breadon, president of the Cardinals, made an impassioned plea for his farm system, which still was meeting with Landis' displeasure, while Ernest Barnard, the new American League president, gave out a statement in which he said, "The major-minor league farm system will run its course."

Earlier in the year, the Judge had slapped around some of the major league clubs for covering up ball players, and in one of his findings the Detroit club lost one of the best catching prospects then in baseball and a major league star for 17 years, Rick Ferrell. A Detroit farmhand, Ferrell had been with Kinston, Va., and Columbus, Ohio, in 1926–27–28. Ferrell's name wasn't placed on the Columbus club's 1928 reserve list, whereupon Landis made the young Carolina catcher a free agent. It was a nice windfall for Rick, for after accepting a $1,500 bonus in 1926 for signing with the Detroit organization, he now was in a position to sell his services to the highest bidder. Phil Ball gave him a $25,000 bonus for signing with the Browns.

On March 15, 1929, Landis had served notice he didn't intend to stand for any shenanigans in the way of "cover-ups," and made his first wholesale liberation. Ten players were made free agents.

They were men of lesser ability than Ferrell, but most of them were able to sign with big league clubs for tidy bonuses. The men were Pitcher Claude Jonnard of the St. Louis Browns; Pitcher Harold McKain of the Cleveland Indians; Pitcher Guy Cantrell and Outfielder Mel Simons of Washington; Pitcher Ernie Wingard of Milwaukee; Catcher Roy Spencer of Indianapolis; Pitcher Ralph Judd and Infielder Jay Partridge of Birmingham; and Infielder Kyle Anderson of Columbia, S.C. The Browns, Pirates, Washington Senators, Philadelphia Athletics and several of the minor league clubs also were fined from $500 to $1,000 by the irate Judge.

Landis also slapped a $500 fine on the Yankees and ordered Catcher-Outfielder W. A. (Chick) Outen to return a Ruppert-signed check for $1,200 for signing with the New Yorkers. It seemed Outen already had taken a $600 bonus from the Charlotte, N.C., club. This was one of those "I do" and "I don't" sort of verdicts, as Yankee Scout Johnny Nee was exonerated of having any knowledge that Outen previously had taken Charlotte's money. And cracking down on Branch Rickey's farms, the Judge strongly "recommended" that the Cardinal organization sell its Dayton club of the Central League. The Commissioner suspected Brother Branch was interested in the Fort Wayne club of the same league.

23 : Phil Ball Takes the Judge to Court

Every now and then the major league club owners took a surprising slap at Judge Landis. Such a move was made at the joint meeting in New York in 1930, when the big leaguers refused to accept their own Commissioner as an arbitrator in a dispute they had with the minors. That probably was one of the reasons he had a disdainful attitude for many of the men who employed him, a state of mind to which I already have referred.

I've mentioned Landis' battles for a free and unobstructed draft. Well, the majors and minors continued wrangling about it in the Commissioner's first decade in office. The Class AA draft price then was $5,000 and the scale ran down to $1,000 for Class D selectees. The minors wanted $10,000 for AA players and a higher scale for all classes. Landis already had won an earlier point that any player who had once been in the majors and dropped back should be subject to the draft. The minors, however, insisted that no Class AA league player without major experience should be subject to draft unless he had played at least four seasons in minor league ball. The majors wanted to make that three seasons.

The minor league committee then suggested: "Gentlemen, we are getting nowhere. Suppose we leave it up to Judge Landis to arbitrate the differences between us."

To their surprise, the big leaguers, perhaps fearing the Judge would decide against them, turned down the suggestion, whereupon the minor league committee stalked angrily out of the room.

The major leaguers might just as well have taken the Judge as an arbitrator, as they eventually accepted the four-year condition for Class AA men, three years for Class A and A-1, and two years from Class B down. The draft prices also resulted in compromises, $7,500 for Class AA, $6,000 for Classes A-1 and A, $4,000 for B, $2,500 for C and $2,000 for D. Landis had a lot to do with writing the final ticket; it remained in effect until the 1946 season, when the Triple-A classification, with its $10,000 draft price, was created.

In 1930–31, a club owner finally went to court with Judge Landis, and it should occasion no surprise that the man was none other than that unreconstructed rebel from St. Louis, Phil Ball of the Browns. Of course, it was a horrendous thing to do in the eyes of many baseball men, especially those in the National League. One of the reasons for electing Landis, and giving him so much power, was to keep the games out of the courts. But Ball's suit succeeded in establishing the legality of Landis' autocratic powers and brought about the sanctioning of his Czarship in a Federal court. However, Judge Landis did not emerge with the full loaf, as one of his former Chicago associates, Federal Judge Walter Lindley, also upheld the legality of Landis' pet aversion, the new-fangled farm system.

The case involved an outfielder, Fred Bennett, a player in the zone between a good Class AA minor leaguer and one not quite good enough for the big leagues. Bennett was acquired by the Browns from Ardmore, Oklahoma, in 1924, and from then on was bounced around to Muskogee, Tulsa, Wichita Falls and Milwaukee, clubs owned or controlled by Ball. Every now and then, Bennett was yanked in by the Browns for brief trials. The original bill of complaint was brought by Ball's Milwaukee club, but later a supplemental bill of complaint was filed by the St. Louis Americans.

When the St. Louis club sent the outfielder to Milwaukee after the 1930 training season, Commissioner Landis disapproved of the optional phase of the contract, saying the period whereby the player could be sent out on options ended April 5, 1930. The Milwaukee club then first sought court relief to stop Landis' interference, which explains how the case came to land in Judge Lindley's court in Chicago. By mutual consent the application for an injunction was not pressed while Bennett played the 1930 season with Milwaukee, but the Browns "recalled" him in September, and Judge Lindley's finding indicates the Browns asked for waivers on him September 3, when the Pirates claimed him for $7,500. However, the St. Louis club withdrew the waiver. In the meantime, Bennett had got fed up on being pushed around, and asked Landis to make him a free agent. The Commissioner granted the request, which brought the Browns into the case as one of the plaintiffs.

In the supplemental bill, the plaintiffs (the Milwaukee and St.

Louis clubs) sought "to restrain the Commissioner of Baseball from interfering with the relation between Bennett and the plaintiffs or either of them, or with Bennett's contract with the St. Louis club and any assignments thereof previously or subsequently made."

The Commissioner answered that his action and what he proposed to do, if not enjoined, were clearly within his authority and in accord with the rules governing Organized Baseball.

Judge Lindley apparently saw it the same way. He ruled that as the baseball people had actually made Landis a czar, they had to take his decisions whether they liked them or not, and play ball under his rules. They had made their bed; let them lie in it. He even ruled that his former fellow jurist of the Chicago Federal Courts Building was the absolute despot of baseball.

Said Judge Lindley in his finding of April 25, 1931: "The major-minor league agreement recognizes the office of the Commissioner and the jurisdiction aforesaid and provides that in case of any dispute between any major club and any minor club the disputants may certify the dispute to the Commissioner for decision and that the determination shall be final.

"The various agreements and rules, constituting a complete code for, or charter and by-laws of, Organized Baseball in America disclose a clear intent upon the part of the parties to endow the Commissioner with all the attributes of a benevolent but absolute despot and all the disciplinary powers of the proverbial pater familias."

Lindley recognized the legality of the baseball farm, when he ruled there was nothing in the code to prevent a major league club owner from owning minor league properties, but felt that right should not be used to bottle up a player indefinitely in the farm system. It was covered in the following paragraph:

"It is apparent that Ball, by controlling the St. Louis, Wichita Falls, Tulsa and Milwaukee clubs, and in addition Springfield, Mo., is, and has at all times since April 5, 1928, been able at his own discretion to direct the transfer of Bennett at any time from any one of these clubs to any other of them without asking for waivers from major league clubs. Though there is nothing in the rules to prohibit an individual owning control of a major league club from likewise owning control of minor league clubs the intent of the code is such that common ownership is not to be made use of as to give one individual, controlling all of the clubs mentioned, the absolute right, independent of other clubs, to control indefinitely a player acquired and switched about by apparent outright purchases."

Ball didn't take the decision kindly; he still was full of fight and didn't intend that this should be the last round. He immediately announced that he would appeal Judge Lindley's decision, and instructed his attorneys to fight it all the way to the United States Supreme Court if that was necessary.

Landis, by this time, was pretty much fed up with Ball, and irked about his conduct. Again it looked like a showdown with the American League. He called a group of American League club owners, including Ball, to his Chicago office, and again laid down the law. Were they going to live up to their agreement with the Commissioner, or, even with Ban Johnson dead, were they to permit Ball to continue his guerilla fighting?

As Ball was coming down in the elevator with Alva Bradley, then the comparatively new president of the Cleveland Indians, the St. Louisan remarked: "Did you ever see a more stubborn man than Landis?"

"Yes, I have," replied Bradley, looking Ball right in the eye.

"You don't mean me, do you?" asked the Brown president.

"I don't mean anyone else," said Bradley.

Ball reflected a moment before replying. "Well, if I am more stubborn than Landis, I must be the most stubborn man in the United States. If that is so, I'd better call my lawyers and tell them to drop the appeal."

However, it wasn't until the last week of 1931 that Ball finally agreed to accept Landis' decision on Bennett and withdraw his appeal. In the meantime, Clark Griffith, president of the Washington club, and Bob Quinn, then president of the Red Sox and Ball's former business manager in St. Louis, had put additional pressure on him, and pointed out that Landis was likely to toss up his job any moment unless the appeal was withdrawn. Thus ended the first and last attempt to have one of Landis' decisions reversed in the higher courts of the land.

The depression was biting deeper and deeper into the nation, also baseball, in that harassed season of 1931. It didn't help things to have the Athletics and Cardinals win in runaway races in their respective leagues. However, the season had an exciting climax, when the Cardinals, helped by Pepper Martin's wild ride (he hit .500 and stole five bases), downed the great Athletics in an exciting seven-game Series.

Despite his role as a strictly neutral Commissioner, the Judge couldn't hide his admiration for the galloping Wild Horse of the Osage, another of Martin's appellations. And I think he really enjoyed Pepper's great show. With his chin on the rail, and his battered hat almost down to his ears, he really "ate it up." "Did you ever see anything like that Martin's performance?" he asked with enthusiasm. "Why, there were times when I thought he would steal Mickey's (Cochrane's) underwear."

During the 1931 season, Landis had continued his battle with the gamblers—carried it to a point many considered silly. Gabby Hartnett, the Cub catcher, was partly to blame. The big, red-faced, jovial Massachusetts Irishman, one of Landis' favorite ball players, was foolish enough to have his picture taken as he was chatting with Al Capone in front of the Cicero Bootleg King's box at Wrigley Field, Chicago. Capone already had had pretty much of a "bad press," and the picture, first printed in Chicago, was reproduced in newspapers from coast to coast. It caused much annoyance to Landis, also to the two major league executives, Heydler and Will Harridge, who had become American League president early in the year.

At Landis' direction, both league presidents issued instructions that no player could hold any conversation with a fan before or during a game. The offending player suffered an automatic fine of $5.00. Umpires were assigned to the parks long before game time to see that the rule was enforced. The idea was to prevent players passing on any information, especially in regard to a possible starting pitcher, to a gambler. But it also prevented Joe Blong from saying "How-yah" to a neighbor, or from coming up to the rail and greeting the delegation from Kalamazoo. The move was by no means popular, and kept away fans who had a particular interest in some particular player at the time when the game needed every fan it could entice through a turnstile.

Landis also gave orders that no manager or other club official should give any advance information on the starting pitcher. The idea also was to prevent such information from reaching the ears of the gamblers, though they are a rather crafty, canny breed, and can figure out likely pitching starters better than many baseball men.

This last edict vexed many of the baseball writers, especially men on afternoon sheets. It had been their practice to ascertain the likely pitchers from the two managers, and they often built their leads on likely pitching combinations such as Carl Hubbell, Giants vs. Bill Hallahan, Cardinals; Burleigh Grimes, Cards vs. Charley Root, Cubs; and Lefty Grove, Athletics vs. Goofy Gomez, Yankees. Grove had a winning streak of sixteen straight that season. After he had run off around twelve of these victories, he met Gomez, who also had piled up something like ten straight, at Yankee Stadium. The game was a "natural," and had it been properly built up, with full play on the two great lefthanders tangling together, it would have been good for a midweek crowd of 35,000 —even in those depression times. As it was, the two just stumbled into each other, and some 7,000 New York fans attended.

New York writers pointed out that any other sport, amateur or professional, would have exploited such a contest all over the sports pages. They also pointed out that Mack and the Athletics, with their big pay roll and lean home receipts, badly needed their "take" from such a New York crowd. Some said Landis was unquestionably a strong and able Commissioner, but a poor baseball business man.

The Judge didn't take kindly to such criticism. "I'm battling to keep this game clean, and away from gamblers, and some of these writing fellows are trying to make it harder for me," he said.

However, his critics were as hostile to the gambling fraternity as he was. But, they called for a more common sense attitude. They

202

said if it was necessary to be so secretive, why not be consistent and refrain from printing that the Athletics would meet the Yankees? Then, the gamblers wouldn't know a game was on— unless they had a pocket schedule in their trouser pockets.

The order against giving the names of pitchers before games gradually faded out. I don't believe the Commissioner ever rescinded the order, but after a time it no longer was enforced. After a few years, the order against fraternizing with the fans also was first modified and then practically discontinued. Then, after the gambling fraternity preyed on all professional sports in 1946, the rules were made still more rigid in 1947.

"Economy" was the watch-word at the 1931 joint meetings, with Judge Landis casting the deciding vote with the more economically-minded National League. In the Heydler circuit, the majority of the owners voted to reduce the player limit from twenty-five to twenty-three. In the American League, most of the owners voted to continue the old twenty-five limit. Landis broke the deadlock by siding with the twenty-three-player men. Another depression-inspired resolution called for a reduction of players' salaries, all down the line.

An effort, which had Landis' support, sought to wipe out what then was called the "synthetic double-header," with Breadon and Rickey of the St. Louis Cardinals being the culprits who started the vogue. Bob Quinn of the Red Sox had the American League go on record against the practice, and it was brought to the attention of Landis at the joint meeting. It was pointed out that Section 1, Article 5 of the Major League Agreement provided that after the schedules have been made and issued they must be observed and that there could be no change without the concurrence of both league presidents. On questioning the club owners, Landis learned that this rule had been suspended in the National League.

Commissioner Landis then ruled: "From now on, I shall insist that this rule be enforced."

That seemed to dispose of it. A news item of that time read, "As it is considered unlikely that the league presidents will permit arbitrary moving up of games, except in extraordinary cases, that seems to dispose of artificial double-headers."

However, the synthetic double-header—especially the former St. Louis Sunday twin-bill—was here to stay. And it wasn't long before there was no need of moving up games to create them; they were included on the regular schedule.

24: The Judge Takes a $25,000 Cut

There was no improvement for baseball as the game reached the Hoover-Roosevelt election year of 1932. Many big league clubs were having a difficult time finding banks which would extend loans to meet operating expenses, while minor league clubs and minor leagues were blowing up almost daily.

Paul Mickelson, Associated Press writer, bearded the white-haired jurist in his Chicago den, and inquired why some help hadn't been extended to some of the stricken clubs.

"Yes, yes, I know the minor leagues, especially those of lower classification, are having their financial worries," Landis replied. "But what can I or the major leagues do about it? It would take an act of Congress and the United States Treasury to pull them out.

"Baseball is suffering just like all other business. It just seems that it can't be helped. They'll all get along all right in time. Five B and C leagues already have suspended, while a lot of the others, AA and A leagues included, are caught in the general depression, but a lot of business houses are in worse shape than some of the weakest and sickest of our minor league clubs."

"What about the big surplus the majors have stored up, supposedly for a rainy day?" persisted Mickelson. "It has been suggested that the majors turn over some of that surplus to the minors to tide them over the bumps."

The Judge looked at Paul most disapprovingly. "Surplus! Surplus!" he yelled. "Now, I know that you are talking foolish. Sometimes I don't know who is in the craziest profession, you or I. Goodbye!"

At the 1932 Yankee-Cub World's Series, Landis again showed he ran the game above any consideration for gate receipts. But he again was soundly panned by many baseball men for his poor business judgment in handling the first two games at Yankee Stadium. "He can't adjust himself to the fact that there is a depression on, and that we must act accordingly," was one of the complaints.

He rather bungled things at the first game, with the result that only a 41,459 crowd was out in a stadium seating 65,000. Those 25,000 vacant seats looked like a black eye for baseball, but there were mitigating circumstances. It was at the depth of the depression, and Ed Barrow, the Yankee president, still had many reserved box seat and lower grandstand tickets left when his mail sale was over. These tickets were sold in strips of three, for the three games likely to be played at Yankee Stadium.

The sensible thing then seemed to be to sell these $5.50 and $6.60 seats at the windows on the day of games, but Landis ruled a fan still would have to buy a strip of three at $16.50 and $19.80 at the booths. There also were some 35,000 unreserved $3.30 upper grandstand and $1.10 bleacher seats placed on sale on the day of the game.

However, in the morning and early afternoon of the first game, September 28, a steady rain fell all over New York. In fact, it rained so hard in nearby Westchester County that Lou Gehrig, the Yankee captain, didn't think there was a possibility of a game. The Iron Horse didn't gallop into the Stadium until just five minutes before the start of the game.

Few persons thought there was any likelihood of a contest, and the sale of the unreserved seats was practically killed, while the $16.50 and $19.80 three-game windows did no business at all. The Commissioner could have called off the game any time during the morning, or later because of wet grounds, but when the rain stopped around 1.30, he ordered the game played before the poor crowd and all those empty seats.

Landis vigorously defended his action. "The schedule called for the Series to open in New York on a Wednesday, September 28," he said. "That meant that Saturday and Sunday games were scheduled for Chicago, even if the Series ran to only four games. I wanted nothing to interfere with that arrangement. Many of the Chicago fans purchased their three-game strip tickets to see these week-end games, and I wanted to play fair with them, even though some New Yorkers had to sit on wet seats."

However, the next day the Commissioner rescinded his order on reserved seats, and permitted Barrow to sell $6.60 box and $5.50

lower grandstand tickets for only the second game at the booths. The attendance increased to 50,709, still far below capacity.

The Series brought about the novel situation of a ball player complaining to Landis about an umpire, and one of the best arbiters in the game at that. Lou Gehrig made the charge against Bill Klem. "He called me something that wasn't called for, and I won't take it," said Lou.

In one of the earlier games, Lou, who was Yankee captain, came tearing in from first base to protest about a called ball on one of the Cub players. Lou insisted it was a strike. Now, if there was one thing Bill was touchy about, it was his calling of strikes and balls. In his book, he was perfect in that department. "Get back there, you big lout; you take care of your job, and I'll take care of mine," bellowed Klem.

From there on the feud smouldered all during the Series. Gehrig had an amazing Series; he batted .529, scored nine runs in four games, drove in eight, and pretty near ran the Cubs into the ground. In the fourth game in Chicago, Bill—umpiring on the bases—stood on the first-base side of second as Gehrig was at bat. Lou waved to him several times to get over to the other side of the bag or park his dogs elsewhere on the infield. Bill never budged; he wasn't going to let any American Leaguer, even a .529 hitter, tell him where he was going to stand. Gehrig smacked one of his machine-gun drives right at Klem, and Bill had to jump quickly to keep his legs from being cut from under him. On the bases, the pair exchanged other compliments. Lou told Landis that Bill had insulted him; he also objected to where Klem stood on the infield, but the Series ended with that game, and Gehrig soon forgot his peeve in the joys of another Yankee four-straight victory. As for Landis, he chuckled over the incident, but did bring it to Klem's attention.

Shortly after the Series, Landis made an adverse ruling on a claim by Rogers Hornsby, the great slugger, for a Cub World's Series share. The fiery Texan's penchant for betting on the races had put him in the Commissioner's doghouse long before this. Hornsby was to remain in it until Landis' death.

Hornsby was player-manager of the Cubs until August 4 of that season, when he was succeeded by the team's aggressive first baseman, Charley Grimm, now again the Chicago manager. Hornsby had had trouble with some of his players, and Landis had information that some of them had made loans to their manager. The club perked up under the leadership of Grimm and beat out the Pirates for the pennant.

In their clubhouse meeting before the World's Series, the Chicago players voted against cutting Hornsby in for any share of the players' pool. It was the same meeting at which they voted only a fraction of a share to Mark Koenig, the former Yankee, who had been a valuable player in their drive for the pennant.

In view of the fact that Hornsby had been with the club for almost two-thirds of the 1932 season and went to no other club after his release, he felt he was entitled to a share. Many sports writers thought the Cubs might have been a little more liberal and voted Hornsby a share. In a rather lengthy statement, the Commissioner upheld the players and turned down Hornsby, ruling that he hadn't been "a bonafide member to a qualifying team on or succeeding August 31," and further quoted: "It is specifically provided that 'no other person shall receive any part of said funds except . . . pursuant to written recommendations voluntarily made and signed by all the players entitled to receive a full share.'" As no such recommendation was made, Landis ruled Hornsby had no case.

The Cubs were Hornsby's third managerial venture in the majors, as he formerly had led the Cardinals and the Braves. He was to get another chance, this time in the American League with the Browns. He eventually lost this job in midseason of 1937, partly because he just couldn't keep from wagering on horse flesh. Landis frequently had him on his carpet, but he wouldn't take heed. Though Rogers later got managerial posts in the minors, and was general manager of the Fort Worth club when the war suspended operations in the Texas League in 1942, Hornsby always felt—rightly or wrongly—that Landis blocked his way to another big league managerial post. This probably was true, as Landis was irked by Hornsby's refusal to discontinue his horse playing.

"That fellow never will learn," the Commissioner once said with a display of impatience. "His betting has got him into one scrape after another, cost him a fortune and several jobs, and still he hasn't enough sense to stop it."

Hornsby countered with: "No one ever accused me of a thing in baseball. As a player I hustled with the best of them, and as a manager I made every effort to win. I don't drink or smoke, never did, and racing is my recreation. I enjoy it and get a kick out of it. Racing, and betting on races, is permitted by law in many of the states, so I was doing nothing illegal. Some of the best people in the country, including Cabinet ministers, attend races and bet on races. I always gave full time to my baseball jobs, and if I bet money on the races, it was my own, honestly earned. I could see no difference from betting a horse would win and a lot of the club owners playing the market and betting a stock would go up or down."

Maybe the forthright Hornsby deserved some credit for having the courage of his convictions, but his stand was unwise and kept him continually in hot water.

Further economies were put into effect at the December, 1932, meetings. The leagues voted to continue the 23-player limit, sidetracked one of Landis' pet projects, the annual appropriation of $50,000 for American Legion baseball, and voted a salary cut for umpires all the way down the line. And the depression also caught up with Kenesaw Mountain. It was announced at the joint meeting that the Commissioner made a gesture of "tremendous generosity," and declared that if the funds for carrying on his office proved insufficient, he would make it up from his salary.

Landis' cut wasn't announced at the time, but it later developed that he had voluntarily reduced his annual stipend from $65,000 to $40,000. This cut remained in effect for five years.

That cut came in for a lot of publicity after Commissioner Landis' death. In the June 28, 1945, issue of *The Sporting News* we ran a Washington story on the condition of the treasury, which the newly elected Commissioner, Senator A. B. Chandler, was taking over.

The story contained these paragraphs: "It is said the treasury now contains little more than $100,000. The regulations provide that the office of the Commissioner shall be financed from receipts collected in the form of a 15 per cent levy on World's Series and city series games, which, averaging around $144,692 annually, had been more than enough to finance the administration of Judge Landis and build up a surplus in addition. It is reported part of this surplus was diminished some years ago through investments that turned sour, including Insull stocks.

"Contributions to war relief funds the last three years have reduced the amounts received by the Commissioner's office from World's Series. In 1942, the office received $92,299.16; $102,079.80 in 1943 and only $68,826 in 1944."

We treated it as strictly a news story from a Washington correspondent. As to Landis' losing some money in Insull investments, that long had been common knowledge among those in the know of the game. I didn't intend to make a point of it. For who didn't have investments in those difficult years in the early 30's that turned sour?

However, Leslie O'Connor, who for years was Landis' secretary-treasurer and then served as Chandler's Chicago adviser, seemed considerably annoyed at the story and wrote a letter to Chandler. Apparently O'Connor thought the story was inspired by the new Commissioner. He sent some figures on the $767,589.20 surplus entrusted to the Commissioner under the Landis regime.

Gene Kessler, sports editor of the Chicago *Times*, got hold of the letter and wrote in his column of June 30, 1945:

"These figures did show a loss of $29,000 through investments made for the Commission by a bank in interest-bearing Insull securities. Such a loss, over a period of 23 years, is rather small in handling such funds, as any banking institution will verify, but when Landis learned of it he immediately made amends.

" 'That was the reason Judge Landis took a voluntary reduction in salary,' explained O'Connor. 'And his act repaid the loss 400 per cent, since he took a total reduction of more than $100,000 salary.'

"What seemed to irk O'Connor, who idolized Judge Landis, was that this small figure leaked out, especially through a source close to Chandler, and immediately was built from a mole hill into a mountain. . . . We doubt very much if Chandler ever knew about the reports on Landis' handling of funds. One thing which hasn't been emphasized is that Chandler is receiving only his $10,000 salary as Senator. He won't start receiving the 50 G's until he quits Washington and moves into the Cincinnati office as Commissioner. Financing usually doesn't interest the baseball fans, unless it concerns a player's salary. But in this case there is definite interest."

Chandler didn't appreciate O'Connor's letter, nor the interview with Kessler. Without exactly using the phraseology of Judge Landis to Barney Dreyfuss in 1924, he admonished Leslie to keep his shirt on or tender his resignation.

There also was some clipping of the Commissioner's wings at the December, 1932, meetings, and the big leaguers supposedly took from Landis the power to mess up their farm deals. A resolution was passed by the unanimous vote of all sixteen clubs to remove from the jurisdiction of Commissioner Landis the authority to rule against player transactions solely because they were made between farms of the same major league club.

A year before the American League had passed the same resolution, but the National League, fearing Landis might resign, refused to go along with it, though men like Breadon and Rickey of St. Louis strongly favored it. But, by 1932, conditions were so chaotic in the minors that the National League swung into line, and also backed the resolution to the limit. Landis didn't resign, and he found other ways of getting at the "farmers" when their manipulations were too much for him to swallow, as the present Brooklyn president, Branch Rickey, and Jack Zeller, now chief scout of the Braves, may well attest.

25: World's Series Boys Play Rough

The Commissioner's next few years were fairly peaceable. That farm business continued to irk him, and every now and then he would slap down on some operator, especially Rickey of the Cardinals. But they were years for lots of golf and relaxation. In December, 1933, Judge Landis was re-elected for a third seven-year term by the major league club owners. This, however, was a cut and dried program at the Chicago meeting, with no Ban Johnson or Phil Ball to disturb the serenity of the baseball waters. Battling Phil of St. Louis had died shortly after the 1933 season. The Commissioner's new contract was extended a month, so that it would run out at the December meetings, 1941. No announcement was made at the time as to the salary in the new contract, but Landis continued to take his voluntary cut of $25,000 until 1937, when times and baseball again became more profitable.

The first All-Star game was played in Chicago on July 6, 1933, as one of the sports events of the Century of Progress Exposition. First suggested by Arch Ward, Chicago *Tribune* sports editor, it had the strong support of Landis, and it was largely through his insistence that this game has developed into a dramatic midseason spectacle, secondary on the baseball calendar only to the autumn World's Series. "That's a grand show, and it should be continued," said Landis, after the first Comiskey Park contest. Some of the club owners were lukewarm to the contest, especially in the early years, but the Judge was the game's foremost and most influential champion. He never missed one of them, and one of his last public appearances was at the twelfth All-Star game in Pittsburgh, July 11, 1944.

Starting with 1933, Landis had three successive World's Series in which the rambunctious young men of the diamond caused him to take some dramatic action. Actually, he wasn't so riled over some of these flare-ups as appeared on the surface. In discussing them in his hotel room, after the incidents, he often gave a sly wink, indicative that the conduct on the field hadn't been so terrible.

In the 1933 Washington-Giants World's Series, he set the precedent that he, alone, could put a player out of a Series game, and no umpire was to toss out an obstreperous athlete until first getting the Commissioner's okay. The edict came after National League umpire Charley Moran gave Heinie Manush, hefty Washington left fielder, the air at the fourth game of the event played in Washington, October 6. It was a tight pitching duel betwee Carl Hubbell, the Giants' lefthanded ace, and Monte Weaver and Jack Russell, working for Washington, with New York taking the game in the eleventh inning by a score of 2 to 1.

In the sixth inning, Moran, the first base umpire, called out Manush on a slow grounder to Second Baseman Hughie Critz, Pitcher Hubbell having run over to take the throw at the bag. Moran soon was surrounded by a circle of raging Washington players, who protested loudly and vehemently at the decision. Heinie was in the forefront, and during the argument tried to shove around Moran, a burly football coach during the offseason.

After some minutes, the Washington team took the field, with Manush going out to left field. Then Moran angrily waved for him to get out of there. During the loud talking and shoving, he had ordered Heinie from the field. Heinie wouldn't go for several additional minutes, and stayed in left field, while the Washington fans booed their displeasure. Eventually, the two American League umpires, Moriarty and Ormsby, induced Manush to leave.

Heinie was the first player tossed out of a World's Series game since Tommy Connolly bounced one of Landis' old Cub idols, Frank Chance, out of the third game of the Cub-Athletic series in Chicago 23 years before. As a fan-Commissioner, Landis always felt no player should be put out of a World's Series game unless his offense was grievous. So perhaps, he sympathized with Washington fandom in having this big gun out of the line-up in such a close and important game. Though he fined Manush $50, he also called in the umpires, and said they were to oust no players without his permission, a ruling which remained up to the time of his death.

Yet, a year later, in the final game of the 1934 World's Series between the Tigers and the Gas House Cardinals in Detroit, October 9, Landis ordered Joe Medwick, former St. Louis left fielder, out of the game when Ducky Joe was guilty of nothing more than being a target for a Detroit vegetable and fruit shower.

After a knock-down, drag-out Series, the Cardinals had come from behind by winning the sixth game, and then ran roughshod over Cochrane's club in the grand finale, scoring seven runs in the third inning and eventually winning by a score of 11 to 0. It put the Detroit fans, especially the occupants of the left field bleachers, in a nasty mood.

The Medwick incident came to a head in the sixth inning, with St. Louis already leading, 7 to 0. Ducky hit a triple, scoring a team-mate and slid hard into third base. Medwick and Marvin Owen, the Tiger third baseman, were kicking at each other on the ground when the play ended. They both got up swinging, but the umpires rushed between them before any punches landed. That seemed to close the incident until the Tiger half of the inning, when Medwick went out to left field for the Cardinals. He was bombarded with a shower of apples, oranges, rolled up newspapers and score-cards and any other litter the fans could get their hands on. After a groundkeeper's crew cleared the field of debris, and the game was about to be resumed, a second shower, more intensive than the first, came out of the stands. The crowd, in the meantime, booed Medwick incessantly.

When the shower first started, Landis left his box and retreated about three tiers from the rail, where he soon was engaged in an animated conversation with Charles Hughes, a Chicago friend, who was his guest at the Series. When the second shower came, the Judge returned to his box, held court, to which he summoned the four umpires, and the two players, Medwick and Owen, whose shadow boxing at third base started the row. After some spirited gabbing, the Judge gave his decision; it was that Medwick should leave the game. Manager Frisch of the Cardinals didn't like it, but Chick Fullis went to left field for St. Louis; the Detroit fans were pacified and the game was resumed.

Landis later said he took the action partly to protect Medwick from physical harm. Many persons, including pressbox critics, were not in sympathy with the Judge's handling of the situation. They felt he should have been stricter with the Detroit management, ordered the club to police the stands and eject the throwers, on the threat of forfeiting the game to the Cardinals. Of course, a World's Series forfeited game also would have given baseball a black eye. However, had the score been close, instead of 9 to 0, he hardly could have removed Frisch's best batter from the game when the offenders were unruly Detroit fans.

There was an interesting sequel to the incident. Warren Brown, Chicago *Sun* sports editor and columnist, had observed the conversation between Landis and Hughes while super-heated fans were threatening to take the park apart, and asked Hughes what the Judge had been talking about.

"The Judge had made an important discovery," Hughes said, "and he rushed up to tell me about it. Most of his other guests were ladies, you know, and I guess he realized I was the only one who would appreciate his discovery. All his life, he told me, he had been trying to master the art of spitting tobacco juice through his teeth. While watching Pepper Martin give a demonstration, he had suddenly learned the trick."

During the Series, the young Cardinal catcher, Bill Delancey, had been called out on three straight strikes by Brick Owens, the American League umpire. Delancey had been pretty rough on Owens; the matter was reported to Landis and the Commissioner summoned the Cardinal catcher to his hotel room.

In relating the incident in the privacy of his hotel suite, the Judge said solemnly, "I said to Delancey: 'Young man, what did you say when Owens called the first strike?'

"Delancey replied: 'Well, I'll tell you, Judge; I was pretty much upset. I said: "Why, you ———— ———— blind so-and-so, you surely missed that one!" ' "

A mischievous smile played around the corners of his mouth, as Landis continued the impersonation. He added: "I next asked Delancey what he said when Brick called the second strike."

"Delancey replied: 'I stepped out of the box and said: "Why you blankety-blank blind son of a so-and-so, can't you see the ball?" '

" 'And what did you say after the third pitch?' I inquired.

"Delancey continued: 'By this time, Judge, I was good and mad, so I said: "Of all the sightless ———— lousy ———— of Oriental origin, you are the limit. And with that he said he would report me." ' "

The Judge didn't lose a word in the retelling. As the profane phrases rolled off his tongue, he was convulsed with mirth.

Later he added: "You know that boy came clean with me, so I fined him only $50 and told him he shouldn't talk that way to umpires."

The Judge used to have a similar story on Donie Bush, the former famous Tiger shortstop and now president of the Indianapolis club. At a time when Bush was an American Association manager, his abuse of umpires became so bad that it reached the attention of Landis. He summoned Donie to his Chicago office.

"Now, Donie, I've always liked you, and when you were on the Tigers, you were one of my favorite ball players," said the Judge sternly. "But I've heard some comment about your conduct toward umpires, and I've called you here to tell you that it's got to stop."

"My conduct towards the umpires!" said Bush in surprise. "Who could be saying such things about me?"

"My informant is Umpire Blotz himself," said Landis. "He said that your remarks not only were profane, but also obscene."

"That's a darn lie," exploded Bush. "I never said a profane, obscene thing in my life. All I called him was a blankety-blank-blank." The Commissioner also would rock with laughter as he repeated Bush's conversation.

During the 1934 Series, Bill Klem, the veteran National League umpire, exchanged a few uncomplimentary words on the field with Goose Goslin, picturesque Tiger outfielder, and when Bill later was caged with Goslin in a hotel elevator in downtown Detroit, he couldn't resist the temptation to tell off Mr. Goose in unmistakable terms. I've forgotten Bill's exact words, but it was a Klem gem, bristling with barbed-wire adjectives and Klem satire at its best. The incident was considered to be one of the best laughs of the Series, but certain baseball people were in the car and it soon reached the Commissioner's ears.

I am sure the Judge got a good chuckle out of it, but he called Bill Klem to his suite, put him on the griddle for his loose language in a public conveyance and fined him $50. For sometime thereafter Bill wouldn't accept his check for his World's Series chores, because it was $50 short.

It was around this time that Landis expressed his strong displeasure over Bill Klem's daily presence at the Miami horse tracks during Florida's winter racing season. Ever since he was a young umpire, Bill has been an inveterate track fan, and he still feels he can beat the ponies. Landis didn't mince his words in letting Bill know he didn't like it. "When I attend the races during the off-season, I violate neither the laws of the land, nor of my resident state of Florida."

Whether it was the Goslin incident or his defiance of Landis on his race track attendance, Bill was finished as a World's Series umpire. And it almost broke the old fellow's heart. He had been the particular prince of umpires in getting World's Series assignments, working in seventeen Series from 1908 to 1934, inclusive. For a while, he would work every fall, and after that, every other Series. But after 1934, Landis would not okay him when his name was presented by the National League president. Finally in 1940, Klem's last year as an active umpire, Ford Frick made a personal plea to Landis in his behalf, asking that Klem be permitted to round out his great umpire career with one more Series, and Landis relented.

The boys continued to play rough the following fall, 1935, when the Cubs, fresh from their September winning streak of twenty-one straight, played the Tigers. In the first game, played in Detroit, the Cubs, with a pretty good coterie of bench jockeys, were rather crude in riding tall Hank Greenberg, the Bronx Jewish first baseman of the Tigers. When they carried it into the second game, Moriarty, one of the two American League umpires, told the Cubs they were going too far and would have to cut it out. In the meantime, Moriarty was compelled to call one close decision after another, and almost invariably he decided in favor of Detroit. He was a former Detroit third baseman and manager, but I believe he called them without any bias, and as he saw them.

However, the Cubs were frantic about his work, and bitter language passed between Moriarty, an old two-fisted fighter, and the Cub bench. I've been told it was the worst ever heard at a

World's Series. Finally, in one of the latter games of the Series, Moriarty tossed Chicago Manager Grimm, and two of the Cub substitutes, Outfielder Tuck Stainback and Infielder Woody English, off the Chicago bench. He apparently could do that without consulting with Landis. When the Commissioner reviewed the case, he fined not only all three of the offending players, but also Umpire Moriarty, sums of $200. He pitched especially into Moriarty, saying that he was there as one of the representatives of the Commissioner, should have kept his head and not indulged in a battle of Billingsgate with the Chicago bench.

26: The Saga of Alabama Pitts

In midseason of 1935, Judge Landis reversed a decision of Judge William G. Bramham, the little Czar of the minor leagues, permitting Edwin C. (Alabama) Pitts, the paroled convict from New York's Ossining prison, to play International League ball in a controversy which rocked the nation at the time. Regardless of the sentiment in the matter, I always thought Landis yielded to popular outcry in this case, and I know Judge Bramham always felt the Commissioner left him out on a limb and holding the well-known bag.

Pitts, who did several small stick-up jobs, was convicted of second-degree robbery in New York State in March, 1930. In sentencing Pitts' twenty-year-old lookout to the reformatory, Judge Morris Koenig, passing sentence, said: "There is no evidence before me that he (the lookout) was in any other robbery than this, while Pitts has been in at least five other robberies."

In sentencing the then nineteen-year-old Pitts to New York's Big House on the Hudson for a term of eight to sixteen years, Judge Koenig remarked: "I should think Pitts was very fortunate that he was not compelled to plead guilty to robbery in the first degree, where the mandatory sentence would have been 20 years."

Pitts, apparently a harum-scarum kid, had been in the Navy before his New York adventures, and his past record as a rather tough egg was pretty well forgotten when he developed into the star athlete at Ossining in the next five years, starring on the institution's baseball and football teams and on the track squad. Inasmuch as professional and strong amateur clubs frequently played exhibitions at Ossining, tales of Alabama's athletic fame were not confined by the high prison walls. In June, 1935, Johnny Evers, one of Landis' heroes on the old Cubs and at this time general manager of the Albany club, announced that Pitts soon would be released on parole and that he would sign him to an Albany contract.

Johnny's statement caused quite a ripple of excitement, especially in New York, where Pitts' athletic prowess was known to the readers of metropolitan dailies and there was conjecture whether the

219

former home run hitter of the Big House could hit Class AA pitching.

Then Judge Bramham, down in Durham, N.C., set off the bomb which exploded editorial writers, columnists, sob-sisters, and syndicated feature writers into a wrath of outraged indignation. Bramham decreed that he would not accept the contract of Pitts with the Albany club, or with any other minor league organization.

In connection with Judge Bramham's decision, the National Association gave out the following press release: "The decision of President Bramham in the 'Alabama' Pitts case expressed solely his policy in the interpretation of his duties toward the game.

" 'When the subject was first broached,' Bramham said, 'I considered it of such importance that it was taken into conference with the Executive Committee.

" 'We went into it thoroughly, considering the sentimental angle, as well as the effects upon the game.

" 'While my decision was based upon my personal judgment, the three members of the committee were in accord with my feelings in the matter.

" 'There is no one more in sympathy with Pitts than myself, but in a position where I am expected to safeguard the interests of baseball, nothing else could be considered. The game was confronted with a policy and it was a duty to make a decision. I acted in this duty as my judgment dictated, there being no other course to follow.' "

However, there was one point that Bramham didn't bring out in this explanatory statement, namely, that he had called up Judge Landis in Chicago and had obtained the Commissioner's views before he rendered his verdict. "I wanted to get the Commissioner's viewpoint before making any decision, and thought I was expressing it when I ruled against Pitts," Bramham later confided to a newspaper friend.

However, this is a sympathetic nation, and Pitts became baseball's No. 1 Martyr. Alabama was termed the American Jean Valjean, and from William Allen White's editorial sanctum at Emporia, Kansas, to important pulpits in the East, Judge Bramham was fried to a crisp and pleas went up to the high heavens for justice for Pitts. Charles Evans Hughes, Jr., New York lawyer and son of the former Chief Justice, wired Landis that anyone who opposed Pitt's plea was un-American. Clarence Darrow, the great Chicago criminal lawyer, said there was only one word for Bramham's decision: "Rotten." The East Side Ministers' Council of Buffalo, in a resolution, urged that Pitts be given "a fair chance to establish himself as a law-abiding member of society." Sports writers and fans were unanimous in demanding not only a break, but justice, for the under-dog.

"It is not a question of the individual, Edwin Pitts," Bramham said in reply to this volume of criticism, "but the question: 'Shall the ranks of Organized Baseball be opened to ex-convicts?' I construe it to be my duty to answer in the negative." And all the time he thought he had Landis in his corner.

The fact that Pitts had been in more than one stick-up was completely lost sight of. He was described as just a poor kid, who had gotten hold of some bootleg liquor, listened to bad associates, and got himself into a jam. The New York District Attorney of 1930 was even panned for having highpressured the then 19-year-old youth into a second degree burglary plea. Pitts' life story was syndicated in serial form throughout the country.

After Bramham disqualified Pitts, the Albany club appealed to the Executive Committee of the National Association, which met in New York and upheld Bramham. They pointed out, however, that Pitts had the right to appeal to Landis for a final verdict. This Pitts and Evers, spokesman for the Albany club, proceeded to do. Johnny was most bitter, and said if Bramham wasn't reversed it would be a blot on America's sense of fair play and sportsmanship. Parole officials declared that if Landis would sustain the Bramham ban, it would undo the work of years of parole. Landis' Michigan Boulevard office was bombarded with thousands of wires, letters and telephone calls, asking that Pitts be made eligible. It is doubtful if any previous Landis case—either in his old Federal Court or in his Commissioner's Office—brought such a deluge of mail and telegrams.

It got so that Landis stayed away from his office, and ducked reporters. However, one of them managed to get to the Judge and showed him the proof of an editorial which his newspaper intended running on the following Sunday if the Judge did not rule in Pitts' favor. It was one of the strongest things yet written, and intimated the Commissioner would be tarred with the same brush as Bramham, unless he immediately removed the ban. I've been told that this unprinted editorial was the final straw in Landis' decision to reverse Bramham. I know the Carolinian felt so. "The sentiment for Pitts was so strong, and those wishing to give him a chance in baseball were so unanimous, that no one could resist this tide," Landis later allegedly told Bramham.

In his decision of June 17, 1935, permitting Pitts to play with the Albany club, Landis was quite fair and didn't paint Pitts as a guy who had been wronged, or as a white lily. And he tried to support the original decision of Bramham and the minor leagues' Executive Committee as best he could, considering his verdict.

In going into Pitts' background, the decision said: "In the course of the considerable publicity in this case there have been created erroneous impressions which require correction. It has been represented that the offense committed, which is the basis of the National Association ruling, grew out of an 'escapade' wherein Pitts, 'drunk' and 'hungry,' was misled into accompanying 'an older man' (or 'a tough guy') into a store, only to discover that his companion's purpose was robbery, which the companion accomplished by using a gun, while Pitts, unarmed and merely obeying his companion's orders, took '$5 or $10' from the cash register; that this was the only offense in which Pitts ever was involved; and that Pitts pleaded guilty out of consideration for his companion's wife and children and to lessen his companion's punishment by 'taking the rap' for him.

"The official record, certified by the court which sentenced Pitts, establishes that it was Pitts who entered the store, held up the clerks with his loaded revolver, and took $76.25 from the cash register. (The amount is not important—it depended upon what the cash register contents happened to be—but $5 or $10 is more consistent with the 'drunk' and 'hungry' and 'escapade' representations.) Pitts' accomplice (one year older than Pitts) acted as 'lookout' and was unarmed."

After quoting the New York judge, Morris Koenig, in passing sentence, Landis continued in the finding: "The official record contains no evidence that either Pitts or his accomplice was either 'drunk' or 'hungry.' Apparently the robbery was just a typical illustration of the moral disorder afflicting that portion of 'modern youth' whose desires for 'easy money,' 'thrills' and 'high life' have brought about the pathetic and tragic fact that the great majority of crimes involving use of weapons now are committed by youths of 17 to 27.

"Considering that Pitts was a minor and never before convicted (notwithstanding he had been, according to the court's statement, in at least five other similar robberies), the court committed him to prison for 'not less than eight nor more than 16 years.' Having served the five years' statutory minimum for use of the gun, and his conduct having been good, Pitts has been paroled."

The finding then quoted the ruling of the minor leagues' Executive Committee, in barring Pitts, of which the closing sentence was: "We are of the opinion that the interests of players in our Association will best be served by not admitting players who have been convicted of a crime which is considered by society a much greater offense than offenses for which our own Association rules permanently disqualify a player."

With a little inconsistency, in view of Landis' latter finding, the report says: "The Commissioner is in entire accord with the above quoted views and with the action of the President (Bramham) and Executive Committee of the National Association. (In this connection it may be added that in the only case of this nature heretofore presented for action by the Commissioner, a major league club was prohibited from signing as a player a man terminating a prison sentence for forgery.)

"There is no objection whatsoever to baseball clubs assisting paroled convicts by employing them in any other capacity in the business of the club. But employment connected with the playing of the game, as player, coach, manager or umpire, presents a wholly different situation. It vitally concerns other clubs, other players, and baseball generally, and decision of the questions involved cannot be left to the individual club."

Landis then discussed disqualification of persons guilty of crimes from employment in public office or under civil service, in military service (lifted during World War II), or from occupations and professions requiring a license or certificate of moral fitness. And then fitting it to the national game, said: "And so far as concerns the general fitness of service as a professional baseball player, practically the same question is presented. There can and will be no change in the general policy respecting character qualifications for such employment."

And then with a final pat on the shoulders for Bramham and his minor league associates, the Judge went into his decision: "As originally presented to the President and Executive Committee of the National Association, this case involved only a general question, which they decided properly, as their duty required, and as the Commissioner would have been obliged to rule. Since then, however, a new situation has arisen. Conditions have been created as the result of which there can not be much doubt as to the destructive effect, upon Pitts' effort toward rehabilitation, of not permitting him to enter baseball employment. This was not contemplated by, nor is it due to, the ruling of the President of the National Association. And in this situation, reputable people have expressed to me their belief that there has been a complete reformation in Pitts' character, and their confidence in his earnest intent to regain an honorable position in society. Solely for these reasons, Pitts will be allowed to play, on condition that a new contract be executed by the Albany club and Pitts containing a covenant that during the year, 1935, Pitts shall play only in regular league games and shall not appear in or at exhibition games, this condition being imposed because it is distinctly in Pitts' interest that mere notoriety be not exploited and capitalized."

The decision was most popular, and was applauded all over the country, though a few remembered that Benny Kauff, acquitted by a Bronx County court, was barred from baseball for life because the Judge did not think him a fit associate for other Giant and National League players.

I do not say that Landis erred in overruling Bramham on this celebrated case; no one wants to kick a guy that is down, and certainly all well-meaning citizens would give the parolee every opportunity. It would be nice to report that Pitts became an exemplary citizen and a diamond star, but that was not the happy ending of the story.

Pitts' baseball ability had been much overrated, and Manager Al Mamaux of the Albany club soon had to bench him because of light hitting. Alabama hit only .233 in 43 International League games in 1935. Albany farmed him to York, Pa., in 1936, where he was suspended in June. Later he played briefly for Charlotte, Winston-Salem and Hickory, N.C. He was divorced after coming out of jail, and then remarried.

And then on June 7, 1941, at the age of 30 and almost six years after Landis gave him his bill of clean health, Pitts died of stab wounds at Morgantown, N.C., after a roadside tavern altercation. At a combination filling station, tavern and swimming pool at Valdese, N.C., Alabama tried to "cut in" on a couple that was dancing. The girl's escort resented his intrusion, pulled a knife and stabbed the former convict-player through a shoulder artery. Alabama literally bled to death.

27: The Judge Awards Feller to the Indians

On December 10, 1936, Judge Landis made what was the most important player decision since the old National Commission awarded George Sisler to the St. Louis Browns in 1915. The Commissioner validated the Cleveland contract of Pitcher Bobbie Feller, then an eighteen-year-old kid of great promise. Signed by the Cleveland organization in 1935, Bobbie had flashed like a meteor in the baseball skies ever since he broke in with the Indians in July, 1936. In his first appearance in a Cleveland uniform, he pitched three exhibition innings against the St. Louis Cardinals and struck out eight of the nine men who faced him. Bobbie quickly demonstrated this was no freak or accident, giving early indications of developing into one of the pitching sensations of baseball. In one game, Feller struck out fifteen St. Louis Browns, and followed it up with a seventeen-strikeout game against the Philadelphia Athletics, one above the old American League record. At the time, he was only seventeen, so he had one strikeout for each of his years.

In some respects the Feller case was similar to that of Sisler, as Bobbie was signed to two minor league contracts without ever having thrown a ball in the minors. On July 22, 1935, when Feller was only sixteen and still attending high school at Van Meter, Iowa, he was signed by the Fargo-Moorhead club of the Northern League, which in 1936 transferred the contract to New Orleans, then a Cleveland affiliate. The Pelicans, in turn, transferred the player to Cleveland in July, 1936.

It looked at the time like one of "Slap" Slapnicka's "coverups," and for years Landis had despised and rebuked this business of major leagues covering up players in the minors, though it since has come to be a common practice and permitted under the present code. I can say that most baseball people feared Landis would set Bobbie free and give Slapnicka, the former Cleveland general manager, a boot; and we expected to see a wilder scramble for Feller than for any other free agent in the game's history. Ruppert of the Yanks, with his fat bank roll, was ready to go higher than anyone else.

The situation was brought on by the Des Moines club of the Western League, which operated not too far from Feller's home pasture. Immediately after Feller pitched those three sensational exhibition innings against the Cardinals, July 6, the Des Moines club protested to Landis that it had sought to contract Feller in the summer of 1935, but that its efforts had been thwarted by the action of the Cleveland club in signing Feller in violation of the Major-Minor League Agreement and Rules. The violation allegedly was the signing of a sand lotter, other than a college player, by a major league club.

However, in his finding Landis called attention to legislation relating to "recommended" players, adopted by both the National Association and the major leagues in their 1936 annual meetings, which the Commissioner said "precluded" him from nullifying the Cleveland-Feller contract.

Even though it might have proved profitable for Feller to be declared a free agent, the Commissioner pointed out that both the young pitcher and his father had "zealously sought" validation of the Cleveland contract. Then he pointed out that nullification would be futile, as far as the Des Moines club was concerned, because the only result would be "to recreate precisely the same situation through Feller's signing a new contract in the name of some other minor league club acting for some major league club." The Des Moines club, however, was awarded a $7,500 windfall, that amount having been offered for Feller's contract as a free agent prior to the promulgation of the Fargo-Moorhead contract.

The Commissioner made no bones about it that it was a Slapnicka transaction all the way, and that the Fargo-Moorhead club served only as a handy means of getting Bobbie's name on a baseball contract. "The case has been thoroughly investigated," said the finding. "It turns out that, in reality, Fargo-Moorhead had nothing whatever to do with signing Feller, which was done by the Cleveland club, its agent Slapnicka, using for that purpose a minor league contract because he could not sign him to a Cleveland contract."

The Commissioner then reviewed legislation by both the majors and minors on the subject of free agents, how the major league owners had agreed to stay off sand lotters, exclusive of collegians, as an inducement to the former anti-draft leagues, one of which was the Western League. In this connection Landis said that the idea was "that there should be genuine, bona fide signee of such players exclusively by and exclusively for the minor league club whose contract was signed, not that such clubs should merely act as a catspaw for some major league club owning, controlling or otherwise dominating it, or as an accommodation to some major league club with which it had friendly or agreeable relations not involving ownership, control or domination."

He then called attention to the fact that two years after this understanding, the major-minor league rule was changed so that agreements and transactions involving players "should have the same force and effect for all and every purpose, notwithstanding the stock ownership or control, either directly or indirectly, by any one club or by a stockholder or stockholders of any one club in or of any one or more other clubs."

Landis felt this completely changed the principle of the old sand-lotter rule, and added: "Under this rule, had Cleveland taken the precaution to become the owner of the Fargo-Moorhead club, and to have Slapnicka designated as vice president of the Fargo-Moorhead club, before he signed Feller, there never would have been a Feller case, because the minors adopted the foregoing rule with full knowledge that it enabled major league clubs to sign sandlot players if they merely had them signed to contracts of their own minor clubs by persons designated as officials of such clubs."

He then dwelled on the "recommending method," later approved by both the majors and minors, and was at his satirical best in relating the many recommendations in the then brief career of the 18-year-old Feller. "This was the procedure followed in the Feller Case," he said, "wherein Cleveland 'recommended' that Fargo-Moorhead contract Feller, 'recommended' that New Orleans offer and Fargo-Moorhead accept $200 for the contract, 'recommended' that Feller 'retire,' 'recommended' that he go to

Cleveland, where he was given employment by Cleveland in its concessions department and 'recommended' for semi-pro ball in that vicinity, 'recommended' that he be gotten off the retired list (after Cleveland used him—ostensibly a New Orleans player 're-tired' from baseball—in the exhibition game with the Cardinals), and finally 'recommended' that New Orleans transfer him to Cleveland for $1,500, the $200 New Orleans-Fargo-Moorhead and the $1,500 Cleveland-New Orleans transfer considerations being mere fractions of the then market value of the player's contract."

There is no doubt that Landis' personal disapproval and private scorn for this "recommending method" subterfuge, approved only a short while before by the minor leagues, was largely responsible for the Commissioner approving Feller's contract with the Cleveland club.

If Judge Landis gave the Cleveland club, and its former vice president, C. C. Slapnicka, a break on the Feller case, he slapped down on them less than a half year afterwards, when he freed a promising 21-year-old Cleveland outfield farmhand, Tommy Henrich, and made it possible for the young Ohioan to pick up a neat $25,000 bonus for signing with the Yankees and subsequently star with five championship clubs at Yankee Stadium. Tommy was the brilliant and hard-hitting right fielder of the Bronx Bombers when he went into the Coast Guard late in the 1942 season. He was back with the club in 1946.

A Massillon, Ohio boy, Henrich first was signed in 1934 by the Zanesville club of the Middle Atlantic League. From there he went to Monessen, Pa., back to Zanesville, and then to New Orleans. All three clubs were affiliated with the Cleveland organization. In fact, Tommy had been picked up by Bill Bradley, the Cleveland club's scout, after playing with the Acme Dairies, an Ohio semi-pro outfit, and he was signed to his first professional contract by Billy Evans, formerly general manager of the Indians and now filling the same role at Detroit.

Henrich had a sensational season with the New Orleans club in 1936, hitting .346, scoring 117 runs and driving in 100, while he hit 48 doubles, 16 triples and 15 homers. He was regarded as one of the crack rookies of the country, and there frequently were

229

reports in the New Orleans newspapers that this or that scout had been looking the boy over. However, the following winter, the New Orleans club transferred his contract to the Milwaukee American Association club.

Tommy trained with the Brewers in the spring of 1937, but both he and his father appealed to Judge Landis, and accused the Cleveland club of blocking Henrich's advance to the majors. The Cleveland club always believed that Billy Evans, who had left the Indians under strained circumstances, started the bees buzzing in the Henrich bonnets that if they brought Tommy's transfers before the Judge, they might come out of it with a free hand. During the Landis investigation, Alva Bradley, the Indian president, threatened to press charges against Billy for what he termed a "breach of ethics."

Landis heard the case at New Orleans, March 31, to which he summoned Bradley, Slapnicka and Scout Bill Bradley of the Cleveland club; President Henry Bendinger and Business Manager L. M. Nahin of the Milwaukee club; Manager Larry Gilbert of the New Orleans Pelicans, and Henrich, himself. The session lasted three and a half hours. Henrich expressed the belief that he was the property of the Cleveland club, even then as he was training with the Milwaukee team, while the Indian officials supposedly argued that the Cleveland club at no time had held title to Henrich. The Indians' case, however, was weakened when Landis closely interrogated Bill Bradley, who admitted being a full-time Cleveland scout, that he had scouted Henrich and was instrumental in that player signing his first Zanesville contract.

The case became known as "Tommy Henrich's April Fool joke" on the Indians, as it was tried March 31, and the general impression was that Landis liberated the young player on April Fool's Day. Actually it was April 14, 1937 before Landis rendered his verdict. In his decision making Henrich a free agent, the Commissioner said: "Investigation of the status of Player Tom Henrich, initiated at his request, discloses that he had been 'covered up' for the benefit of the Cleveland club and that his transfer by New Orleans to Milwaukee was directed by the Cleveland club and prevented his advancement to a major league club under the selection clause. Because of the violation of the player's rights under his contract and the major-minor league rules, he is hereby declared a free agent."

Landis said further that if the Cleveland club had desired to retain legal control of Henrich's services, it should have signed the player to an American League contract and optioned him to the various clubs. However, he said the Indians clearly had failed to do this, and his decision served notice on other clubs that despite the "recommending method," he would stand for no shenanigans and would ferret out anything under the surface that he thought wasn't for the best interest of the players. He also barred the Cleveland club from entering the bidding when major league teams joined in the scramble to put the young free agent under contract. Three years later, when Cleveland lost the 1940 American League pennant to Detroit by a single game, Henrich, who hit .307 for New York that year, unquestionably could have thrown the balance in favor of the Indians.

28: Landis—The Great Emancipator

While Landis permitted the Cleveland club to keep Bobbie Feller in 1936 because the minor leagues had approved the so-called "recommending method," the old Judge still heartily disliked both the farm system and Branch Rickey, the man responsible for it. He always seemed to think that Rickey, a Sunday School teacher, was trying to put something over on him six days in the week. As a player, Rickey refused to play Sunday ball, and as a manager he turned his team over to a coach on Sundays. One of the Judge's favorite references to Branch was "that sanctimonious so and so."

Through the years, he had been on Rickey's neck. The present Brooklyn head—at that time still vice president of the Cardinals—always worked on the basis that the more players he controlled the better the opportunity to develop talent. At one time he had all the teams in the Nebraska State League; therefore, all their players became Cardinal prospects, and during another season, he had a finger, directly or indirectly, in most of the teams of the old Arkansas-Missouri League. Branch started these leagues, so he felt that he should get the cream of their players. But the Judge did not think so, and blocked Rickey's wholesale operations. Branch repeatedly was being hauled into the Judge's court, but most of the times he succeeded in squaring himself.

Apparently, realizing Rickey's propensities Landis bided his time, and waited for the proper moment to strike. There was a little leak during the training season of 1938, when the Cardinals trained in St. Petersburg for the first time, and the Judge golfed at his usual winter quarters in nearby Belleair. Breadon, Rickey and some players had been summoned over to Belleair, and there were strong rumors along the Grapefruit Circuit that something big was about to break and that the Judge was getting ready to crack down on Rickey.

Breadon, the Cardinals' owner, was worried, and questioned Rickey about his operations.

"I'm absolutely in the clear, Sam," Branch replied. "I've kept within all the rules and regulations. Landis has nothing on me."

However, the old Judge thought he had plenty, for in the last week of March, 1938, he gave his verdict in what came to be known as the Cedar Rapids case, slapping down hard on the Cardinals, especially on their farm director, Branch Rickey. He set free 91 Cardinal farmhands, including Pete Reiser, who two years later was to become National batting champion with Brooklyn, and Skeeter Webb, 1945 shortstop of the Detroit Tigers and Manager Steve O'Neill's son-in-law.

Landis had Leslie O'Connor work on the Cedar Rapids case for weeks, digging deeply into Rickey's Class D and C farms and doing the preliminary spade work. No penalty was inflicted on Farmer Branch, but the Sacramento Pacific Coast League club and Cedar Rapids of the Western League were each fined sums of $588 and Springfield of the Western Association $1,000. The Commissioner permitted clubs having players declared free agents to dicker again for the services of these players, but added the provision that none could be transferred to a St. Louis club, or affiliate, or to Cedar Rapids within a period of three years.

In his findings, Landis asserted working agreements were being perverted "into arrangements for complete control of the lower classification clubs through secret understandings" and flayed clubs in the Breadon-Rickey chain for violating orders "that no club should contract away its right and obligation to get competitive playing strength as needed and whenever obtainable" and for circumventing the rule against one club having a working agreement with more than one organization in a league. With his customary satire, he tore into so-called "wash sales" by the Cardinals' Sacramento club.

Among the clubs affected by Landis' thunderbolt, in addition to the Cardinals, Cedar Rapids, Sacramento and Springfield, were Fayetteville and Monett of the Arkansas-Missouri League, Newport in the Northeast Arkansas League, Crookston in the Northern League and Mitchell in the Nebraska State League.

Landis gave out pages of Rickey's testimony taken at his hearing, including an interesting colloquy between himself and Farmer Branch as to whether or not Rickey's manipulations were "big as a house." The Judge decidedly felt so; in fact he thought they were "big as the universe." As these verbal tiffs give some idea on

233

the diametrically opposite views held by the two men on farm club operations, several passages of the colloquy follow.

Rickey had an agreement with the Springfield, Ill., club of the Three-I League whereby he agreed to pay $2,500 for the privilege of selecting one of its players, while the Cardinals operated the Danville club of the same league as a farm.

Commissioner: You have this arrangement which obligates Springfield to take optional players only from the owner of the Danville club, its competitor. The same principle is involved as if the agreement provided that they would look to you for all their players. It is only a difference of degree, because one recognized source of supply for minor league players is optional players, and another source is players they get outright; those two kinds of players make up every club. Your ownership of Danville, in the same league, with that limitation they (Springfield) impose upon themselves that they will take optional players only from you, involves that principle.

Rickey: I cannot assume that there is any violation of any rule, that the whole underlying structure of good sportsmanship which must be preserved in professional baseball is infringed upon, when you take a club in one league and own it and then say to another club in the same league you shall not take optional players. What can happen when it is done? Is there a hazard in the games? . . . Is there any overlapping of interest? . . .

Commissioner: Suppose Springfield and Danville are in first and second positions, making a fight, and that Springfield can get an optional player who will strengthen Springfield? Have you a right under this agreement to say to Springfield, "You shall not take that player"?

Rickey: I think we have.

Commissioner: Is that good?

Rickey: It is not good for Springfield.

Commissioner: Is it good for that league? Is it good for the whole institution?

Rickey: Many a club makes an agreement that is bad for itself. It is entirely a question of can a man make a deal for himself.

Commissioner: I am not dealing with the question of the selfish interest of Springfield in the deal. I am dealing with this question: Here is a pennant race in the Three-I League that is, as far as the principle is concerned, just as important as if it were a pennant race in the National or American leagues. They are fighting your club. You have the power to say to them: "This avenue of strength to your club we shut off." It is pretty plain that would be bad for the league, wouldn't it? Not merely the club that was thus deprived of strengthening itself by its own acts with its eyes open, but that would not be good for the league. Springfield has agreed with the owner and operator of Danville that Springfield will not strengthen its club from this source.

Rickey: I get your point: Danville and Springfield are contending for the pennant in the same league. All right. Suppose they have left as the only avenue that they can take optional players from St. Louis and then we withhold the benevolent hand and say, "You can't have any optional player from us, and other sources of supply are stopped; therefore, that will leave you in second place and Danville will win, because you cannot contend with us and we will not give you any players?" Yes, that is in it; you are right.

Commissioner: That is in this (the agreement with Springfield); isn't it?

Rickey: Yes, that is in there.

Commissioner: Big as a house; isn't it?

Rickey: It is not big as a house.

Commissioner: I think it is as big as the universe. This is just as important in the Three-I League as it would be in the National or American leagues. You two fellows are in a fight for the pennant and Springfield says: "Here I have a chance of getting a player." You have the power to say: "You can't do it."

In his decision dealing with this particular Rickey agreement, Landis said: "The provision that Springfield will not accept optional players other than those offered by St. Louis is utterly illegal. In the first place, it violates the essential that all clubs must be at liberty to acquire strength wherever available under the rules; and secondly, inasmuch as St. Louis owns and operates Danville in the I-I-I-League and Springfield is in the same league and the two clubs are therefore competitors in the pennant race, certainly the owner of one of these clubs cannot be allowed the veto power on the other club's acquisition of players."

Though it later was reported that the Cedar Rapids case, costing the Cardinal organization ninety-one young ball players, was one of the things which started the breach between Sam Breadon and Branch Rickey, the St. Louis club owner and president rushed to the defense of his farm director. In a lengthy statement, giving the St. Louis club's answer to Landis' allegations, rebukes and criticism, Singing Sam lauded Rickey as the savior of the minor leagues. By inference, he included Landis among the "do nothings" as far as the plight of minor league ball was concerned. Sam's statement read in part:

"There was a time in baseball history when there were over 50 minor leagues. About 1930, the number had dropped to 13 or 14. The ten years preceding had been boom years, yet the minor leagues reached the low mark when only seven or eight leagues could be counted on to start in the spring of 1931. Minor league baseball was dying and was almost a thing of the past. What was done about it? Was anything at all attempted? Nothing at all.

"Mr. Rickey started the so-called 'farm system,' and it has had, as everyone knows, the constant opposition of the Commissioner's office.

"This farm system idea has proved to be the salvation of the minor leagues. The minors were in great need of complete reorganization and everyone knows that the man who reorganized the whole minor league system and who, to my knowledge, worked day and night for months on that job, was Branch Rickey.

"After this reorganization and later, the added interest of other major league clubs in the minor leagues, the minors took on new life and their rebirth took place during the dark days of 1931 and 1932 on down to the present time, and today there are approximately 40 leagues that will be ready to go at the start of the 1938 season. Branch Rickey should receive a vote of thanks from the Commissioner's office for what he had done for baseball, and not censure.

"I regret more than anything else that these small leagues may now be seriously embarrassed to operate again this year, and I regret, too, the loss of jobs of a number of young players in these days of unemployment. I do not understand how the Commissioner could take these players from the Monett club if he knows the facts."

The general feeling in baseball in 1938 was that the Cedar Rapids case, costing the Cardinals a raft of young ball players, had cleared the atmosphere. It was felt that big league club presidents would closely watch their P's and Q's. Despite Breadon's defense of Rickey and the farm system, the Judge had let it be known that he still didn't like it and would look at all future dealings with a magnifying glass.

There was, however, a school of thought that believed the Commissioner had been out to get Rickey, and would be satisfied to make an example out of Branch, listed for years in his bad boy book. However, such views were dissipated two years later, when Landis cracked down equally hard on the wealthy Detroit club. On January 14, 1940, he also made free agents of ninety-one young Detroit players, and ordered payments of $47,250 to 15 other players with whom the club had had dealings. At the time it was reported that the property damage to the Detroit club was around $500,000, while a Tiger official was quoted as saying that "the Tiger farm system has received a blow which it cannot repair in years." It is interesting, however, that the Tigers won the American League pennant the same year, breaking a four-year pennant monopoly by the Yankees, and then won the world's championship in 1945.

Only four players on the Detroit club were directly affected. They were Second Baseman Benny McCoy and Outfielder Roy Cullenbine, who had been with Detroit in 1939, and two young pitchers just brought up, Lloyd Dietz and Steve Rachunok. The McCoy angle was further complicated by a trade engineered by Jack Zeller, the Tiger general manager, at the American League's annual meeting a month before. Jack traded McCoy to the Athletics for Outfielder Wally Moses. Detroit had to return Moses to the Athletics, and Connie Mack later obtained McCoy by paying him a $45,000 bonus, outbidding Larry MacPhail, then with Brooklyn. MacPhail, however, landed Cullenbine, paying him $25,000 to sign with Brooklyn. After a series of wanderings around the big league map, Cullenbine returned to Detroit in 1945, while McCoy, released by the Athletics after failing to regain his prewar form on returning from service in 1946, also rejoined the Tigers, on a trial basis. McCoy, however, was unable to make the grade.

The one break that Detroit got out of it was that Paul (Dizzy) Trout, the colorful pitcher, originally was on Landis' list of free agents, but the Judge later restored Dizzy to the Tiger roster, saying that the Detroit club's purchase of Trout and the pitcher's later releases to Toledo and Beaumont on optional agreements passed his inspection. Trout, of course, developed into one of Detroit's pitching aces, and today is a $100,000 player. He won a vital game for the Tigers in the 1945 World's Series.

The tossing around of the Detroit club was somewhat different from the Cardinals' "Cedar Rapids Case." Rickey, the Cardinal vice president, had built up a great minor league empire, which at one time took in thirty-three teams, with Breadon owning three Class AA clubs, Rochester, Columbus, O., and Sacramento, Houston in the Texas League, and other valuable properties. The Tigers then owned nothing outright above Beaumont, Texas, but Zeller operated teams of lower classification and had working agreements and affiliations with a dozen minor league clubs. For some time before Landis freed the Tiger serfs, I heard in private baseball discussions that the Commissioner was suspicious of some of Zeller's player deals, and was looking under the surface to see what was going on. His particular complaint was that Jack was holding strings to players, even though they never appeared as Detroit Tiger property. This beat the rule on the number of times a player could be sent out on option; it was the Tommy Henrich case with Slapnicka all over again.

Several league presidents were blamed for allowing such violations to go on; the Judge mentioned J. Alvin Gardner of the Texas League; Tom Fairweather of the Western Association; Walter Morris of the East Texas League and Milton Price of the West Texas-New Mexico League. While both Jack Zeller and

Cecil Coombs, business manager of the Fort Worth Wildcats, were censured, Landis put no other penalty on them, explaining his course by saying he did not ban officials in previous cases along the same line. That referred particularly to his old friend, Rickey.

However, both the Chicago Cubs and St. Louis Browns were penalized for trying to jump the gun and approaching two of the anticipated free agents before Landis set them free. The Cubs were set back $1,000 because Clarence Rowland, then their head scout, contacted Cullenbine before January 14. The Browns were charged only half that much because Fred Haney approached McCoy before the Judge rendered his finding. Both clubs then were barred from bidding for these free agents. The Detroit club was barred from rehiring any of the ninety-one free agents for a period of three years.

In assigning blame for the irregularities in the Detroit set-up, Landis mentioned specifically only Jack Zeller, long-time scout of the Tigers and general manager following the front office's reorganization after Mickey Cochrane was deposed in midseason of 1938. The Commissioner charged that Zeller abused the working agreement privilege by making "secret arrangements" and that, contrary to baseball law, Detroit controlled more than one club in a minor league, another old charge against Rickey. He held that the Detroit club controlled both Beaumont and Fort Worth in the Texas League and Alexandria and Lake Charles in the Evangeline League.

Jack took the full rap, and in a public statement assumed all responsibility, and completely absolved Walter Briggs, the multimillionaire Tiger owner, who took control of the club after the death of Frank Navin in 1935. "The decision handed down by Commissioner Landis is in no way aimed at President Walter O. Briggs, owner of the Detroit baseball club," said Jack in his statement. "The handling of all the minor league affiliations was my job and he did not attempt to familiarize himself in any manner with those operations until after Commissioner Landis started his investigation."

While Landis did not punish Jack Zeller, other than freeing his ball players, the Commissioner served notice that his patience was at an end and that he intended to be tougher. Baseball had been given a strong object lesson in the Cardinal and Detroit cases, and he served notice it mustn't happen again. He warned that all club officials and employes henceforth "found to be involved in any such misconduct will be placed on the ineligible list and that maximum fines will be imposed upon each club concerned."

Although the Landis decision in the "Cedar Rapids case" did not serve as a deterrent to Branch Rickey, who went in for bigger and better farms, Zeller, having his fingers burned, cooled off on the entire farm idea. He eventually sold all of the clubs which Detroit owned, and one of his last suggestions to Judge Landis before the latter's death in 1944 was that the entire supply of young ball players be pooled and then distributed among the sixteen major league clubs.

Between the years of the famous St. Louis and Detroit decisions Commissioner Landis, in 1939, devoted himself whole-heartedly to the celebration of baseball's one hundredth anniversary. From the start, when a season-long series of celebrations were planned, the Judge pitched into baseball's centennial with both fists and did much to make it a red letter year on the game's calendar.

The big moment of the celebration was the dedication of baseball's National Museum and Hall of Fame at Cooperstown, N.Y., the game's birthplace, June 12, 1939. It was a three-day picnic in Cooperstown, and Judge Landis was in the forefront of the activities. The special train which brought the Commissioner and other notables to Cooperstown was the first passenger train to be run into the pretty up-state New York town in eight years.

The Judge's car led the procession in the parade down Cooperstown's main stem, and wearing an old baseball cap, Landis purchased the first strip of a special three-cent Baseball Centennial stamp from Jim Farley, then the nation's Postmaster General. Judge Landis was one of the most interested fans as they introduced the living "Immortals"—Connie Mack, Honus Wagner, Grover Alexander, Tris Speaker, Napoleon Lajoie, George Sisler, Walter Johnson, Eddie Collins, Babe Ruth and Cy Young. Due to a train delay, Ty Cobb did not arrive in Cooperstown in time for the main ceremonies. "What I would give to see all of those fellows play a game while still in their prime," said the Judge, "but I am fortunate that I should have lived to see all of them play ball."

The Commissioner made the leading dedicatory address, and said in part: "It gives me a great deal of pleasure to be present at the dedication of the National Baseball Museum and the Baseball Hall of Fame. Since, for one hundred years, this game has lived and thrived and spread over all our country and a large part of the world, it is fitting that it should have a national museum. And nowhere else than its birthplace could this museum be appropriately situated.

"To the thirteen pioneers who were the moving spirits of the game in its infancy, and to the twelve players who have been nominated to the Hall of Fame by the Baseball Writers' Association, we pay just tribute. But I should like, and I think all these immortals of baseball would agree with me—I should like to dedicate this museum to all America, to lovers of good sportsmanship, healthy bodies, clean minds. For those are the principles of baseball. So it is to them, rather than to the few who are honored here, that I propose to dedicate this shrine of sportsmanship."

The white-haired Judge later proudly threw out the first ball in an All-Star game in which the National and American League teams were managed by two of the immortals, Hans Wagner and Eddie Collins. Such illustrious big leaguers as Hank Greenberg, Charley Gehringer, Dizzy Dean, Lefty Grove, Mel Ott, Billy Herman, Stanley Hack, Johnny Vander Meer, Johnny Allen, George Selkirk, Arky Vaughan, Wally Moses, Joe Medwick were exhibited in Cooperstown. Old Bill Klem put on his breastprotector and umpired behind the plate, and to give the crowd an extra thrill, Immortal Babe Ruth batted for Danny MacFayden.

"What a day! What a day!" said the Judge as he left Cooperstown. "I'll never forget it." A little more than five years later, Judge Landis himself was elected to "the Hall."

In recognition of the fact that Cincinnati had the first professional ball club, the Reds of 1869, and that the Reds of 1939 won the National League pennant, the city on the Ohio River was awarded both the minor and major league meetings in December of the Centennial year. This was quite a distinction for Cincinnati, inasmuch as the major league joint meeting annually rotated between New York and Chicago.

Judge Landis took advantage of the Cincinnati meeting to array himself against any further extension of farm systems and working agreements. He cast a vehement "No" to all amendments previously passed by the National Association that sought to tighten the bond between the big and little fellow of baseball. At one point, Ford Frick, the National League president, asked for a poll of the clubs, and Landis retorted with feeling: "Don't you know how the National voted, Mr. Frick?"

He ridiculed the fact that the legislation seeking closer ties had originated in the annual meeting of the minors, which preceded the major meeting. He intimated it was the work of the Cardinals, Yankees, Dodgers, Browns and other clubs having big chains. "That legislation originated in the majors," asserted the Judge, with scorn. "The minors are just the pawns of the majors. There's no use talking about the minors enjoying anything."

A year later, at the annual meeting of the majors held in Chicago, December 11, 1940, Judge Landis' term was extended to January 12, 1946, the date of the expiration of the National Agreement, at the old salary of $65,000. The Commissioner rather surprised the meeting by relenting on his former stand, and accepted the right of associated clubs to recommend and sign players for each other. Landis sought to add a provision that such recommendations should be reported to him and the president of the National Association, but the Commissioner's proposal was rejected by the minors on the ground it would require too much detail work and that failure to report even conversations about a player might be construed as a violation.

And the Judge cast his first vote against unlimited night games. The National League, which had started night ball, supported the original idea of a seven night game limit for any club, but the

American League, led by Don Barnes of the St. Louis Browns, sought league autonomy on the question. In the final showdown, the Commissioner settled the matter in favor of a seven night game limit by casting his vote with the National League.

29: The Judge Okays the
Baseball Guide

My only contact with the Judge after the 1920 meeting was when I asked him about publishing his findings, as we had done with the old National Commission. *The Sporting News* received $1,000 a year for this, which was our original proposition, and for years we went along with the same arrangement. It was a service we were in a position to render, as the press associations and newspapers gave space only to the Commission's important decisions, and passed up routine cases. As club owners, players, umpires, as well as fans were all readers of *The Sporting News*, it helped keep them abreast with the old National Commission's findings and they could act accordingly.

The Judge never replied to that letter, though I heard later he thought I was trying to get money out of the Commissioner's office, merely in the form of a "plum" for *The Sporting News*.

For years we ran into each other at World's Series, league meetings, etc., but we never exchanged any recognition, though he was head of baseball and I was head of baseball's weekly newspaper. Of course, I knew that back in the twenties he regarded me as a Ban Johnson man, which I was, and still am. In the conduct of *The Sporting News*' editorial and news policy, I always had dictated a constructive policy toward the Commissioner. No one seemed to bother to bring us together. I sat near him at the Joe Louis-Battling Levinsky fight on August 7, 1935, at Chicago's White Sox park. The fight lasted only 60 seconds, and that seemed to amuse him. He softened up considerably, and we had an amiable chat.

Some years ago, I would make periodical trips to the Pacific Coast. It was my custom to return on the Super Chief, which would get me into Chicago around 2 o'clock. I would have time on my hands until I could catch a train after 4 o'clock for St. Louis. On one such trip I decided to see Landis' and ascertain his reaction to me after the years. I went to the wash room on the floor of his offices at 333 North Michigan Boulevard, and the Judge was in there. He immediately recognized me, smiled, made one of his jovial quips about our place of meeting and offered his hand. I told him I had come up to see him, and asked whether he had time for me to visit with him. He said, "Sure Spink, come in"; he treated me nicely, and we had an interesting talk about many things in baseball.

From that time on, I had my most pleasant association with him. If he once had it in for me, because I had been a Johnson supporter, he apparently had forgiven me. I made frequent visits to him after that, at his offices in Chicago, the Hotel Roosevelt in New York and elsewhere. He seemed glad to see me, and treated me cordially and courteously. I recall the All-Star game in Cincinnati on July 6, 1938, when I was having breakfast in the Netherland Plaza. The Judge came in, sat down at my table and breakfasted with me. An outspoken man, he neither pulled his punches nor took much care of his language when discussing someone who had irked him. I do not know how much I was in his confidence, but he gave me a few discourses on some of the men who had brought on his farm decisions which were classics in expression and metaphor.

Frequently I would take duck and quail to Chicago, and leave some of it at his office. It was just a friendly gesture. Several times when the Judge wasn't there, I gave it to one of his men, Phil Piton. I always liked Piton, even though his loyalty to Judge Landis, if that is what he would call it, later resulted in a most unpleasant experience for me.

In the meantime, Spalding's, which had been publishing annual baseball guides since the very infancy of the sport, decided to give up this form of publication. An old friend, Charley White, who had done much of the work in gathering material and compiling it for these guides, died, and no one in the Spalding organization seemed to care to carry on this activity. The last Spalding-Reach *Guide* came out in 1941. The Reach *Guide*, almost as old as Spalding's, made its last appearance in 1939, being combined the next year with Spalding's; so instead of two annual guides, collected through the years by baseball lovers, there suddenly was none.

Having taken up the publication of sports books, including a baseball record book, I felt we had an ideal organization to continue publication of an official guide. I heard that Landis had approached Earle Moss, of the Heilbroner Bureau, on the subject of a guide, and it was discussed at the minor leagues' annual meeting in Jacksonville, December 3–5, 1941, just before Pearl Harbor. Through Ed Brands, editor of *The Sporting News,* and minor league friends I was able to put a halt to any dickerings which the minors may have contemplated with Moss.

In the meantime, Pearl Harbor came on that fateful Sunday, December 7, and the American League, National League and joint meetings were scheduled for Chicago on December 9, 10 and 11. I already had my train reservation for Chicago, but went there with a heavy heart. When everyone thought and talked of war, it wasn't easy to get much interest in a baseball guide. And having a son and son-in-law who soon would be in service, it was one time that I was no super-salesman.

It was on that grim Monday morning, December 8, the day the nation was recoiling from the shock of Pearl Harbor, that I called on Landis about the guide. It was 9.30; the Judge hadn't come in yet, but I waited. It was a very cold morning, and when Landis came in he was almost submerged in a big overcoat. Because of the cold and the excitement of Pearl Harbor, there was water in his eyes. The eye dew may have been due to the blustery winds, but I think they were tears of anger and mortification. He took off the great coat, went over to the window and for a long time stared out at Lake Michigan and said nothing. Eventually he walked over to me, gave me a characteristic poke in the stomach with his bony index finger, and remarked: "Do you realize, Spink, that we now are a secondary power in the Pacific?"

He then admonished me and told me that a "colleague" of mine was responsible for the situation. I didn't get it at once, but later it dawned on me that he spoke of Secretary of the Navy Frank Knox, who then was the owner of the Chicago *Daily News.* Landis was bitterly anti-Roosevelt, and may have resented Knox, candidate for vice president on the 1936 Landon ticket, for entering Roosevelt's cabinet. However, Landis was no pacifist or appeaser. His criticism of the Roosevelt Administration was that it didn't come to grips earlier with Hitler and the Japs, and for not being better prepared when the big blow came.

Finally I got Landis around to the subject of the baseball guide. He suddenly turned to me, and asked what sort of an outfit was Barnes. "Do they publish dancing books and similar publications?" he asked. A. S. Barnes and Co., Inc., of New York also had been mentioned as a possible publisher of the guide. I told him I knew nothing about it—that Barnes was a reputable firm, published rule books and had purchased certain rights from Spalding, but that we were prepared to go ahead with a 1942 *Guide* if we got the proper authorization. If we obtained this okay from the baseball powers, I hoped to make an arrangement with the Barnes Co. to distribute the book.

In the meantime, Landis had me go to both of the major leagues. Will Harridge, the American League president, told me the book primarily was up to Landis, and that he also would have to discuss it with his own steering committee. Later he told me it was all right with his league. I then appeared personally before the National League club owners at their meeting, made a talk on our facilities for getting out an official baseball guide, and feel I made a favorable impression.

After the joint meeting of the majors on December 11th, I called again on the Commissioner. He then told me that he understood that the minor leagues would give us $3,333 as their part for getting out a 1942 official guide and each of the two majors would give the same amount. In return, I was to supply them with such books as they needed.

I started to thank him, but he interrupted: "Do not thank me; I had nothing to do with the arrangement." However, he was quite cordial, and before I left I told him I would submit to him material which we would put in the Guide. "That isn't necessary; I am sure you can do a good job."

Despite the gloomy world picture, I was pleased that I had accomplished my mission. With a private collection of Spalding and Reach *Guides* since their first editions, I felt keenly when these histories of the game were discontinued. I had only one thought when I went back to St. Louis; it was to make a Spink *Guide* as good as any of the Spalding and Reach *Guides* which preceded it, better if we could make it so.

It was middle December; the war now was on full tilt, and daily we were more aware of it. We didn't have much time, but we plunged into the job and we worked very hard. I arranged with a man who had worked on the Spalding book in New York to work with us so nothing would be overlooked. We finally got the book out in the early spring of 1942 shortly before the opening of the baseball season. I thought we did a good job, and so did many of the nation's top-ranking sports editors and sports writers: Arch Ward of the *Chicago Tribune*, Ed Bang of the *Cleveland News*, Ned Cronin of the *Los Angeles News*, E. A. Armstrong of the *Winnipeg News*, Jimmy Powers of the *New York News*, Elmer Ferguson of the *Montreal Herald*, Charley Young of the *Albany Knickerbocker News* and a host of others from all parts of the United States and Canada.

Tributes came from people high up in baseball, in the majors and minors. I was amused when I received one of these complimentary letters on the stationery of the House of Representatives, State of Tennessee. It came from Herman (Hank) DeBerry, representative for Hardin County and scout for the Giants. Hank kindly wrote: "I believe this to be the best record book I've ever seen."

A letter from Judge Landis' righthand man in the Commissioner's office, Leslie O'Connor, also made me feel pretty good. I reproduce it:

April 11, 1942

Dear Mr. Spink:

Congratulations on your fine performance in publication of the 1942 Official Baseball Record Book. It seems to be very complete and should be of much interest and service to all who are interested in baseball.

Yours very truly,
(signed) Leslie O'Connor

About a week after I received the O'Connor letter, I had another pleasant gesture from the Commissioner's office. The Judge called me up by long-distance telephone from Chicago. In his jocular way, he said he was sorry he hadn't called me up before as he had a faint suspicion I had gotten out a "damn fine book." Well, coming from the big baseball boss in Chicago himself I was surprised and impressed. Judge Landis wasn't the type to call up people and offer compliments. I told him our greatest concern in getting out such a book was that errors might creep in—of which we were unaware, but that we had taken every precaution to keep them down to a minimum. "Oh, don't worry about that," he said; "you've got out a fine book, and one of which you may all be proud."

Naturally, I thanked him and considering the fact that at one time our relations weren't overly cordial, I was greatly pleased, I thought I really was in his good graces. I could tell by this time that the book would cost us approximately $14,000, of which baseball had contributed $10,000. Books of this type are not profitable; in fact, that is why Spalding's gave it up. We were going to lose some money on it, but I was quite happy. We not only had gotten out a "damn fine official Guide," in Landis' own words, but everybody else also seemed to like it.

30: Bible of Baseball

On June 20, 1942, the *Saturday Evening Post* printed an article entitled "Bible of Baseball," by Stanley Frank, then a sports writer on the *New York Post*. It was the story of *The Sporting News*, how it had been founded in 1886 by my father and uncle, Charles and Al Spink, respectively; it gave something of our history, our battles for clean baseball. Several times I was referred to as "Mr. Baseball," especially in advertising on the piece, under the heading: "Meet Mr. Baseball."

The article led that particular issue of the *Post*, and while I felt flattered, I was pleased particularly because a great national magazine had so featured a baseball publication. I thought it was quite a plug for the game, and that the people in Organized Baseball also would be pleased. Never was I so wrong. I quickly learned that there was only one Mr. Baseball, and assuredly I was not the man. There were immediate repercussions from the Commissioner's office, and overnight I landed back in the Judge's doghouse. The article raised so much hell, completely changed my relations with the Judge, and showed his many-sided character that it is reprinted here: *

BIBLE OF BASEBALL

By STANLEY FRANK

"*Wrapped in the history of* The Sporting News *is the saga of our national game—its punks, its heroes, its loyal fans. Taylor Spink is its bellowing Boswell, Mr. Baseball himself.*

"It sounds screwy today, but in 1885 the St. Louis Browns actually won a pennant. This was in the old American Association, and it was a warm summer, with the beer and *Schmierkäse* gardens doing a heavy business. Gaseous praises to Manager Charlie Comiskey's heroes rose from stein-laden tables as the fans debated how to capitalize culturally on the new eminence that had come to the

* Copyright 1942, The Curtis Publishing Company. Reprinted by permission.

brewing capital. Only one citizen did anything constructive, a fellow named Al Spink, who was a sports and theatrical promoter. In 1886, as the second season of glory got under way, Spink began publication of something called *The Sporting News*. With the new paper hobbling along obscurely, the Browns that season won the pennant a second time, taking the postseason interleague duel from the Chicago National League team, and in 1887 and 1888 ran their pennant string to four in a row.

"When the American League opened in 1901, the Browns graduated to it, and since 1888 the only honor they have acquired has been a negative one—they are the only club in either circuit which has never won a major-league pennant. *The Sporting News* proved to be of tougher stuff. Its circulation spread beyond the confines of the beer barony and in time it became the national paper of baseball. It has come down to our own era a solid and unique weekly of full newspaper size, a bible and handbook of the great American game and an institution rivaling in power that of Judge Landis himself.

"Throughout its fifty-six-year career, *The Sporting News* has been strictly a Spink family enterprise. The present publisher, J. G. Taylor Spink, is a nephew of the founder. Born when *The Sporting News* was in its second year, Spink today is an energetic, plumpish, bull-voiced man of excellent digestion, and his furious labors in behalf of his favorite sport have earned for him the nickname of Mr. Baseball, a tag he likes so well he will probably have it chiseled on his tombstone. Spink is the game's unofficial conscience, historian, watchdog and worshiper; and, happily, he has made a nice piece of change in these public-spirited roles. The fans begrudge him this no more than they begrudged Babe Ruth the immense income he got from the diamond.

"To fix Spink's true position in the baseball cosmos, it is necessary first to comprehend the scope of *The Sporting News*' truly remarkable influence. Every Thursday more than 100,000 fans pay fifteen cents for its latest number.

"Although its sixteen pages are awesome masses of fine type containing up to 100,000 English and semi-English words, *The Sporting News* is devoured by the fans with religious absorption, down to the last comma. Players read it for ammunition which can be used on the firing line when the dugout jockeys are unloading. Baseball executives watch it for trends. Managers and scouts study it to trace the progress of rookies in the deepest bush. It is the only organ that carries percentages, box scores and weekly reviews of every team in every loop from the Class D, leaky-roof leagues, with their sixty-five-dollars-a-month salary limit, to the plushy majors. For a great many baseball-loving Americans, *The Sporting News* is their only extracurricular reading material.

"Before the present war, *The Sporting News* was sold in virtually every foreign land, with Japan and, surprisingly, South Africa among the larger overseas centers of distribution.

"Despite the loss of its foreign market due to the war, *The Sporting News* sends more copies abroad than ever. Virtually every convoy carries copies of *The Sporting News* which are handed out, free, among the members of the A.E.F.'s. Spink and the major-league club owners share the cost. In the same way, servicemen still in this country get their *Sporting News*. *The Sporting News* is a prime morale booster for men cut off from their beloved ball parks.

"The A.E.F. to the Rescue

"With Spink this is a sentimental as well as a patriotic gesture, since the first World War saved his baby when it was close to failure. Baseball was classified as a nonessential occupation, and interest in the game dwindled. Circulation fell off to 5,000 copies. In France, Capt. Tillinghast L'Hommedieu Huston, co-owner of the Yankees, saw that the boys were starved for baseball news, and he persuaded the American League to buy 150,000 copies of *The Sporting News* for free distribution. It proved to be the most popular publication in the A.E.F., except for *The Stars and Stripes*, even outdrawing *La Vie Parisienne*.

"The Spink masterpiece never backs away from a crusade, and in 1890 the National League, annoyed by the fledgling paper's militant sniping and fearless exposure of 'the interests,' attempted to break the Spinks by bank-rolling an opposition sheet, *The Sporting Times*. The venture cost the league a young fortune, and the

Times, like all other competitors of the Spinks, folded quickly. Today the National and American Leagues would dip into the sinking fund to subsidize Spink, in the extremely unlikely event he should need assistance. The owners recognize the value of *The Sporting News* in promoting the game, sustaining interest during the off season and, above all, as a barometer of cash-customer opinion. *The Sporting News* readers are inveterate letter writers and devoted partisans, and Spink editorially reflects their anxiety for the welfare of the game.

"Last winter, Ted Williams' application for draft deferment threatened to start a *cause célèbre* that might have ruined the good will acquired by professional baseball during the course of a century. Before Spink could get an editorial into print on the Williams case, he received more than 300 letters from fans defending Williams' right to appeal for deferment. This flood of unsolicited letters was the earliest and most encouraging assurance given the club owners that they would not have to suspend operations for the duration of the war.

"Although Spink is the big shot of the sports publishing business, he counts a sixteen-hour trick a normal working day. For years he has opened up his office at Tenth and Olive streets in St. Louis at seven o'clock, seven days a week. When he is not on the road drumming up advertising or plugging a scheme to promote baseball, he reads every line of the galley proofs and struggles with the composition of gaggy, breezy headlines. They are his particular pride and joy, and the funnier they are the louder he laughs at them.

"Like most old-time baseball men, Spink has a passion for accuracy. He loathes sloppy reporting and will drop everything to track down the score, date, pitchers and circumstances of ball games played forty years ago.

"It has been suggested to Spink that the customers would derive more pleasure from *The Sporting News* if the paper were sprinkled carefully with factual errors. Dyed-in-the-wool fans are statistical hounds who dearly love to catch the experts in a bobble, but Spink seldom gives them the opportunity.

"The most indefatigable user of the telephone and telegraph

since Ziegfeld, Spink thinks nothing of phoning his correspondents in San Francisco or New York when he rises at five A.M., just to pass the time of night. He seems unable to understand why the party at the other end of the line is not on top of the ball and ready to greet the new day with an idea for the ages. It is not unusual for him to send one man six wires a day, adding up to a thousand words. The tenor of his remarks ordinarily can be confined to five words: How's your local club doing? Spink's telegraph toll runs to about $10,000 a year and his telephone bill averages $6,500. Western Union long ago installed a branch office at *The Sporting News* in order to have some messenger boys available for other duties in Greater St. Louis.

"Spink's brief vacations from baseball always find him in a sporting atmosphere. He likes to invest an occasional two bucks on a horse race, to scout the talent in the night clubs and to cut up old touches with the mob, but in general he has a constitutional inability to relax in anything but work. In addition to his duties as publisher, salesman and bright-idea man for the paper, he writes two long columns a week under the titles of Looping the Loops and Three and One. In his spare time he appears on the radio—on the average of twice a week during the season—and writes the scripts for three other fifteen-minute broadcasts which are furnished free to 250 stations throughout the country.

"*The Sporting News* is not Spink's only enterprise. He publishes the *Sporting Goods Dealer*, a monthly magazine for the trade; the official record book, formerly issued by the Reach and Spalding companies; the *Baseball Register*, an elaborate compendium of the records of current players and old stars; and *The Sporting News Dope Book*. He has printed scores of pamphlets on how to play the various positions, how to bat and how to score, as well as booklets containing biographical sketches and a welter of valuable historical data on baseball.

"*Baseball by the Pound*

"The chief characteristic of a volume issued under the Spink imprimatur is its size. A Spink opus expands with each successive issue until it can serve splendidly as the doorstop for a bank vault.

If a competing firm puts out a product rivaling a Spink publication in heft, he sees to it that his next edition tops it in the number of pages and wordage. His first *Baseball Register*, in 1940, carried 224 pages; this year it has 288 pages and has sold 100,000 at one dollar the copy. The official record book is a 588-page affair and has fractured all previous records with a circulation of half a million.

"The staggering impact of Spink's weight-by-pound baseball literature has led people to suspect it is a manifestation of an inferiority complex springing from his short stature. The amateur psychologists don't know Spink, who is completely without inhibitions, or the fans' insatiable appetite for figures and words in bulk. Spink was the first to discover that you can choke a horse, but never a baseball fan.

"He must be right, for *The Sporting News* is the only nonfiction periodical devoted exclusively to sports, apart from racing sheets, that has ever made important money. It has survived longer than any other straight sport publication, and it dominates the field so completely that no attempt to invade the lucrative territory has been made in a quarter of a century.

"A typical Spink service that helps to promote baseball interests is the awarding of fifteen trophies to the most valuable players in the various leagues. Years ago, before he took it over, much wire pulling verging on scandal was mixed up with the designation, and for a time it was abandoned.

"During the 1920's each league had a rather hit-and-miss system for selecting the outstanding players. In 1930 *The Sporting News*, in conjunction with the baseball writers, took over the Most Valuable Player award and put an abrupt end to suspicions of skulduggery.

"*The Sporting News* started off as a combination sports and theatrical paper. It was the second publication that gave the up-and-coming game more than casual attention, a paper called *Sporting Life* having preceded it by three years.

"Uncle Al, the founder, was an inveterate promoter, and in his zeal to get rich in a hurry he ignored the one potential meal ticket he had ever launched, and rushed to establish the St. Louis *World*, a daily newspaper that rolled over and played dead dog after a year and a half. He also organized the South Side race track and made the first attempt to popularize night racing. The ruination of Uncle Al, however, was a misbegotten inspiration which prompted him to write *The Derby Winner*, a throbbing melodrama of the race track. It was a turkey by any standard and even the home town gave it a lukewarm reception.

"But, fascinated by the glamour of the theater, Al decided to take his epic on tour. Unable to leave the struggling *Sporting News* high and dry, Al offered his younger brother, Charlie—Taylor's father—fifty dollars a week to become business manager of the paper. Charlie, who was then homesteading in the Dakotas, blew a kiss to the prairie dogs and took a train for St. Louis. Al met Charlie at the station and promptly promoted a ten-dollar touch from him with which to celebrate the partnership at the best restaurant in town. The playwright then took his production on the road, and it proceeded to splatter omelets over the surrounding countryside.

"Improving a Diamond in the Rough

"*The Sporting News* was no howler either. Its subsequent growth was due to Charlie's acumen. From the beginning, Charlie perceived that *The Sporting News* could survive only as a straight baseball paper. He dropped the racing, boxing and theatrical news and threw out the patent-medicine ads. The paper plucked feebly at the coverlet and circulation fell below 3,000 a week. Baseball was gaining in popularity, but it was regarded as a disreputable, back-alley form of entertainment frequented only by low, coarse characters. It was impossible to get advertising, and more than once Charlie Spink's diamond ring was hocked to meet the paper's slim pay roll.

"The future looked dark, but Spink was determined to make the paper go—possibly to avoid a return to homesteading—and he did it in a tried old journalistic way—by attacking 'the interests.' His first target was Chris Von der Ahe, the president of the Browns, who was then baseball's most powerful figure as a result of his club's great showing in the 1880's. Von der Ahe was a vaudeville-type burgher, who liked to speak of himself as 'der poss bresident,' and his love for baseball seemed to stem largely from an intense desire to sell lots of beer. Von der Ahe owned a saloon on the North Side, and when Sportsman's Park was built he saw to it that it was located near his establishment. The fans, after paying at the turnstile to cheer his team, flocked to his saloon to slake their thirsts, to celebrate the victory or to drown the memory of a defeat. Von der Ahe pulled considerable political weight locally and it seemed suicidal when Charlie Spink took out after him. But *The Sporting News* chased Von der Ahe out of baseball, then ran a benefit for him which raised $6,000. During his happier days, Von der Ahe had taken care that posterity would not forget him by having a life-size statue of himself, in frock coat and statesmanlike pose, hewn out of marble. The image of der poss bresident still adorns his grave in Bellefontaine Cemetery.

"Charlie Spink next turned to a campaign against syndicate baseball, or control of more than one team in a league by the same individual. This was a pernicious evil, and Spink alone realized it had to be stamped out if the game was ever to gain the confidence of the public.

"The success of these crusades, combined with the changing nature of baseball, helped to consolidate the paper's position. Circulation rose slowly but steadily, and baseball men were beginning to recognize *The Sporting News* as the clearinghouse for authentic news of the business.

"For a time, the paper served as an intermediary between players and owners, but ceased to do so after a harrowing experience with Mike Donlin, who had been plugged extravagantly by the Pacific Coast operative. Stanley Robison, owner of the Cardinals, asked Spink to arrange for a state signing of Donlin in St. Louis after the conclusion of the season. Donlin came on from the Coast, made a grand entrance into *The Sporting News* office, observed the pictures of famous players on the walls and flew into a terrible rage.

" 'Where the hell is my picture?' he cried dramatically.

"Donlin deigned to favor St. Louis with his presence after the signing and Charlie Spink more or less adopted him as a protégé.

The relationship was hurriedly disavowed when Donlin, filled with Christmas cheer, playfully set fire to an elderly citizen's whiskers in a public place. A bystander, who resented Donlin's sense of humor, pulled a knife and inflicted a permanent scar upon the fun-loving fellow. Donlin was an actor at heart and later became one.

"Birth of the American League

"*The Sporting News* was catching on with the public, yet as late as 1896 Charlie Spink was doing odd jobs around Brother Al's South Side race track to make ends meet. His connection with racing terminated only when the St. Louis cyclone of '96 leveled the track. And then Charlie went overboard for the radical idea put forward by a newspaperman from Cincinnati who was to make baseball and its bible big business.

"That man was Ban Johnson, the founder of the American League, and the moving spirit in the game until he was superseded by Judge Landis. They laughed when Johnson sat down and tried to prove that baseball was ready for a second major league. They smiled indulgently when Johnson got up and went out to raise financial backing for eight teams which were to compete against the well-established National League.

"Johnson organized this league, forced the haughty Nationals to meet his champions in a postseason set of games which, as the World Series, was to become America's premier sporting event. He lived to see his ridiculed scheme surpass the National League in popularity, and *The Sporting News* was an indispensable weapon of support. Johnson always acknowledged his debt to the Spinks, admitting he would have been unable to establish the American League if the paper had not been on his side.

"*The Sporting News*' prestige was given tremendous impetus when the warring factions asked Editor Flanner to write the national agreement, the pact which ended the war and served as the foundation of organized baseball as it is known today. This historic document was set in type by hand in the Spink composing room and submitted to Harry Pulliam, president of the National

League. Pulliam was so impressed with its fairness that Flanner's document was adopted without a change.

"An aftermath of the bitter struggle, almost as enduring as the American League itself, was the friendship between Johnson and the Spinks. In the case of Taylor Spink, it practically amounted to idolatry. It was only recently that Taylor broke down and confessed that Judge Landis, rather than Johnson, was the first-ranking benefactor of baseball, and he still feels uncomfortable about it, as though he has betrayed a sacred trust or something. Spink refuses to make appointments which will prevent him from going to Spencer, Indiana, on March twenty-eighth each year to lay a wreath on the grave of Johnson, who died in 1931. His son, now in the Coast Guard, was christened Charles C. Johnson Spink, but the only name by which he ever has been called by his father is Johnson. In important issues of editorial policy, Spink tries to shape his course in accordance with Ban Johnson's ideas and philosophy.

"Taylor was twenty when he went to work alongside his father on *The Sporting News*. He had left high school in his second year to take a job sweeping out a local sporting-goods store and then, through his father's influence, had got a place on the St. Louis *Post-Dispatch* sports staff. When a *Sporting News* office boy resigned, Taylor quit the *Post-Dispatch* and took his place.

"He was an office boy with unusually exalted ideas which, at the time, encompassed a broader world than the family property. One day he sent a telegram to Ban Johnson asking to be appointed official scorer for the 1910 World Series. Every baseball writer in the country wanted the plum, and our hero, who was only twenty-one, had never scored a game in his life, but that did not deter him. He bombarded Johnson with so many telegrams that the league president gave him the assignment in self-defense.

"That was the beginning of Taylor's passion for telegrams and his worshipful admiration of Johnson. Just for the record, he was so satisfactory as a scorer that he held the post for eight years, when he voluntarily withdrew to give a baseball writer a crack at the fee which went with it.

259

"At about the same time Taylor was making Johnson's life miserable with wires, Charlie Spink was shopping for an editor to succeed old Joe Flanner, who was resigning to accept an important position with the National Commission. In September, 1910, on Hugh Fullerton's recommendation, Spink hired a solemn young baseball writer out of Chicago. The new editor lasted less than a year, but while he was with *The Sporting News* he gave his first evidence of possessing a talent which was to make an imperishable contribution to American letters.

"*You Know Me, Al*

"The solemn, sometimes morose editor was Ring Lardner. He never was particularly happy working for Charlie Spink; he chafed under the confinement of handling copy and he missed the excitement of the daily baseball beat. Taylor, who was familiar with the editor's work as a traveling correspondent with the Chicago teams, suggested that Lardner do a series of humorous articles dealing with the off-field activities of ballplayers. Lardner wrote the series under the heading of Pullman Pastimes. This was the genesis of the *You Know Me, Al* yarns which established Lardner as a master of the short story. Strangely, nobody but Taylor Spink and a few baseball writers thought Lardner's stuff was good at that time. There was increasing friction between Charlie Spink and his editor, and Lardner quit to take a job in Boston.

"During Lardner's regime the paper slumped badly, but Taylor believed that the publisher, not the editor, was at fault. He agitated for a drastic reorganization of the paper, and Charlie Spink finally gave in when circulation fell to 22,000 in 1912.

"Until that time the paper had only two staff correspondents—W. M. Rankin, who rewrote the major-league news from New York, and H. G. Merrill, who covered the minors from Wilkes-Barre. *The Sporting News* was at least ten days behind developments and Taylor realized that its copy was stodgy, run-of-the-mine stuff, sadly lacking in originality and freshness. He instituted the system of lining up a correspondent in each city which had a team in organized baseball, and the paper soon came out of its coma. Circulation doubled and for the first time in a quarter of a century the paper assumed the scope of a national publication. Spink, who claims to know more sports writers than any other man, today has more than 300 correspondents and carries the occasional contributions of perhaps fifty free-lances.

"Mounting differences between father and son came to an angry boil in 1914 with the formation of the Federal League. Old Charlie Spink believed baseball was ready to embrace a third major circuit. Taylor opposed the Federals on the ground that the prospective owners were backing the teams only to cash in on publicity for other activities in which they were financially interested. With Taylor rooting ardently from the side line, Joe Vila satirized the Federals as the 'Lunch-Room League,' a nickname inspired by Charles Weeghman, owner of the Chicago franchise, who ran a chain of restaurants. The entire affair became something more serious than a family dispute. It was turned into a fight for survival when the paper's strongest competitor, *Sporting Life*, of Philadelphia, came out in strong support of the Feds.

"A League Flies Out

"At the height of the intrafamily controversy, Taylor got married and left on his honeymoon. He was recalled hurriedly on April 22, 1914. Charlie Spink had died suddenly after attending the Federal League inaugural in Chicago. Taylor, now in complete control of *The Sporting News*, blasted the Feds unmercifully. The outlaw league dissolved after the close of the 1915 season when the National and American leagues agreed to pay the backers $700,000. Robert B. Ward, who financed the Brooklyn Feds, is reputed to have lost more than $3,000,000 on the venture. Spink came off handsomely, though. *Sporting Life* collapsed with the Federal League and the Spink paper dominated the field.

"Taylor Spink was rapidly gaining recognition as a smart young baseball man, and in 1917 Ban Johnson entrusted him with a delicate diplomatic mission. Johnson wanted to place Miller Huggins, then managing the Cardinals, in New York to build up the Yankees, a chronic second-division team. The Cardinals were in a precarious financial position and Johnson believed Huggins could be induced to shift to the American League, but it was hardly cricket for Johnson to negotiate personally with a manager of the rival organization.

"Both Johnson and Jake Ruppert, owner of the Yankees, agreed on Spink as the man to approach Huggins and sound him out. Huggins expressed interest. Spink arranged for a secret meeting between Ruppert and Huggins when the Cardinals were playing in New York, but nothing came of it. Huggins was eager to sign on the spot, but Ruppert, mysteriously evasive, said he would withhold his decision until the end of the season. Johnson invited Huggins to New York as his guest at the Giants-White Sox World Series. Huggins accepted and was considerably embarrassed to find Branch Rickey, general manager of the Cardinals, on the same train.

" 'When Huggins, in response to Rickey's question, said he was going to take in the World Series, Branch's sensitive nose immediately smelled a rat,' Spink relates. 'Rickey knew it was highly improbable that Huggins, who was canny with a dollar, would spend a dime to see the coronation of the King of England and the eruption of Mount Vesuvius if both were billed on the same program.'

"A good deal of comic-opera hocus-pocus followed. Spink registered Huggins at a hotel under an assumed name and led him through devious back alleys to clandestine meetings with Ruppert. Johnson thoughtlessly spoiled Spink's stratagem by giving Huggins a World Series ticket in a section of the Polo Grounds occupied by the American League delegation, and the supposedly secret deal got to be common gossip.

"*New Huggins Headgear*

"Huggins finally was appointed to the Yankee job in January, 1918, and then Ruppert revealed to Spink his reason for stalling so long. It seems that Huggins had appeared at interviews wearing a cap, and the colonel, an urbane gent who was fond of the amenities, frowned upon grown men who wore caps. Huggins bought himself a proper hat and went on to establish the Yankee dynasty with the help of Babe Ruth, who wore caps when the colonel was paying him more than the President of the United States was getting.

"The 1918–1920 period was a critical one for Spink and *The Sporting News*. Saved from extinction during the war by the American League's free distribution of the sheet in France, the paper suffered, along with the sport, from the Black Sox scandal. Public confidence in baseball was at a low ebb and, worst of all—in Spink's view—Ban Johnson was through as the dominating personality of baseball.

"The downfall of Johnson was the Carl Mays case. In 1919, Harry Frazee, owner of the Red Sox, was deep in debt and he began to sell his stars to Ruppert, who was spending fabulous sums in his effort to build the Yankees into a winning team. Johnson denounced the ruinous raid on the Boston club, then the best franchise in the league, and refused to sanction the sale of Mays, a Frazee star, to the Yankees. That was the final straw for the club owners, who had been showing increasing resentment of Johnson's autocratic control of the league.

"On November 18, 1920, eleven club owners met in secret at Chicago. Their intention was to adopt the Lasker plan, which provided for the formation of a new, twelve-club league. The eight National League teams already had agreed to the proposal and the Yankees, Red Sox and White Sox were ready to secede from the American League. Tipped off to the meeting, Spink belabored the insurgents so vigorously that the scheme was abandoned, but the opposition to Johnson mounted steadily. A new National Commission, designed to curb his powers, undoubtedly would have been proposed even if the Black Sox scandal had not precipitated the appointment of Judge Landis.

"Democracy at Work

"The sellout to the gamblers was a blow from which Johnson never recovered. The shock of learning that a ballplayer, and particularly an American Leaguer, could actually be dishonest broke the old man. He ruthlessly explored every clue of crookedness and demanded a public trial of the seven accused players.

Serving as Johnson's special investigator, Spink unearthed much of the evidence which later barred some of the players for life.

"With baseball a model of honesty for the past couple of decades, *The Sporting News* seldom has occasion these days to pick up its old crusading cudgel. Its chief function for years has been to enlighten and amuse rather than to agitate and excoriate. But Spink insists that the old cudgel is still in his office and will be used in the near future on a few issues. One is the perennially hopeless state of clubs like the Phillies, Athletics, Braves and Browns, who, Spink says, are ruining the essentially competitive nature of the sport. The owners, he says, have got to cure this condition or face increased apathy.

"Another is the down-at-the-heel facilities which are provided for the minor-league fans.

"And something will be done, for Spink's gripes are the fans' gripes. Hearing him talk about baseball, you can't doubt his authenticity or his sincerity as a spokesman.

" 'Baseball is the American success story,' he says with pious intensity. 'It is the only avenue of escape for thousands of boys born into a dreary environment of poverty. It is, moreover, a great common ground on which bartenders and bishops, clergymen and bosses, bankers and laborers meet with true equality and understanding. The game has proved in everyday language that democracy works.' "

31 : A Baseball Moses Gets Told Off

The *Saturday Evening Post* story vexed the Commissioner sorely, but I later learned its aftermath. A two-column review of the Frank article by Dan Daniel, our New York correspondent, in *The Sporting News* issue of June 18, 1942, was the composition which really put me in solid with the Commissioner. It surely added a tankful of fuel to the flames.

I suppose Dan did spread it on, but he only agreed to write the review, provided I ran it as he wrote it, so we were pledged not to change a comma. Yet Dan, in his kindly way, meant only to solidify the new friendship between the Commissioner and myself. Near the end of his review he wrote:

"One of the most pleasant features of the family life of *The Sporting News* is the friendship between Spink and Judge Kenesaw Mountain Landis. I think I had something to do with this. In any event, I am taking a bow, justified or not.

"Landis and Ban Johnson did not like each other. It was a natural antipathy. Spink was very close to Johnson and his loyalty made him feel that if Johnson doesn't like the Judge, I cannot like him.

"But in time, Spink came to recognize the value of this man, Landis, and his human side. Now they are pals. And as the story in the *Saturday Evening Post* points out, if you catch Spink in a weak moment over his spaghetti, in Garavelli's restaurant, he will confide to you that this man Landis stands out EVEN ABOVE JOHNSON. Spink will whisper this, so Ban can't hear it.

"I imagine that one of the things Spink has to fight is the ingratitude of the baseball magnates. They know what *The Sporting News* means; they know what Spink stands for. They won't deny that the Bible of Baseball and the Moses on Mount Sinai with the Ten Commandments of the game, which he will not permit to be violated, are paramount in the major picture. But they are human, and they forget, and they slip."

Daniel learned through me and through others that the Commissioner was furious over this column of his, though I think he knew it even before I did. Daniel wrote and wired to Judge

Landis several times, asking what was wrong, but received no response. On his next visit to Chicago with the Yankees, he called on the Judge, and it wasn't long before he realized he had caught the white-haired jurist in one of his most irascible moods. Though Daniel had known him quite intimately during Landis' twenty-one years in office, his greeting was frigid.

"What's the trouble, Judge?" asked Daniel.

"Do I have to ask you what the trouble is?" snapped Landis.

"Well, that's what I'm here to find out about," insisted Dan.

"That article in a recent issue of *The Sporting News*," said the Commissioner, without changing his belligerent tone. "There are a lot of things in that article which you never should have written. How about: 'Now we [Spink and Landis] are chummy.' Don't you put me to bed with that kind of company."

After a few more passages along similar lines, the Judge blurted: "Since when is it necessary to have a watchdog for baseball?"

Daniel countered with the remark: "Well, I think Spink does a great job in the field that he operates in."

"Wherein does he do such a wonderful job?" asked Landis.

"What I mean is that he hollers out against bad practices, wherever they occur in baseball," continued Daniel.

"A man with a paper can put in whatever he likes if he thinks he hollers out about bad practices," snapped the Judge.

"That's the way I look at it," insisted Dan.

"Well, we just don't see eye to eye," said Landis, terminating the interview.

By the time the All-Star game was played in New York, July 6, 1942, the *Saturday Evening Post* article and the later Daniel column had receded into the background of our first war season. Personal stories and articles, no matter how laudatory, are a one-day sensation in a busy newspaperman's life and then soon are forgotten. Naturally, I had heard of Landis' peeve over me being called Mr. Baseball, the baseball Moses and a watchdog, but I felt it was one of those storms which quickly would blow over. There even was an element of humor in it, as I realized the Judge was baseball's No. 1 watchdog, and at various times I had thought of him, Connie Mack and Clark Griffith as "Mr. Baseball."

266

I didn't go to the All-Star game in New York, but the night of the following day, July 7, the American League victor of the New York contest played the Service All-Stars in a never-to-be-forgotten patriotic spectacle before 62,094 at Cleveland's great Municipal Stadium.

I went to Cleveland for the game, and while I was there took advantage of the opportunity to call up Judge Landis to ask whether he would discuss with me the subject of getting out baseball's official guide for 1943, which covered the 1942 season. He made a date for me to call at his suite in the Cleveland Hotel. When I arrived at the appointed time, Sam Breadon of the Cardinals and Larry MacPhail, then still with Brooklyn, were having a misunderstanding about a player—I think it was Don Padgett, who went into the Navy after the Cardinals sold him to the Dodgers. I saw the argument was likely to go on for some time, so excused myself and told Leslie O'Connor I would see them later.

When I called again, the Commissioner and Leslie O'Connor were alone in the room. I asked whether *The Sporting News* again was to publish the *Guide*. They told me they would let me know in three weeks. We sat around for a while and had a friendly discussion about the All-Star game, baseball's problems in the first year of war, and other matters pertaining to the game. Everything was friendly and cordial, and there was no intimation that there was any concern, or annoyance, about the story in the *Saturday Evening Post* of June 20, and our review. In later correspondence, Landis wrote me he did not know of either article at the time, though that seemed unlikely.

When three or four weeks went by without receiving any word, I wrote to the Commissioner but received no reply. I then contacted Will Harridge, president of the American League, and asked him what we should do about the book. He told me that he would speak to Judge Landis. Still no answer. On the afternoon of August 28, 1942, I flew to Chicago to see the All-Star football game. I left St. Louis at 2 o'clock, and the plane got in around 4 o'clock. It later developed that the clock on the automobile bringing us in from the field was wrong. I went to Will Harridge's office, hoping to see him—thinking it was 4.30, but it was nearly five and Harridge had gone home. Miss Hummell, Harridge's assistant, told me that the Commissioner was in his office, deciding on the distribution of 1942 World's Series money. She called up to find out if he would be in and whether I could call.

Landis had had a meeting with a press committee on the distribution of Red Cross money. Ed Prell of the Chicago *Tribune* was at this meeting, as was Hugo Autz of my organization. He greeted Autz with: "Oh, you're the fellow who works for Mr. Baseball." It was evident to Autz that the *Saturday Evening Post* article still lodged in his craw.

I waited until Judge Landis got through with these men, and then sat down for a talk. Immediately the Commissioner began to berate me and with ironical emphasis, started calling me, "Mr. Baseball." He told one of his men: "Be very careful what you do. That's Mr. Baseball; he'll watch everything you do in this office."

He talked about some other things, including some matters in which he was interested, including two men, one of whom still is in baseball today, about whom he once wondered why he ever allowed him to remain in the game. We raked over the whole matter of the *Saturday Evening Post* article, and I advised him that not only was I without knowledge of the statements made in the article but that my mother had become quite angry that she was not given more credit in the piece for what she had done in connection with *The Sporting News*. "Your mother is absolutely right on that," he said.

The Commissioner's attitude continued most unfriendly. One of his employes came into the room for the moment and Landis sarcastically referred to me as "the conscience of baseball," and said even then I was "looking over that man's shoulder—other men's shoulders, in his employ."

He continued to insist that I had seen the *Saturday Evening Post* story in advance of publication. He then went on to his pet peeve, Daniel's review. He pointed out that Daniel's story said that I read every line that went into *The Sporting News*, and I told him that was correct. But, I also told him of my promise to Daniel to run his copy as he sent it in, but he brushed that aside. He got

268

particularly wrought up over Daniel's reference that we were pals. I told him that was incorrect, as was Daniel's statement that he had anything to do with bringing us together.

I then broke in and asked whether we might print the *Official Record Book and Guide* again. He replied, "No," giving as his reason the *Post* article, and saying that its publication by us would tend to bear out some of the things in the article. He then left in a huff, put on his coat and walked out on me. I was overcome with emotion, and felt as though a truck had run over me. It was probably the most uncomfortable half hour in my life. I, too, burned up, inasmuch as the Judge had let me come to his office, knowing in advance that he intended to browbeat me.

I sat down on one of the benches in the outer hall. I thought Piton was friendly, and I suppose in a situation like that I was looking for sympathy. I might have let out my pent-up emotions to most anyone who was listening. I remarked to Piton that after having done so much for baseball and having tried to please Landis through the years, he now had turned on me because of a complimentary article in one of the leading national magazines. I did not know at the time that Piton was a shorthand expert. He apparently made notes of all the things I said, and reported them to his chief the next morning.

That next morning I called up Will Harridge and told him what had happened in Landis' office. He told me that he thought it would blow over and that he would call the Judge. I went to the Cub park that afternoon with Albert Mitchell, the "Answer Man." I sat down, but my thoughts still were on my visit to Landis' office the afternoon before. Finally, after two innings, Mitchell reminded me that he was my guest at the ball game. "You surely aren't a very loquacious fellow," he said.

But I remained on edge, and after 4 o'clock I called up Harridge's office again and asked Will whether he had heard from the Commissioner. He told me that he had talked to Landis, and the Judge wanted to see me. Excusing myself, and leaving the "Answer Man" at the park, I got into a cab and paid another most unpleasant visit to Landis' office. This time I really got the third degree.

Arriving at the office, I told Piton I understood that the Commissioner wanted to see me. "That's right," said Piton, "have a seat." I sat next to a German-looking fellow with a brief case; I didn't know that he was another stenographer who soon would take down notes on me. From his inner office Landis seemed to be trying to make a telephone connection. He called three or four numbers and finally poked his head through the door and asked me: "Have you any idea where Will Harridge might be at this moment?" I said if he wasn't at his office or his home, he might be at a restaurant downstairs in the building in which the American League made their headquarters.

The Judge tried that number, failed to get Harridge, and apparently gave up. He told me to come in, and the fellow who had been sitting next to me entered with me. He was apparently a court stenographer. This time the Commissioner really gave me the works. He had four questions written down, and asked me to answer, as the stenographer took down my replies. Some of these questions had to do with some of the remarks I had made to Piton the day before.

Before I had concluded my conversation with the Commissioner, Piton came into the room, smoking a cigarette. He sat beside me, and with some hesitation tried to explain to me that he had only repeated what he had heard. I told him that it was all right. "You work for Landis, and did what you thought was best," I said. He sort of shrugged his shoulders as if to say, "Well, what could I do?"

I asked the Commissioner if he would send me a copy of our conversation. He asked the shorthand expert he had called in to make an extra copy and assured me that I would receive it. But, up to the time of the Judge's death, I never received it.

He opened a door containing a washstand and started to wash his hands. As he did so, I said: "Well, where does this put us now? Am I still a friend of yours, or am I not a friend?"

He replied: "I have no friends, and you're just the same as you were before."

I then asked him if he would shake hands with me. He dried his hands, extended his right and shook with me. As we shook hands on my departure, he said: "Remember me to the lady." He always

270

had been very thoughtful of my wife, who held him in high regard, and for a moment this little gesture assuaged my feelings. But deep down, I left his office hurt and humiliated, as I never had been before.

There was some other correspondence with Landis and others high up in baseball before I gave up in our battle of the *Guide*. But a sequel of the August conversation, which I got smack in the teeth, came in the form of a letter from the Judge the following January.

BASEBALL

Kenesaw M. Landis
COMMISSIONER

333 North Michigan Avenue,
CHICAGO
January 16, 1943

Mr. J. G. Taylor Spink,
The Sporting News,
10th & Olive Sts.,
St. Louis, Missouri

Dear Mr. Spink:
Acknowledging receipt of your letter of January 14 and its predecessors, you are informed that your Sporting News *issue of June 18, 1942, has made it impossible for me to acquiesce either in your being authorized by the Major Leagues to get out the "official" guide or to be paid money by them for getting out a guide. Should you have any doubt as to the why of this, go back and read Dan Daniel's article in the June 18, 1942, issue of* The Sporting News, *having in mind the proposition "subsidy" when you read that article.*

Very truly yours
(signed) *K. M. Landis*

Copies to Messrs. Harridge and Frick.

We did get out a *Guide* in 1943, and though it didn't have "official" on the cover, it was a replica of our splendid effort of 1942, and *The Sporting News* has been getting out a guide each year since then. In August, 1943, Landis finally came out with an "official guide," when the season was two-thirds over, long after baseball writers, scouts, managers, etc. have a need for such a volume. It was edited by Leslie O'Connor, and was a weighty, pompous tome of 736 pages in a war year of paper shortage.

The Judge going into the publishing business was not greeted with any great hallelujahs by members of the writing fraternity.

Over a heading, "Landis Batting .125 as Pinch-Hitter for Alphabetical Spink," Red Smith wrote in the March 22 Philadelphia *Record* from the Wilmington, Delaware, training camp of the Athletics:

"Judge Kenesaw Landis is a fool. And if that be treason, let him go ahead and fine me $29,000,000.

"Here we are stuck away down here in the Delaware bayou country with orders to write baseball, and there isn't a copy of the 1943 *Baseball Guide* in the Athletics' whole camp, and how the hell is a guy supposed to write baseball when he doesn't know how many assists Bernard Zook made last year at first base for Greeneville, Tenn., in the Appalachian League?

"The 1942 guide was published by Mr. J. G. Taylor Alphabetical Spink with a $10,000 subsidy from organized baseball. It was the most accurate, the most complete, in all respects and by all odds the best ever put out.

"Last December the major leagues voted to continue the subsidy. Later Landis decided he didn't like the way Mr. Spink parts his name on the side and he called the deal off, announcing he would publish the 1943 guide himself, when he got around to it.

"The Judge's deep and abiding disaffection for Mr. Spink is strictly personal and has been attributed to various causes, all of them petty. The Judge himself never gave any reason for going into the publishing business. Maybe he noticed how the newspapermen he deals with quake and cower at the mention of the sports editor's name and decided he'd like to be an editor so he could be all-powerful, too. The old guy has got a dictator complex."

In the same vein, Joe Williams, well-known sports columnist of the New York *World-Telegram*, wrote in his column of March

9, 1943, under the heading: "Landis Shows Baseball Fans He's Real Dictator":

"It is about this time of the year the annual baseball guide comes rolling off the presses. It is a pleasant and surefire harbinger of spring. The guide will be late in arriving this year, and not without reason.

"You see, Judge Landis has decided to go into the publishing business. In short, he has taken over the *Guide* himself. From now on it will be edited and issued from his office in Chicago.

"To the addicts at large this is not a matter of importance, but to the press box historians it is scarcely a trivial thing, because a record book, to have any value at all, must be complete and foolproof.

"It is possible the Judge and his office workers, despite their lack of specialized training in editorial and publishing fields, may be able to come up with an acceptable issue, but that isn't the way we'd want to bet.

"Indeed, the manner in which the new publisher is going about the initial phase of the assignment is ground enough for pessimism. He has made reporters of the club owners. They are to furnish him with the material for the issue. They are to compose what they want in the issue and send the copy, along with photographs, to his Chicago office. After which the editor and his assistants presumably will majestically weave the text and plates into a finished whole. This is going about a professional job in an amateurish way, and it's difficult to contemplate the results without shuddering.

"There is a story back of all this, and it has to do with personalities. The Judge, who bruises easily, has formed a distaste for J. G. Taylor Spink, the man who gets out *The Sporting News*, which is loosely referred to as the 'bible of baseball.' The 1942 issue of the guide was produced by Spink, who in turn had taken it over from the original publisher, a sports manufacturing house. The latter agency, undergoing the rigors of a stern retrenchment policy, had decided to abandon the guide. There is no money in sports literature of this sort.

273

"Meanwhile Spink and his bible were featured in a national magazine piece. The author didn't make Spink look too unimportant as a baseball figure, nor did he present the bible as an organ of minor influence in the development of the sport.

"Among other things Spink was presented as a staunch Ban Johnson man who had only recently been converted to the Landis pulpit. This may have been the thing that caused the Judge to bristle. Johnson as president of the American League had been the biggest man in baseball until the Judge. The feeling was mutual.

"So this could have been it: The admission by Spink that he had been a Johnson man. At any rate the Judge decided to take the guide away from Spink and publish it himself, and that's why the club owners around the country, abruptly cast as reporters, are tearing their hair and gnashing their teeth and wondering what in the hell goes on in the Chicago office these days.

"It is almost inconceivable the Judge would use an old hate as a device of retaliation, but there are times you never can tell about him. Whatever the purpose and motive the action is both childish and unbusiness-like. It would be different if Spink had turned out an inferior issue last year, but, on the contrary, it was the best of all time, far superior even to the original issues.

"The Judge can't possibly hope to improve it, and there is every indication, in view of the amateurish start, that it will be pretty sloppy and probably woefully inaccurate. It takes an expert to turn out record books, and while the Judge may be an expert in many fields there is nothing in his record to show that he knows anything about this kind of operation.

"Happily, there is no law by which the Judge can prevent Spink from getting out another record book of his own, and this we understand the gentleman intends to do. In which event, of course, the Judge's 'official' book will be spectacularly ignored by the press box historians. It will have little more than curiosity value, although the manner in which it is edited and put together may be the source of some unexpected humor.

"Spink and his dad before him made a life's work of the factual history of baseball. Spink has records in his keeping which date

274

back to the birth of the game. It naturally follows then that he is in an enviable position to handle the book which the Judge has decided his office will publish from now on."

I believe the humor of the situation came the next year, 1944, when after the Commissioner's belated 736-page volume of 1943, government officials would not release the Judge any paper to publish an "official" guide of 1944. So, if it hadn't been for our enterprise in getting out our "unofficial" effort, there would have been no guide at all that year, and a year's break in the game's history and records. In 1945, Landis' office partly caught up with the game, when its "official guide" included the averages for both the seasons of 1943 and 1944.

32: Three Seasons of War

In the last nine years of Judge Landis' life, his health was a source of considerable concern to Mrs. Landis and his many friends. He had quite a serious spell in 1935 and early 1936. A report around that time was the Commissioner was in poor shape, and wouldn't live six months. However, like the report of Mark Twain's death, the seriousness of the Judge's malady was grossly exaggerated.

He left his old Florida winter headquarters at Belleair for several winters to take advantage of the drier climate at Phoenix, Arizona. And he had a prostate operation, which performed miracles. He was a new man after the operation.

"Don't ever let anything get wrong with your prostates," he told a sports writer in his typical positive language. "That's the damnest thing that can happen to a man."

For some years after the operation, the Commissioner again was in pretty good shape, resumed his golf, got considerable fun out of life, and smacked down on Rickey or anyone who wandered off his reservation. John Heydler, the veteran National League president, three years younger than Landis, had retired because of failing health in 1934, and several times it was suggested that the Judge step down, play a little in the years he had left, and get from under the strain and pressure of running baseball. But he pooh-poohed any such suggestions. He really loved his job, the publicity, prestige and prominence which went with it. He knew what it meant to be an ex-something, and he didn't mean to be the ex-Commissioner. He loved to have his fingers on the baseball pulse, and I always felt he never would resign, and literally would die with his baseball shoes on. That actually came to pass.

The Judge had a close call shortly after the Yankee-Dodger World's Series of 1941. The last game was played in Brooklyn, October 6, and Landis rushed from the World's Series to a cabin at Burt Lake, in northern Michigan, for a fishing trip and some needed relaxation. However, it gets pretty cold in that part of the world in October, and the Judge, tired from too much hiking, got numb with cold as he put in a day of fishing on the lake. At first, Landis thought he only had caught a heavy cold, but when he quickly ran up a temperature and his breath came in quick gasps, his associates became alarmed. The fishing trip was hurriedly called off and Landis was rushed to a hospital at Petoskey, Mich. He entered there, October 10, only four days after the final Monday game of the Series, and the physicians quickly diagnosed his condition as bronchial pneumonia. It was said at the time that if the Judge had been left at the fishing lodge a few more days it would have been fatal.

The trouble with the Commissioner was that he didn't appreciate that the years were catching up on him. By this time he had reached the ripe age of 75. He hated the thought of age, and disliked making any concessions to it; he thought he could tramp in the woods and suffer exposure as when he was a tough "young man" of 50. The Petoskey physicians gradually pulled him through and late in the month, he was well enough to sign the World's Series checks for the lucky Yankee and Brooklyn World's Series players.

When Landis returned to Chicago, and took up his crowded desk at 333 North Michigan Avenue, it wasn't difficult to see that he had been through an ordeal. The illness in the woods had taken a severe toll on his small physique and waning strength. He had aged much in the few months since the 1941 World's Series. The Commissioner missed the annual meeting of the minor leagues in Jacksonville in the week before Pearl Harbor, and I already have related how I called on him in Chicago the Monday morning after that "Day of Infamy."

Frail, but as mentally alert as ever, Landis presided at the joint meeting of the majors in Chicago, December 11. Lacking any word from Washington, the Judge promptly took the stand that baseball would go on, subject to any subsequent restrictions or requests by the Government. A sum of $25,000—$20,000 from the Commissioner's office—was made immediately available for an Equipment Fund—to buy bats, balls and athletic paraphernalia for service men, and at Landis' recommendation the proceeds of the 1942 All-Star game, at increased prices, would go to this fund. The sum of $20,000 to Landis' old pet, American Legion baseball, again was voted. The subject of night ball also came up again. Clark Griffith and Don Barnes of the American argued for unlimited

277

night ball, in view of expected war conditions: an increase to fourteen nocturnal games was permitted, but Landis again tipped the scales against any move which would permit an individual club to exceed those figures. Landis felt well enough to have the big leaguers as guests at a luncheon, and quipped about his recent illness. "Gentlemen, I am as good as ever," he told the big leaguers.

It was early in 1942 that Judge Landis obtained from President Roosevelt the Chief Executive's famous "Green Light" letter for baseball. I've told before that in politics Landis was bitterly anti-Roosevelt. I do not know whether the late war President knew of the political views of the former Judge of the Northern District of Illinois, but I do know Roosevelt responded magnificently to an inquiry by Landis on the war status of professional baseball. I always have felt that most baseball people were not sufficiently grateful for this letter; it served as baseball's wartime Magna Charta, and made possible the four difficult war seasons which followed. The letter read as follows:

THE WHITE HOUSE
WASHINGTON

January 15, 1942

My dear Judge:—

Thank you for yours of January fourteenth. As you will, of course, realize the final decision about the baseball season must rest with you and the Baseball Club owners—so what I am going to say is solely a personal and not an official point of view.

I honestly feel that it would be best for the country to keep baseball going. There will be fewer people unemployed and everybody will work longer hours and harder than ever before.

And that means that they ought to have a chance for recreation and for taking their minds off their work even more than before.

Baseball provides a recreation which does not last over two hours or two hours and a half, and which can be got for very little cost. And, incidentally, I hope that night baseball can be extended because it gives an opportunity to the day shift to see a game occasionally.

As to the players themselves, I know you agree with me that individual players who are of active military or naval age should go, without question, into the services. Even if the actual quality of the teams is lowered by the greater use of older players, this will not dampen the popularity of the sport. Of course, if any individual has some particular aptitude in a trade or profession, he ought to serve the Government. That, however, is a matter which I know you can handle with complete justice.

Here is another way of looking at it—if 300 teams use 5,000 or 6,000 players, these players are a definite recreational asset to at least 20,000,000 of their fellow citizens—and that in my judgment is thoroughly worthwhile.

With every best wish,
Very sincerely yours,
(Signed) Franklin D. Roosevelt

Hon. Kenesaw M. Landis
333 North Michigan Avenue
Chicago, Illinois

From the start Landis stressed the fact that the game made no suggestions to President Roosevelt, asked for no favors, and would ask for none. He insisted, and in that all baseball agreed with him, that no preferment would be asked for a single man in the game. Outside of his fine patriotism, Landis realized that the only way the public would tolerate baseball as a war activity was if its stars took the same chances with their draft boards as did Mrs. Quinn's son, Jimmie; Mrs. Piekarski's Sigmund, and Mrs. Cohen's boy, Benny. But Landis did stress, back there in the early months of the war, a statement he repeated right up to the time of his death in 1944: "We'll play as long as we can put nine men on the field."

The teams trained at their customary spots in Florida and California in 1942, but the travel situation, and the general war picture, had changed perceptibly by 1943. As early as November 30, 1942, Joseph B. Eastman, Director of War Defense Transportation, sent a letter to Judge Landis and to the major league presidents, Will Harridge and Ford Frick, asking that they curtail transportation, especially as it dealt with long training trips. East-

279

man said later he did not "dictate" to baseball; "merely sought its cooperation."

He got full-hearted cooperation from the now aged Judge Landis, showing his years but still full of fight and fire. He was as bitter and truculent against the Axis heads as he was against the Kaiser in 1917–1918. To the Judge the war was all-important, and baseball entirely secondary, which is as it should have been. In January, 1943, he went to Washington for a conference with Joe Eastman. Out of it grew the so-called Eastman-Landis line for training. Under it clubs were restricted from training south of the Potomac and Ohio Rivers, and, with the exception of the St. Louis clubs, west of the Mississippi. It meant training in such cold spots as Bear Mountain, N.Y., Wallingford, Conn., Asbury Park, N.J., and Cairo, Ill., where the Ohio River had a habit of backing into the training field, but then war is hell.

However, at no other time during the war did the Judge go to Washington to present baseball's problems before the government. As these problems multiplied, and became more serious as the war dragged through 1942, 1943 and 1944, there were hints and suggestions from baseball people that their aged Commissioner go to the capital, if only to present baseball's picture to the proper authorities. But the Judge was adamant. "I'll not go to Washington, nor will I ask a favor for baseball from anyone," he insisted. And he persisted in this stand until his death. And even after Judge Landis passed from this life, and the major league presidents, Ford Frick and Will Harridge, went to Washington in the winter of 1944–1945 to get some clarification on the game's then complicated status, Leslie O'Connor, the Judge's old secretary-treasurer, didn't like it, and expressed himself accordingly. That wasn't playing ball up to the Judge's old code and holding fast to his memory.

Landis saw to it that nothing happened to the World's Series. He was a World's Series fan long before he ever became Commissioner, and considered the Series an American event only a little secondary to the Fourth of July. "The World's Series is a national institution, and those fellows fighting out there in the stench and dirt want it just as much as we do," he said. Both the Series of 1942 and 1943 involved the New York Yankees and the St.

Louis Cardinals. They were both short Series—five games; the Cardinals surprised the nation by winning in 1942, stopping the Yankees after they had won eight straight Series, but the powerful Stadium Bombers snapped back strongly the following October. Landis' big regret about these short Series was that it limited the amount of money he could turn over to the Red Cross and war charities. Nothing gave him greater pleasure than when he signed his name to a USO check for $362,926.50 from the 1942 Series and one for $308,375.40 to the War Relief and Service Fund of 1943.

Landis had a disagreeable task in the war season of 1943. Not since he tossed out Jimmy O'Connell and Cozy Dolan of the Giants in 1924 was it necessary for the Commissioner to give a player such an extreme penalty—permanent expulsion from the game—but at the end of this season he was forced to take such action against one of the major-league club presidents, Bill Cox of the Phillies.

Cox's offense wasn't so terrible, nothing that would put a stigma on him among his business associates. But he fell a victim to one of the edicts Landis put into effect shortly after the Cobb-Speaker and Gandil-Risberg cases of 1926 and 1927. Cox bet on ball games of which his club was a participant, and ran smack into Major League Rule 21 (d) 2: "Any player, umpire, or club or league official or employe who shall bet any sum whatsoever upon any baseball game in connection with which the bettor had a duty to perform shall be declared permanently ineligible."

Cox, a New York lumber man and a former Yale catcher, had a turbulent season in baseball. He once owned a race horse, liked to bet on races and played cards for fairly big stakes. He was a man who enjoyed making a bet. He came into the Philadelphia baseball picture early in 1943, when the National League decided it had enough of Gerry Nugent; and Cox, heading a fairly responsible group, made Ford Frick, the National League president, the best offer for the property. Cox engaged Bucky Harris, the former successful Washington pilot, as his manager and for several months seemed to make considerable progress in lifting the club out of its rut.

However, Cox proceeded to get into arguments with Ford Frick and others and in midseason got considerable unfavorable publicity by the manner in which he fired Manager Harris and put Freddy Fitzsimmons in his place. After the story of Harris' release broke elsewhere, the former popular manager was fired by telephone, and the Philadelphia players almost staged a strike before a night game in St. Louis, July 28, with a 17,883 Red Cross benefit crowd in the stands. The players consented to take the field after considerable persuasion and only after addressing a statement to Cox expressing resentment over the manner in which Harris was fired, especially that news of the release should have come out before the club president officially took up the matter with Bucky. Harris struck back with a vitriolic interview against his former boss, accused Cox of interference, second-guessing players in the clubhouse, and, as late as July 20, of assuring Bucky in Pittsburgh that no changes were contemplated in the management of the club. Harris' midseason release was of considerable importance, because it was on Bucky's testimony that Landis found Cox guilty of baseball gambling.

There were rumblings that Cox was in Landis' doghouse in early November, 1943. The Judge fined the young club owner $100 for an alleged undercover agreement with the Trenton club, and gave a warning that a repetition of the offense would bring a fine of $500. However a fortnight later, November 23, Landis really slapped down on Bill Cox, recited the charges against him, and notified him to be present at a hearing in New York on December 4.

The official finding in part, handed to the press, follows:

"In August, 1943, it was rumored that William D. Cox, president of the Philadelphia National League club, had bet on baseball games during the 1943 season, in violation of Major League Rule 21 (d) 2.

[The rule is given.]

"At that time, Mr. Cox asserted that such rumors had no basis, except that an associate in his lumber business had placed such bets on his own account; and that when Mr. Cox first heard about such bets in May, 1943, he requested his lumber associate to discontinue them, which request had been immediately complied with.

"However, an investigation was made and on November 15, 1943, Mr. Cox was notified that a hearing upon the charge would be held at New York on December 4, and that—

" 'You (William D. Cox) are requested and directed to appear at said time and place to answer fully to such charges and present any and all evidence you may wish to have considered, including the testimony of yourself and of any witness you may desire to have present. You may, if you so desire, be represented by counsel and either you or counsel may present any statements, argument or brief desired.

" 'You are also requested to mail to me a complete statement of bets made by you upon baseball games in the 1943 season, as stated to me by you, including as to each bet the amount, the date of the game, the teams involved, the name of the team upon which you bet to win, the odds, and the name and address of the person with whom the bet was placed.

" 'In view of the statements you have heretofore made to me respecting this matter, I am obliged to inform you that pending the hearing and decision it will not be appropriate for you to participate in any baseball meeting or transaction.' "

The Commissioner then quoted from a letter which Cox had written him on November 18, notifying Landis that he had resigned as president and as a director of the Philadelphia club and that he would dispose of "his large investment in the club" as soon as he could find "a satisfactory purchaser."

Cox closed the letter with this paragraph: "In view of my resignation and the full statements which I have heretofore made to you, I do not see that any useful purpose would be served by my attending any further hearing before you."

Landis replied sharply in a letter of November 22. Skipping several early paragraphs, the Commissioner wrote: "In your interview with me on August 14, and continuously thereafter until November 3, you asserted that any allegations that you had bet on baseball games during the 1943 season were ridiculous and that it was only an associate in the lumber business who had done so. During this period you made fruitless efforts to ascertain from me what results were being obtained in my investigation. Finally, in New York on November 3 (and subsequently in Chicago) you stated to me that you had placed through a bookmaker 'approximately 15 or 20 bets' of from $25 to $100 per game on Philadelphia to win,' on games of the Philadelphia National League club; that this betting began 'about a week after the 1943 season started' and continued 'up to about May 20'; and that about May 20 you learned of the rule prohibiting such betting; that until you saw that rule you did not know betting on games by persons having to do with the sport was prohibited or penalized; and that from the time you learned of said rule you made no bet of any kind or in any way, or amount, on any baseball game. . . . I presume that by 'the full statements which I have heretofore made to you' you mean the statements above mentioned. As you know those were not 'full' statements and my letter of November 15 requested you (as previously requested verbally) to give me a 'complete statement of bets made by you upon baseball games in the 1943 season.' . . ."

The Commissioner's finding ended with a paragraph barring Cox permanently from any club in Organized Baseball: "The proposed hearing, December 4, 1943, was intended to develop fully statements of the facts by yourself and others, and give you an opportunity to present anything you might want to have considered. Therefore, I am not in accord with your view that such hearing would serve no useful purpose. However, you decline to attend such hearing and to answer fully in this matter. This obliges me to notify you that your betting on baseball games of the Philadelphia National League club, as to which games, as chief executive of that club, in charge of operations, you had 'a duty to perform,' which betting is established by my investigation and by your own statements, require me, pursuant to Major League Rule 21 (d) 2, to declare you to be permanently ineligible to hold any office or employment with the Philadelphia National League club, or any other club or league party to the Major League Agreement, or Major-Minor League Agreement."

In a "Goodbye to Baseball" broadcast over Station WOR on

November 23, the night of Judge Landis' finding, Bill Cox admitted he had made sentimental bets before he knew of the rule against it. In closing, he said: "In saying goodbye to baseball forever, I want to say . . . I looked up to, rather than at, my fellow club presidents with a sincere hope that I could emulate the best of their individual deeds. I hope I have not offended them. I have endeavored in every way to lead an exemplary life and conduct myself with the proper viewpoint to this great sport.

"Good luck and goodbye to everyone in baseball."

However, shortly after this talk, Cox had a change of heart. He sought to retract his former admissions of wagering on the Phillies, saying he had circulated the report simply to test the loyalty of an unnamed employe. He called on Judge Landis to hold his December 4 hearing, and went there accompanied by Lloyd Paul Stryker, a well-known New York attorney.

It was an open hearing, lasting six hours, and at its conclusion, Landis reaffirmed his original ruling, stating: "There is no escape from the conclusion, with such intelligence as I am endowed with —or inflicted with—that there is nothing I can do for Mr. Cox. Baseball rules on betting are obligatory on me, as on other baseball men, and the order will have to be that I do not put out a new order."

Miss Elizabeth Massey, secretary to Cox, and Mary Esterbrook, telephone operator at Cox' office, both denied at the hearing any knowledge of money wagered by the Philadelphia president.

However, Bucky Harris, fired by Cox as manager in July, supplied the most damaging testimony against his former club president. He testified that on one occasion when he and Road Secretary Jimmy Hagan were in Cox' office, he heard Miss Massey get betting odds over the telephone, and that she told Harris she kept books for Cox. Bucky related that he replied:

"If Judge Landis ever hears about this, it will be the end of Cox."

In trying to defend his client, Barrister Stryker several times got into Landis' shock of white hair. In arguing his case for Cox, Stryker said: "In the absence of proof, I ask you to clear this man of the charge that he gambled on the outcome of baseball games," and then after a pause: "unless you want to hear Cox' explanation of why he played private detective to test the loyalty of one of his men. I don't think that would be good for baseball."

Landis bristled and then glared at Cox' counsel and spoke through clenched teeth: "If you think it will be bad for baseball, then bring it in. We'll hear it."

At another point in his concluding address to Landis, Stryker attempted to toss a few bouquets in the Judge's direction, addressing him as an "eminent judge of vast experience on the federal bench and I appreciate the time and patience which you have given me—"

Landis cut him short with an impatient wave of his hand, and said in his iciest tones: "Save your energy."

33 : An Eventful November

Landis, by now seventy-seven, went through another difficult war campaign in 1944, the season topped with pennant-winners for both St. Louis clubs. In midseason, he attended the annual All-Star game, played at Forbes Field, Pittsburgh, July 11. The game was played on a particularly hot night after a 100-degree day, but the Commissioner looked chipper and happy when he attended the contest with Mrs. Landis. He complimented Mrs. Barney Dreyfuss, widow of the man he once admonished to keep his shirt on, on her fine show, and apparently had a swell time. He still smoked cigarettes incessantly, but at a cocktail party at Pittsburgh's Schenley given by Bill Benswanger, Pirate president, he merely touched the glass to his lips. Never more than a drinker for politeness sake and at the "nineteenth hole," he practically gave up alcohol entirely in his late years. The game, won by the National League, 7 to 1, was Landis' last appearance at a World's Series or All-Star game.

To inquiries about his health, he replied: "I'm feeling fine. Everything is fine!" but to a few intimates he was admitting that Father Time was closing in on him. "It makes me so damn mad to feel old," he said sadly. "You just find out you can't do the things you want to do, and there are so many things you want to do."

One of his last public appearances was at a game played at Great Lakes, Ill., August 23, between the crack Great Lakes team and the New York Giants, a club the Judge had rooted against in the old days. Perhaps, as they played against a great sailor team in an exhibition, he felt privileged again to root against New York, and the Great Lakes team won, 5 to 1. Landis was the guest there of Captain R. N. Emmet, commander of the naval station, and was one of several influential guests, including the Most Rev. Bernard J. Sheil, senior auxiliary bishop of the archdiocese of Chicago. The Judge, never too robust, looked particularly frail when he had his picture taken with the Captain and Bishop. Perhaps it was a warning the end wasn't too far away.

On August 28, he presided at a meeting in his Chicago office to discuss 1944 World's Series plans with Sam Breadon of the Cardinals and representatives of the three leading American League contenders, Don Barnes and Bill DeWitt of the Browns, Jack Zeller of the Tigers and Charley McManus of the Yankees. In the group picture of this meeting, the venerable Chicago jurist again looked a tired old man. He seemed to have aged several years since the Pittsburgh All-Star game.

As the season went into September, and a remarkable finish in the American League, Landis was much concerned with gambling at Shibe Park, Philadelphia, whether either the Athletics or Phillies were the home team. He fought the baseball gamblers almost to his last breath. In early September he wrote Philadelphia's Public Safety Director, James H. Malone, that gambling conditions were worse at Shibe Park than in any park in the majors. Later in the month, he wrote again to Malone, thanking him for his cooperation.

For years a resident of Chicago apartment hotels, Landis in his late years bought a suburban home at Glencoe, Ill.—outside of Chicago. Still trying to do something to help win the war, he put in his spare time in his Victory Garden, time he had given to golf in former years. There is no doubt that he over-taxed his heart with his spading and digging. He also was subject to periodic colds ever since he had the pneumonia attack after the 1941 World's Series.

The first game of the Cardinal-Brown World's Series was scheduled for St. Louis, October 4, but Judge Landis was not in his customary box, throwing out the first ball before a battery of cameras, when Mort Cooper and Denny Galehouse squared off for the opener. Sorrowfully his faithful assistant, Leslie O'Connor, came down to St. Louis alone two days before, saying the Judge's health made it necessary for the Commissioner to remain in Chicago. Two days before the start of the Series, October 2, the Judge entered St. Luke's Hospital in Chicago, supposedly because of a lingering cold and for a general check-up. He never came out alive.

Mrs. Landis already was a patient at St. Luke's when the Judge was admitted; the Squire's lady was receiving treatment for a broken wrist.

Leslie O'Connor, who presided over the all-St. Louis World's Series as Landis' pinch-hitter, no doubt hoping for the best, turned aside anxious queries about his big little boss's illness by saying: "It is nothing serious. The Judge had quite a heavy cold, and needed a rest. He thought he would play it safe, and go to the hospital. A few weeks there will fix him up fine. When he comes out, he'll be better than ever."

However, those who knew the Judge realized something was radically wrong with Landis to keep him away from a World's Series, the first he missed since coming into office in 1921. The Series was the Commissioner's annual show; he was proud of his perfect attendance record and of the way he ran it. In the language of the late Irvin Cobb, it was "nothing trivial" that kept him away. No doubt Landis would have come, cold or no cold, if his Chicago physicians, knowing the condition of his heart, had not positively forbidden it.

During October, the reports from Landis' hospital bedside were encouraging. A few baseball people were permitted to see him and he told one and all that even if he didn't leave the hospital for the St. Louis World's Series, "there's one day I'll get out of here." That was election day, when he wanted to make sure he would cast his vote against that man Roosevelt. When election day came and went, and the Commissioner didn't come out to cast his ballot, his friends knew that the Judge was a very sick man.

But as late as the Chicago draft meetings, November 1, the club owners apparently felt that the Commissioner soon would be up, and ready to tackle baseball's many problems. In order to make it easier for the Judge to attend the annual meetings, scheduled for New York, December 5, 6 and 7, the meetings were shifted to Chicago, December 11, 12 and 13, even though the change necessitated wholesale shifts of wartime hotel accommodations at that late date. It was written at the time: "Landis is strong enough to wield the gavel at the joint meeting, having remained in the hospital longer than his actual illness required in order to be thoroughly rested."

In addition to the many perplexities as the game finished its third war season, baseball was getting relatively close to the end of the

25-year Major League Agreement which brought Landis into power. The expiration date was January 21, 1946. This also would mark the expiration of Judge Landis' term as Commissioner, and it always had been baseball's practice to re-elect the Judge at least a year before the expiration of a term. This matter had come up as early as the major league meeting held in Pittsburgh, July 11, at the time of the All-Star game, when the league presidents were requested to appoint committees to consider the matter. Here and there, there was some grumbling over Landis' conduct of the game's affairs, his general attitude on the farms, and his failure to go to Washington in the game's behalf. There was even talk of taking away a little of Landis' absolute power in a new agreement, also a few suggestions to go back to a three-man Commission.

November was destined to be an important month as the Judge neared life's goal. On November 17, the joint committee met in Chicago, and decided there was no one in the field to take Landis' place. Advancing years and illness had taken their visible toll, but he was their chief, and they wanted it to stay that way. They recommended that Landis' term be extended another seven years, after his present term expired, which would carry him to 1953, when he would be 86 years old. It was also the sense of the meeting when the Major League Agreement was renewed that there would be no change in any of the Commissioner's powers or prerogatives.

The committee felt that inasmuch as Landis' term expired on January 21, 1946, he would have over a year to decide whether the state of his health and his general strength would enable him to continue. Yet members of the committee seemed to have no doubt that the Judge would go on. Their action recommending Landis for the additional term was not final, as it still had to be ratified at the December joint meeting, but that was expected to be merely routine business. The committee had some of the best brains in baseball. On the American League side were President Will Harridge, Alva Bradley and Joseph Hostetler (the league attorney) of the Cleveland club, Jack Zeller of Detroit and Harry Grabiner of the White Sox. Representing the National League were President Ford Frick, Sam Breadon of St. Louis, Branch Rickey of Brooklyn, Horace Stoneham of New York and Warren Giles of Cincinnati.

Sam Breadon, president of the then new World's Champion Cardinals and vice president of the National League, was one of the last baseball men to call on Landis, visiting him while in Chicago. He found the Commissioner's mind as keen as ever. The Judge joshed Breadon over his inability to be there when he celebrated a new World's Championship, and was in good spirits. But his little body seemed frailer than ever.

Three days after the committee's recommendation for another long term for Landis, November 20, the elderly baseball czar quietly celebrated his seventy-eighth birthday at the hospital. And around that time, there was word from St. Luke's that Judge Landis could have no more visitors, except by special permission of his physician and his family.

Landis no doubt knew he was slipping away, but he tried to the end to keep the general public from knowing the seriousness of his condition. When persons called up to ask about his condition, he requested his nurses to say, "The Judge is doing all right." It really wasn't until November 24 that the press associations got word of the fact that the Commissioner's condition had taken a turn for the worse and was exceedingly grave.

In the early morning of November 25, a Saturday, baseball's first Commissioner breathed his last and the spirit of a stalwart American moved into the Great Beyond. Kenesaw Mountain Landis died peacefully at 5.35 under an oxygen tent.

His family, which he loved so dearly, was with him at the end, Mrs. Landis; their son, Reed G. Landis, the World War I ace, and daughter, Mrs. Richard W. Phillips. Others in attendance were Phillips, his son-in-law; Leslie O'Connor, the faithful assistant of his long tenure in baseball, and Mr. and Mrs. John Stevenson, a niece and nephew. The Judge was conscious and able to speak to his family until shortly before the oxygen tent was required. He died an hour after the tent was placed over him.

Leslie O'Connor issued a short statement, disclosing the late Commissioner's last wishes. The Judge wanted no funeral, no flowers, no one to lament over him. He had left orders that his body be cremated, and he requested no memorial. It was like the old Judge to make such a request; he hated sham and disliked anything that smacked of hypocrisy. "They always can think of the most wonderful things about a man after he is dead."

They did think many wonderful things about Landis when the end came. Organized Baseball would have liked to pay proper homage to a man who had governed the sport for a quarter of a century, a man many regarded as the savior of baseball. But they respected his last wishes.

Perhaps Will Harridge, American League president, expressed the sentiment of his fellow executives and club owners when he said: "He was most sincere in his belief that his friends would have brighter memories of him if there was no funeral. I know he had a definite understanding with his family that his wish would be carried out strictly. He was a wonderful man. His great qualities of honesty and downright simplicity impressed themselves deeply on all who knew him."

The little weazened body that last carried the indomitable spirit of Kenesaw Mountain Landis was cremated the day after his death. It no doubt was a fitting end, the end he wished for. Landis was not a religious man, in so far as creeds, church-going and any outward display of worship were concerned; in fact, some considered him an atheist, but he had a great belief in the supremacy of the spirit over the frail human body. I heard him flay religious hypocrites and persons who went around with pious looks on their faces and larceny in their hearts. He just hated sham. He may not have been a believer in the accepted sense, but he had a deep abiding conviction in some great power or divine intelligence which in some way permitted human beings to work out their destiny. His own inherent honesty and zeal for uprightness in personal character made him critical—and even intolerant—toward some of his fellow men who may not have measured quite up to his standards. As an attorney, a judge on the Federal bench, and as baseball Commissioner, who heard charges and accusations against club owners, managers, players and others in the game, he knew human frailty and had a contempt for many of the human race. He loathed and despised anyone who was even remotely concerned with gambling, and carried it to anyone who was connected in any way with race tracks, as when he prevented the popular crooner Bing Crosby from buying into a big league ball club because Bing raced horses and had an interest in a track. But, in his many sided nature, Landis was always the friend of the underdog, as when he acquitted the young man who stole the Liberty bonds. He also was the friend of the ball player, and while he was Commissioner of all baseball, he always felt he was the ball player's man and the fan's man on baseball's supreme body. "The club owners have their league presidents to look out for their interests," he once said.

Landis wanted no memorial, but persons in all walks of life, men high in the councils of the nation, editors, soldiers, jurists, physicians, scientists, paid him honor. One and all called him "a great American, and the type of man only America could produce." The baseball men were shocked, stunned, dumbfounded at his going.

Only a week before the end, they practically had elected him for another term of seven years, which would have continued him in office until his eighty-sixth birthday. "They seem to think he is like Old Man River, that he'll just keep rollin' along—always," someone said flippantly at the time. But that literally was true; Landis had run their game so long they couldn't conceive of anyone else handling the tiller. Many of the club owners seemed in a daze; they were like sheep who had lost their shepherd. Eventually, they put Leslie O'Connor in temporary charge of their game, and on April 24, 1945, they elected A. B. "Happy" Chandler, then United States Senator from Kentucky, as their new Commissioner. Chandler is in many ways the opposite of the "old Judge" and the smiling Kentuckian already has suffered because he didn't fit completely into the old Landis pattern. However, Chandler, an individualist, insisted on being himself. He no more could try to emulate Landis in all things than Landis in 1921 could have made himself another Garry Herrmann.

While Landis wanted no memorial, he did get one, and one of which he unquestionably would have approved. In August, 1944, he had appointed an Old Timers' committee to select illustrious baseball names to the Cooperstown Hall of Fame, men not named in the annual poll of the Baseball Writers' Association. The committee was made up of three well known baseball officials, Connie Mack of the Athletics; Ed Barrow, former president of the Yankees; and Bob Quinn, former president of the Braves, and two veteran baseball writers, the late Sid Mercer and Mel Webb. Two weeks after Landis' death the committee made its first selection; it was Judge Kenesaw Landis, the man who made the dedication speech when the Hall of Fame formally was opened in 1939. The Baseball Writers' Association also named the plaques given to players winning their annual "most valuable player" designations, the Judge Kenesaw Mountain Landis awards.

So we leave the Hoosier judge, who for so many years was such an important figure in American baseball. I had differences, disputes, arguments with him; in my heart I once sided with Ban Johnson in his battles with Landis, though I never let it color the editorial or news policies of *The Sporting News*. But, I fully appreciate what Landis did for baseball and meant to America's great sport. It is odd that both Judge Landis and Babe Ruth, credited by their rival admirers with having saved baseball after the lamented "Black Sox scandal," blazed forth on the American sports pages around the same time. Just as Ruth left slugging marks in the baseball records which I doubt time ever will erase, so Landis left his indelible marks in the council halls of the game. At times he may have been arbitrary, self-willed, and even unfair, but he "called 'em as he saw 'em," and he turned over to his successor a game cleansed of the nasty spots which followed World War I. He put the fear of God into weak characters who otherwise might have been inclined to violate their trust. And for that, I, as a lifelong lover and proponent of baseball, will be eternally grateful.

Index

Havana race track, 86-87
Haywood, William D. (Big Bill), 22-23
Heilbroner Bureau, 246
Heilmann, Harry, 166
Hendrix, Claude, 62
Henline, Butch, 94
Henrich, Tommy, 229-231
Herman, Billy, 241
Herrmann, August (Garry), 38, 42 ff.,
    51, 59, 70, 71, 75, 92, 98, 101,
    121 ff., 293
  death of, 179
  downfall of, 52-53
  retirement of, 191
Heydler, John Arnold, 13, 43, 44,
    52 ff., 59, 61, 62, 65 ff., 89, 91, 101,
    113, 130, 131, 138, 146, 148, 189,
    192, 201, 211
  decision against, 121 ff.
  for Landis, 48-56
  on George Kelly, 140
  quoted, 55-56
  retirement of, 276
  statement re. appointment of
    Landis, 73
  writes agreement between majors,
    75
Hildebrand, George, 112-114
Hitless Wonder Sox, 19
Hoernschmeyer, Leopold (Lee
    Magee), 34
Hofman, Artie, 15
Hollister, Judge, 34
Hooper, Harry, 44, 45
Hoover, Herbert, 194
Horner, Henry, 21
Hornsby, Rogers, 151, 207-209
Horses, betting on, 85-88, 208, 281
Hostetler, Joseph, 290
Hoy, Dummy, 13
Hoyne, State's attorney, 57, 81
Hoyt, Waite, 102, 103
Hubbell, Carl, 202, 213
Huggins, Miller, 127, 188, 189, 261-262
Hughes, Charles Evans, Jr., 214, 215,
    221
Hummell, Miss, 268
Huston, Tillinghast L., 50, 66, 102 ff.,
    252

Hyland, Robert, 179

Impeachment, motions for, 18
Indianapolis Club, 96-97
Indians, 11, 57
Insull stocks, 209-210
Insurrectionists, 51-52, 67
"Internal affairs" ruling, 118
International League, 126, 144
International League farm, Rochester,
    192
International Workers of the World,
    23, 24
I.W.W., 23, 24

Jackson, Joe, 57, 60, 81, 85, 107, 108,
    151, 166
James, Bill, 166 ff., 171
Jamison, J. V., Jr., 149
Jennings, Hughie, 162
Johnson, Ban, 19, 31, 32, 38, 39, 40, 42,
    43, 44, 46 ff., 57 ff., 65 ff., 75, 101,
    113, 114, 122, 125, 188-189, 258 ff.,
    274
  and Cobb-Speaker case, 173 ff.
  and Milwaukee cases, 107
  and O'Connell-Dolan case, 133-134
  break with Comiskey, 48 ff.
  death of, 179
  denounces Lasker plan, 66, 70
  final resignation of, 178
  gets salary raise, 149-150
  hires detectives, 147
  Judge Landis and, 80-88, 142-143
  loss of power, 49
  makes come-back in own league,
    147
  on betting on ball games, 162-163
  on Pacific Coast League gambling,
    141
  public censure of, 143-144
  resignation from league, 154
  restored to Advisory Council, 152
  statement re. appointment of Lan-
    dis, 73
  vote of thanks to, 189
Johnson, George F., 77
Johnson, Hiram, 15, 64, 65
Johnson, Jack, 36

299

300

303